Terroir of Golf

A Golf Book for Wine Lovers

TABA DALE

Rp
RYAN PUBLISHING

First published 2023 by Ryan Publishing
PO Box 7680, Melbourne, 3004, Victoria,
Australia

Ph: 61 3 9505 6820
Email: books@ryanpub.com   Website: www.ryanpub.com

RYAN PUBLISHING

Terroir of Golf
ISBN(s): 9781876498849 Hardback
9781876498856 Paperback
9781876498863 Ebook

A catalogue record for this book is available from the National Library of Australia

Internal design by Luke Harris, Working Type Studio, Victoria, Australia. www.workingtype.com.au
Editing: Graeme Ryan | Cover design: Luke Harris

Cover photographs.
The 19th (or spare) hole at Kingston Heath Golf Club, Melbourne, Victoria, Australia - Gary Lisbon Golf Photography.
Vineyard at Montalto Winery, Mornington Peninsula, Victoria, Australia – John Mitchell, Owner.

Special thanks to the following people for permission to use their photographs. Helen Keplinger of Keplinger Wines, Mike Aylward of Ocean Eight, Werner Roux of Goose Wines, Kirsten Nicholson, Manager of Shiskine Golf and Tennis Club.

The following photographs were taken by Taba Dale: Pages: 59, 61, 62, 69, 71, 263, 276, 279 281, 286, 287, 292, 295, 297.

For, and with my amazing Kevin,

whose handicap keeps dropping as he gets older.

Contents

Foreword

It was all land for golf

It is always a pleasure to meet or to hear from Taba Dale, the great romantic and lover of golf. She always smiles. She always has a delightful question or twenty and is interested intensely in the diverse answers offered by her myriad of friends and admirers. She opens minds to the great gift of life and to the most amazing elements of golf.

This time she came with a simple question: Tell me what you think about the land for golf?

I was struggling to regain lucidity after months in hospital struggling with sepsis and afloat in a lake of antibiotics. I was just hoping to get back on my feet soon and discover whether I could overcome my weakened state to get my drives past the ladies' tees! Please Taba, don't get me going again.

To make the answer a little less complex than it might be, one must state up front that the only land not suitable for golf, or attractive to the golfer, is a wet and smelly bog, land hanging off the side of Mount Everest, or land submerged under ten feet of snow. Everything else has potential, has promise, or is simply irresistible. Even a beach revealed to the gaze at low tide offers opportunities for play.

As a boy cycling along country roads, I was always captivated by the potential for a drawn fairway wood around an oak growing in the middle of a sloping meadow; the excitement that would surround a long iron over a duck pond onto a wee shelf of low-grazed land beyond; and the magnificence of a valley running far below and just begging for a great, soaring drive to the fairway below.

It was all land for golf.

We revelled in golf just after World War II. The courses were presented poorly for the most part as the game had suffered and machinery was still basic. At our club there was an arrangement that anyone who owned a lawnmower would take turns mowing a green or two. When it became obvious that not all greens were cut each week a local rule was introduced allowing the player to press with his foot a path through the grass from ball to hole so that it could be putted rather than chipped!

The comradeship was terrific. No matter what the score, the talk would be mighty as all retired to the local pub, except for the few swanky clubs with clubhouses, for a sandwich and pint of stout or three. It got boisterous. They knew their drink and how to chat to each other in the pre-television and pre-internet age. They talked face-to-face and shared without thought the great, big gasps of the smoke laden air.

They were worse in Scotland, they tell me, where one famous club, admittedly not today or yesterday, was enjoying its regular after golf dinner upstairs in a local hostelry when a waiter happened to be pushed or thrown out a window. When the head of the house enquired what should be done about the waiter, he was told, "Put him on the bill!"

Okay Taba, I will get back to the question of land for golf and give a glimpse into my mind which is always raging with images of hills, valleys, quarries, plateaus, ridges, meadows, dunes, deserts, gorges, canyons, peninsulas, inlets of sea and lake, ponds, waving grasses, eskers, mountains and vegetation from low grass to towering trees.

The desire to go golfing and the thrill of designing a golf course becomes fun once one realizes the advantages one has in the matter of the raw materials provided by nature.

The number of possible design combinations when creating a golf course is seemingly infinite as compared to the simple board game called chess in which two players with sixteen pieces each go face to face across a little board divided into sixty-four squares. Easy.

"The number of possible design combinations when creating a golf course is seemingly infinite as compared to the simple board game called chess."

Not so, as one realizes when told that there are 400 different positions after each player makes one move; 72,084 positions after two moves each and this explodes to 9-million-plus positions after both players have made three moves. This, in turn, looks puny when one is told that there are 288-billion-plus possible positions later in the game.

One can only believe these numbers while recalling the excitement of world chess champion Garry Kasparov versus the computer back in 1997.

Golf is even more difficult when taking into account the multifarious locations and land types that the game is played upon, the varying weather conditions, the baffling array of equipment available to the players, the range of golf design elements employed by the sport's architects — bunkers, undulating greens, narrow and wide fairways, optical illusions — and the widely varying physical and mental frailties and strengths of the players!

All that having been said, it is unquestionable that golf is best played on links land. On the free draining sandy deposits which link (ergo 'golf links') the seashore to the inland soil. It is here that the ball runs fast, there is bounce in the greens and all the primary elements of ocean, land and sky meet in convulsive grandeur sometimes sublimely calm and beautiful and at other times awesomely angry.

Ireland is blessed with a necklace of golf links dotted around its coastline. Just on forty of them, almost one third of the world supply of golf links, and all within a few hours' drive of each other. Scotland is somewhat the same, while England and Wales have a lesser share. This is the original form of golf and so rare that when one runs the maths taking into account matters of season and access, fewer than 25% of the world's golfers will ever get one game on any one links!

After links my favorite golf land is found in the deserts of Arizona and Nevada. Okay, this will surprise many. The desert courses are presented so beautifully with the contrast of maintained grasslands to the desert simply stunning to the eye, and just to crown this delightful visual cocktail add the stark lines and lovely shades of the mountains. It can't get better.

The American parkland experience, especially when linked to wealth and the urge for excellence, is sublime. Apart from the obvious household names there are hundreds and possibly thousands of wonderfully designed and maintained golf courses with the grasses, the lakes and rivers, and the trees all combining to present a Garden of Eden effect.

So it goes from Japan, through Australia and South America, all over Europe and in 208 of the world's designated 245 countries! They are donning their spikes, their colored pants, their golf caps, and socks in all those places and losing something like 250-million golf balls (luckily, they find some to balance matters a little) a year collectively! Fore!

At the end of it all, however, it comes to terrain that can be traversed, where grass can be grown and where the weather allows players to get out.

Ireland is blessed in this regard with a temperate climate, thanks in large part to the Gulf Stream bringing warm water over from Mexico and Texas, allowing golf most days of the year in relative comfort. At the southern and easterly seaside links the game is played over 320-days annually.

By contrast the season is short in Canada where I had the pleasure of building two, if I may say so in all modesty, fine golf courses for the Montreal Island Golf Club. They stop playing sometime in mid-October and open only in early April. Yet they really open with great enthusiasm as I found to my amazement with full car parks as early as 6 am The skies are put aside, the clubs are gleaming, and the game goes on.

The game is irresistible for today's golfers as it was for the lovely people I shared the fairways with back in the 1950s. Have clubs will play. Long may it be so and let nobody complain about the greens. We are the fortunate ones.

Pat Ruddy

The European Club May 2018

Introduction

A powerful connection with nature

The revelation for this title came to me while I was playing golf at Machrie on the Isle of Islay (pronounced eye-la). Although our recent golf odyssey throughout Scotland was organized as a book tour for my newly published paperback, *A Stroll on the Old Lady,* I had persuaded Kevin, my significant other, to visit some golf courses and locales that were not featured in the stories.

In addition to being a golf writer, I work with Kevin as a tour operator specializing in golf. Convenient, eh? It is essential for our business to keep abreast of new developments with our travel vendors, as well as test out routes to important golf destinations. It's all part of making sure that 'getting there is half the fun!'

Although new course openings are few and far between, we are always tracking new projects and course renovations or restorations which golf architects and developers are implementing around the world. Moreover, we are keeping up to date on new hotel properties or refurbishments and the rare new road or ferry services. Yet sometimes we can devise an extraordinary itinerary that enables us to fit in a visit to a remote course, or one that is just really hard to get to. That's when we experience the thrill of being travelers on a trip, and adventurers!

In 2016, I had my heart set on playing golf at two places in particular — Shiskine (Isle of Arran) and The Machrie. Visiting these golfing gems and many places in between, I discovered parallels between creating a unique wine (one which we savor when we drink), and that of a unique golf experience that we drink while playing a course. As with a fine wine, it is equally intoxicating when a superb golf course delivers a powerful connection with nature. So, while I meandered around the dunes of The Machrie, all the elements coalesced into a single phrase: *Terroir of Golf.*

I borrowed from the world of wine where terroir (French from the word terre or 'land') refers to the specific environment where a particular wine is produced. The concept of terroir, as it relates to a crop of grapes, starts with the physical habitat including soil, climate and topography. This epiphany occurred to me while on Islay, much better known for whisky than for golf, so I'm also loosely borrowing from the world of whisky-making.

"The concept of terroir, as it relates to a crop of grapes, starts with the physical habitat including soil, climate and topography."

I rather doubt that even the most sophisticated distilleries would use the word *terroir* to describe how they craft whisky (or whiskey in Ireland). Perhaps there is a Scottish word for the importance of the ground and the grain that goes into the making of uisge beatha (or *uisce* in Irish Gaelic) which translates into 'water of life'. It was the Irish monks of the early Middle Ages who used the Latin translation of *aqua vitae* to describe distilled alcohol. However, that discussion requires a red, white or brown liquid, poured into a lovely crystal glass, with or without a stem, to be properly and luxuriously explored at great length.

Back to the subject at hand. While I am concocting the philosophy of golf terroir, I am also factoring in the impossible-to-define passion and poetry of the visionary, and in the case of a golf course — the architect — the heart and soul which that person or design group brings to the project.

Another intangible that contributes to the pleasure of drinking a fine wine or playing a fine golf course, is atmosphere. I'm talking about something other than climate. It's more like a mystical aura that links us and the natural world — the living world. This concept subtly illuminates how each detail in course design counts, just like it does in the artistry of properly planting vineyards and bringing a superb wine to fruition.

The wine starts with its sacred place — the site where it is grown — likewise, a phenomenal golf course emerges the same way. The climate, soil, and terrain, blended harmoniously by the course designer, become the key contextual characteristics that come together as terroir does for the winemaker.

So, no matter what you are doing on the golf course — laughing, cursing, breaking clubs, or breaking records — you are doing something else at the same time. You are communing with nature and discovering, or re-discovering, the nature of the game.

In the end, it is all about passion. Passion for the game of golf, yet also for the greatness of the ground it is played upon.

Turnberry Lighthouse.

Turnberry

A total golf experience

My first visit to this magnificent property was in 2005, when I was setting up my own travel venture and my business plan consisted of (1) only using 5-star properties, and (2) getting a partner who knew the lay of the land. Well, I'm pleased to say that often, golf travelers also desire the best of the best, and I chose my partner well. That would be none other than Kevin McGrath, my golf travel partner and now my life partner.

Our first stop on this adventure was to be Turnberry, mainly to see the redesigned course. I had stayed at this grand old resort before, on a couple of different occasions, and was keen to see the latest transformation.

When courses are ranked in the World Top 100, on a list of any kind, the panelists are told to rate the golf course itself. But there should be a separate ranking — that of the total golf *experience*. On that list, Turnberry will stand near the top every time.

Our journey began with the fast ferry from Larne in Northern Ireland. We arrived in Cairnryan bang on time at 6:30 pm. From there it was straight up the road on the South Ayrshire coast — well I say straight, but it's

Turnberry Clubhouse and Hotel in the background.

really a twisty road — through one quaint town or village after another.

One minute you are welcomed to the town of Ballantrae and a minute later you see the sign 'Haste Ye Back'. Sometimes the road runs along the rocky shoreline, then turns inland for a bit where it is carved out of heavily forested mountains. It winds past cow pastures and fields dotted with sheep.

Suddenly, you see it — the big ethereal rock — looming ghostlike in the distance, Ailsa Craig. The giant blue dome-shaped island becomes our constant companion as we wind our way to Turnberry, where at last the towering chimneys of the regal resort peek above the treetops.

At the same time, the magnificent three-storey, red-tiled roof comes into view on your right. What must be the largest blue and white

Saltire flag flies tall on your left, announcing the fact that you have arrived at Turnberry!

The drama builds as you climb higher while the links course spreads out before you. Ailsa Craig looms as if anchored in the Firth of Clyde, and the famous lighthouse, built in 1873 on the remains of the 13th century Turnberry Castle, sits on the very edge of the Ailsa course in the distance. What was once the keeper's apartment has been converted into luxury accommodations.

Eventually you circle around to the hotel entrance on the east side of the cruise-ship-size building. Originally sited this way because when the resort was first built in 1906 it was a railway hotel, and the entrance would have been just steps away from the station.

Before you have shifted into park, the elegant, kilted doorman is there to assist. From the giant pheasant feather affixed to his gray wool cap to his handsome gray wool tartan, woven with a soft blue band, he graciously escorts you to reception, where you check in.

Next, you are shown to your sumptuous room that lacks absolutely nothing. The monstrous flat screen TV was nearly as big as our king size bed. Every piece of carved walnut burl mahogany furniture is trimmed in trademark Trump gold leaf detail. The bathroom was equally opulent, and thankfully they have not done away with the tub like so many other high-end hotels have chosen to do in recent years. Big mistake if you ask me as someone who loves to luxuriate in steaming water and indulge in the personal serenity of relaxing hydrotherapy.

Dinner in the 1906 restaurant was sublime. The view, the food, and the service were all exquisite. Not that we had room for another bite, we ordered a sticky toffee pudding dessert anyway. Wow! How delicious! We decided on the spot that we would taste and rank sticky toffee pudding everywhere we went. Working on a scale of 1 to 10, we gave the Turnberry pudding a 9.5, a tad leeway to see if anything could possibly exceed it by the end of our trip.

We were scheduled to meet with Angus

Sunset over the Irish Sea at Turnberry.

Watson, the golf sales manager of the resort, at 9 am on the following day. We joined him in the lavishly appointed lobby, standing just outside the Grand Tea Lounge. Our eyes were already glued to the jaw-dropping crystal chandelier taking up nearly the whole atrium. Angus pointed upward and jovially informed us, "That is *The Ivanka*. It was designed specifically for this resort!" Laden with 1,000 Swarovski crystals and taking six months to create, it was roughly 10 feet tall and 8 feet wide. Certainly, enormous by most standards. Being able to view it from all angles made climbing the main staircase a breathtaking exercise in more ways than one.

Angus himself seemed to be tailor-made for this Luxury Collection Resort as well. He was one of the most genial and knowledgeable golf sales managers I've ever met. With commensurate composure and a generous dollop of charm, he accompanied us all over the property.

We saw loads of fascinating memorabilia during our stroll down a corridor full of framed newspaper articles and original railway timetables from the days when the resort was known as the Turnberry Station Hotel.

Angus paused in front of one the frames and said, "The resort became quite popular during the formative years of Scottish motor racing. Check out this photograph of Stirling Moss speeding to victory in a 500cc Formula III race in his single-seater Cooper-Norton back in 1952. Isn't that cool?" I could easily imagine those exhilarating days when automobile racing captured the imagination of engineers and drivers alike, following a time of petrol rationing in war-torn Britain.

Even though there was little action on the disused airfields after WWII, Turnberry was still an exceptionally attractive destination for its location on the edge of the sea.

Angus explained, "There were three runways out on the original golf courses.

And later on, during the war years, Turnberry was turned into a military hospital, too."

That was barely part of how Turnberry had been pressed into service to become a military air base. During WWI, the Royal Flying Corps trained pilots and the wounded convalesced in the hotel. Peace did come and repairs were done, but when war was again declared against Germany in 1939, Turnberry resumed the role of an air base and hospital.

Except this time the heavier aircraft and machinery took a greater toll, damaging the courses more severely.

As we progressed down the hallway, several photos of golf played at Turnberry after the war years were a welcome sight.

Kevin gleefully discovered a countryman in one of the photos and declared, "Look, that's Christy O'Connor in a match with Tom Haliburton!" Although the photograph was dated 1957, a few years before Kevin began playing golf, he'd certainly followed Christy's long and illustrious career.

Another precious piece of memorabilia was

a poster of Bob Hope with the caption, 'Would You Like to Swing With a Star?' A charity event broadcast on Scottish Television was created in aid of UNICEF. It was advertised that Bob Hope would be handing out the prize at the World Show/Am Final at Turnberry, 20 September 1981. Bob Hope was resplendent in his colorful blue and red plaid pants, snazzy white loafers, and a dazzling smile. The splendid resort, originally designed by James Miller as the Glasgow & South Western Railway's Turnberry Hotel, stretched the entire width of the poster's background.

From there, Angus guided us into the gigantic Crystal Ballroom, and I gushed, "You could put a car in here!"

With a knowing smile, he replied, "There were actually four cars in here during a race event back in the day!"

The room was so enormous, they could probably have fitted a few railway cars in there as well. No exaggeration, the ceiling was nearly 20 feet high.

I couldn't possibly help noticing that crystal was the dominant theme in this grand dame of railway resorts. Although there are over 300 new crystal chandeliers installed throughout, the one place you'll not find one was the next stop on our tour.

"I couldn't possibly help noticing that crystal was the dominant theme in this grand dame of railway resorts."

When I heard Angus say, "Let's go into the kitchen," I thought it was rather, er, unconventional. Not normally where you'd expect to be taken on a formal site visit such as this. However, when he ushered us through the double swinging doors to the main commercial kitchen, then led us to the Chef's Table, it was an Aha moment! The diminutive room was intimate and cozy, accommodating eight people comfortably around an understated U-shaped hand-hewn wooden table. One end of the room opened to the kitchen and the other walls were adorned with framed menus of lavish six-course meals. Not that you could ever tire of the view from the 1906 Restaurant, but if you want to splash out (it's ultra-pricey), and be treated to a theatrical, culinary performance by the talented chefs, this room is the place to be!

I had only been privileged once before to experience this kind of private dining. Our Canadian friend, Roger Bailes, planned a surprise birthday party for his wife at The Sanctuary Resort in Paradise Valley, Arizona, a few years ago. The invitees arrived appropriately early, and we were served cocktails in a luxuriously appointed private room. Sophisticated lighting and elegant artwork complemented the exquisite table, set for twelve. The guest of honor arrived to a chorus of, "Surprise!" and "Happy Birthday."

Once she'd recovered from her shock, the sumptuous curtains, running unobtrusively down the length of the long wall, magically opened to reveal the state-of-the-art show kitchen, behind a glass wall. At that stage we were all astonished to discover we were being treated to a personalized, interactive journey with the chef. Oh, that Roger, what a clever and classy guy!

So, all this and we hadn't even been to the golf course. The best was yet to come! But first, Angus took us to see a few of the handsomely appointed meeting rooms. They varied in size from less than 200 square feet to more than 2,000. When we entered the Tom Carrick Boardroom, I noticed a hefty hardback book on a side table. I browsed the pages that detailed the marvelous redesign of Turnberry by Tom Mackenzie & Martin Ebert.

Along with adding many course improvements to other Open Championship venues including Royal Troon, Royal St George's, and Royal Lytham & St Annes, Mackenzie & Ebert have designed or advised on sixty courses in sixteen countries. I was so taken by surprise when I saw Askernish included in a separate booklet about their many projects. In fact, I was utterly gobsmacked.

"Askernish!" I exclaimed. "We were trying to figure out how to get there on this trip. But it seemed way too complicated — although we are definitely going to Shiskine on Arran and Machrie on Islay!" I was barely able to contain myself when I saw the photo of Askernish, the most esoteric of all the courses I've ever wanted to play.

I'd read several years ago about the course which was 'lost' and now re-discovered. It was believed to have been laid out by Old Tom Morris during his heyday of the late 1800s.

Getting there takes an extraordinary amount of advance planning though, as it's on South Uist (Scottish Gaelic: Uibhist a Deas) in the Outer Hebrides of Scotland. When Kevin went to map out our journey, he was told that one of the key ferries wasn't running this year. That put the kibosh on our Askernish dreaming — for this year anyway.

Angus, astonished by my excitement, beamed and said, "I'm going there myself in August to play in the Askernish Open!"

Well now I was astonished. How amazing is that? What good fortune. And how does he get there — to this magical sounding island, known to be one of the last strongholds of the Gaelic language in Scotland. This is how:

"Last year we drove up to Skye and stayed overnight," Angus continued. "We caught the early ferry from Uig to Lochmaddy on North Uist (pronounced something like you-est), then it's about a forty-five-minute drive down to South Uist and Askernish."

By the way, after Angus told us his route, I asked him to repeat the whole thing so I could record him on my digital Nikon. He laughed mightily, then accommodated me, with even more detail. He's a star.

Kevin wanted to make sure he understood all the logistics, and asked, "Do you have to take another ferry?"

"No, it's actually three islands joined together by causeways," Angus explained. "Well, that's a relief," I said.

Angus went on to say, "We stayed three nights in the *something-or-other* hotel." I couldn't quite catch the name, but I didn't want to make Angus repeat himself. "It's incredibly good fun — the most natural links you've ever seen. Basically, the story goes like this: Old Tom Morris laid it out for a lady who owned the land. The course was lost over time, but somebody found a letter from this lady to Old Tom Morris saying, 'Thanks for laying out the course and here is your payment of ...."

"Probably one pound," I blurted, stating what I'd once read about Old Tom, "that was his fee!"

"That's right, I think," Angus agreed, then picked up the thread. "Tom Mackenzie and Martin Ebert got hold of this information and decided to go and see if they could find the course. They stood up on this dune and they were like: 'There it is!' They didn't have any plans, they just figured out what Old Tom would have done."

"Tom Mackenzie and Martin Ebert got hold of this information and decided to go and see if they could find the course."

Kevin jumped in, "So when is the Askernish Open? We can't get over this year, but maybe the next."

"It's the last week of August," Angus replied. "The first day they do a Stableford competition. Saturday is the actual Askernish Open. Then they clear out the greenkeeper's shed and have a Ceilidh (pronounced kay-lee)."

This is a custom that usually involves playing folk music and dancing. It can be at a house party or in a larger space like a social hall or any community gathering place. The Irish tradition is spelled Céilí. In olden times storytelling and a poetry recital were part of the festivities.

Angus continued, "Sunday is the International Texas Scramble."

Are you kidding me? I was amazed. *A Texas Scramble on this remote Outer Hebridian* island?

Angus read the surprise on my face and confirmed, "Yeah, they have a Texas Scramble, and everybody gets hungover and near dying. It's great fun!"

That's something to look forward to for sure;

but we had to hustle over to the Ailsa course for today's fun.

"We better get going — it's almost our tee time," I said, moving toward the door. Angus checked his watch to calculate approximately when we'd finish the front nine.

"I'll meet you by the green at the ninth. I want to take you inside the lighthouse."

A shiver of delight went up my spine, and I thanked him for his generous offer.

You'll rarely see a photograph of the Ailsa course that doesn't feature this iconic white building, built on the site of a castle that once belonged to Robert the Bruce. We'd heard it had been converted into a rather ritzy halfway house. Little did we know what we were in for.

As we gathered our golf bags at the clubhouse for our 12:06 pm tee time, we discovered we were paired with Ludwig and Mark, two affable guys who both live in the San Francisco Bay area, but Ludwig was born in Italy and grew up near Lake Como.

"If you go to Italy and want to play golf," Ludwig insisted, "you *must* go to Villa d'Este by Lake Como. It's really special."

"Ludwig, maybe we can work it into a Golf Tour of Italy. I've been thinking about creating a trip to play golf, go to wineries, maybe have a cooking class." I said, as I already began figuring out all the golfers we know who would probably love to travel with us.

Our foursome walked over to the starter's hut and the first tee. Mark warned me, "You ought to know, Ludwig takes the game quite seriously." Truer words were never spoken. The physical evidence? He brought along a video camera (and a tripod, I kid you not!) and even managed to film his own eagle putt on the 7th green.

In the Mackenzie & Ebert coffee-table book about the Ailsa course, Angus had flipped the pages to show us the numerous changes around the turn, starting with the ninth hole, which used to play as a long par 4. It was known for having an unfair hogs-back contour running down the middle of the fairway with the fall-off on each side.

The new ninth has been reborn as a dramatic par 3 over the bay, not unlike the 16th at Cypress Point. Angus added a sweet anecdote, "The new green is where the coastguard used to have his garden and kept his sheep when he lived in the lighthouse." I could easily picture that idyllic scene when we arrived at the spot.

The 'members' tees are more like 185 — 160 yards, and although it doesn't look like it from the tee boxes; there is a bit of run-up in the front.

When our foursome reached the ninth hole, which measures 248 yards from the back tee, both Kevin and Ludwig had to go over what is a very intimidating rocky shoreline. Like two medieval swordsmen unsheathing their weapons from their scabbards, Kevin and Ludwig each boldly drew their drivers from bag, ready to demonstrate their golfing prowess.

"Like two medieval swordsmen unsheathing their weapons from their scabbards, Kevin and Ludwig each boldly drew their drivers from bag."

With daring defiance, they ignored the stern-looking ranger standing on the front edge of the green. Rather than succeeding to intimidate them and put them off, he just proved to be a tempting target. Kevin's tee shot carried to dry land but did not rattle the ranger. Ludwig's bid to carry the water fell short. But both had the thrill of having tried it.

No sooner did we make the trek over to the ninth green and there was Angus, as promised, waving at us, ready to show us the magnificent two-bedroom suite of the Turnberry Resort's exquisite Lighthouse. There was only one hitch. Justin Rose, who was there to do a photo-shoot for one of his sponsors, was upstairs getting prepared.

Justin Rose took to golf at a young age, breaking 70 when he turned eleven. Born in 1980, he turned pro in 1998 and went on to win over 21 tournaments, including the US

Open at Merion in 2013. He became the first Englishman in 43 years to win this coveted Major title.

Knock-knock. Oh, sorry Justin, we just want to have a wee look around. And that's not just the fantasy movie running in my head — it's what really happened! Justin couldn't have been more gracious about us barging in on him. He chatted away with everybody and when Kevin asked me if I wanted to have my picture taken with him, Justin beckoned me to him, put his arm around me, and smiled for the camera.

His height surprised me. The top of my head didn't even clear his shoulder. Justin was not only tall and gorgeous, he was also an absolute gentleman. Meeting him was such an amazing treat. I was so golf-star struck that I practically forgot to take in the view across the Irish Sea to the Isle of Arran or observe the elegant surroundings of the posh suite. After spending so much time hobnobbing with Justin, we missed out on a glimpse of the must-see halfway house. Reportedly on the opulent side, serving soup, toasties, coffee and cappuccino, a big part of the appeal are the stunning views. You can sit outside on the deck on a clear day and see the Irish coastline.

In fact, the shock of having bumbled into what is probably one of the finest hotel suites in the world, replete with a living room, dining table, super king beds, Swarovski crystal chandeliers, and three 65 inch flat-screen TVs, only to find one of the finest golfers in the world awaiting his appointed time to perform duties as a brand ambassador, no less, had all of us discombobulated.

So, the new tenth hole which now plays as a par 5, was kind of a blur. We chalked it up to the euphoria of being in Justin's glow. I vaguely remembered Angus having said that they pushed the green back onto the old 11th tee. I can tell you it was quite a long hole of 565 yards from the back tee.

The 11th hole had a new tee sitting on the shoreline and was a challenging par 3 across the water. Another big change was the 14th, which

9th and 10 holes at Turnberry

became a par 5 and takes you back on top of the hill, with stunning views of the lighthouse and the sea.

At last, we came to the par 3 15th, although it was not the way I remembered it when I had my birdie here back in 2005. I was playing with an affable man, David Wood and his son, David Jr. I learned during our round that David Sr hailed from Des Moines, Iowa, and was a member of Loch Lomond Golf Club. We had that in common. I had the privilege of being a member there myself at that time.

Whatever else happened in the summer of 2005, all the magic for me was on that particular hole. I recalled asking David Sr if I could have my picture taken with him when we finished playing the 18th, with the iconic Turnberry hotel on the hill in the background. He was my Justin Rose on that day, and nearly as tall. We've remained friends ever since, and I've become a devoted fan of his 'Golf Quote of the Day' which he emails to me regularly.

The 17th was now a par 4 because the 14th became a par 5. The final change was the 18th. Mackenzie & Ebert put the tee box back on the dunes, where again, there are stunning views of the sea.

Earlier, before we'd started our round on the Ailsa Course, Angus had declared, "The feedback on the changes has been incredibly good and there has not been one negative comment."

Having seen it and played it for ourselves, I'd have to put the redesigned Ailsa Course right up there as a 9.5 with the sticky toffee pudding!

Turnberry Resort, Scotland.

The Marcliffe

It's Like Coming Home

Did I say I like the 5-star experience? How about *love* the 5-star experience? That's how I feel about The Marcliffe Hotel. It's true love.

After one more sumptuous breakfast at Turnberry, Kevin and I embarked on the three- hour drive to Aberdeenshire. With our destination being one of our absolute favorites, the journey was that much more pleasurable.

Before and after our round of golf, like two honeybees, we wanted to land in the cozy hive that is The Marcliffe Hotel.

We thought we'd be lucky just to be able to check in a bit early and stash our luggage in our room. But who should we bump into on our arrival, but the Monarch of the Marcliffe himself, Stewart Spence.

"I got your book already and I love it!" Stewart exclaimed. "And I already bought ten more."

I was bowled over! I'd brought along a signed copy and figured that would be the first time he ever laid eyes on it. But no, he beat me to it, making me feel like I'd just written the bestseller of the century.

He wasn't kidding either. When arrived at our room, called 'The Blair', Stewart had personalized our Welcome Letter with a handwritten "P.S. The book is wonderful!"

Along with noting that Stewart says he has handicap 8 (I think he was playing off 7 a few years ago), the letter got me to thinking about having Scottish Beef (aged a minimum of 35 days) and 'cut to suit, any weight'.

Mindful that we had an appointment to do a site visit at MacLeod House and then had a mid-afternoon tee time as well, we agreed to reconvene before dinner and have drinks in the lounge.

Kevin and I had been invited to play Trump Aberdeen when it opened in 2012. I had visited the property on a few different occasions when it was owned by Tom Griffin, who ran the estate as a hunting lodge, with Menie House the nucleus of the property. It has now been renovated to a high standard and renamed MacLeod House, after Donald Trump's mother's clan name.

Although the imposing granite Menie House was designed by the esteemed Aberdeen architect John Smith around 1835, the links course is quite new. Spectacular beauty? Check. Challenging for all levels of players? Great variety of holes? Memorable? Check. Check. Check. It's also what I call muscular, in that the course takes you up, down, around and through towering primary dunes so your body (and mind) will know you've been put to a rigorous test. In 2012, both Kevin and I thought it was immense fun and playable, and felt it would be even better when it matured. Well, I'm happy to report that it has.

As it turned out, we didn't tee off until 2.55 pm and only played 9 holes before the wind picked up and the temperature dropped considerably, making that juicy steak seem all the more appealing.

We were positively jubilant to get back into the Marcliffe hive, which was buzzing with activity. We barely had a chance to order a drink in The Drawing Room Bar, when Stewart appeared, impeccably dressed in a perfectly tailored charcoal grey suit, crisp white shirt and dark blue patterned tie to match his twinkling blue eyes. Forthwith, he began introducing us to people, telling them about the book, absolutely effusive in his praise.

Then a most amazing thing happened, although it is really a common occurrence if you hang around Stewart Spence for about ten seconds. The very next people he introduced us to were Walter Ragazzi and his wife. Why is that amazing? Because only the day before, Ludwig, who was born in Italy, had told us while we were playing at Turnberry that we *must* go play golf at Villa d'Este. Now standing before us is Walter, Presidente of Circolo Golf Villa D'Este as it says on his card.

We still hadn't a chance to order drinks. For Kevin it was an easy decision, a vodka tonic. Yet for me, having it already in my head that I'd be ordering that Aberdeen Angus beef, I was leaning toward a glass of red wine. As soon as I stated my preference for a Cabernet Sauvignon, Stewart disappeared into his extensive wine cellar.

"Stewart's wine selection is exceptional. It even includes an entire list of Wine Produced by Golfers for Golfers."

Just like everything else he creates, Stewart's wine selection is exceptional. It even includes an entire list of Wine Produced by Golfers for Golfers. From the Luke Donald Collection to the Ernie Els Signature wines of Stellenbosch, there are dozens of Cabs, Chardonnays, and blends from some of the world's most famous golfers and winemakers.

Stewart returned a few minutes later with a bottle — but not just any bottle. For me, he chose a wine called Balgownie Estate. Although it was not from the famous golfer list, it was highly significant for more than one reason.

Stewart, being a brilliant master of ceremony, remarked, "You know, I'm a member of Royal Aberdeen now for more than forty-four years, but we just call it Balgownie."

There's a tidbit of history behind that. Although the club was founded in 1780, in 1888 the members decided to move across the River Don to play their golf on the links of Balgownie.

Our charismatic host, standing behind the bar, procured a perfect tall wine glass and proceeded to pour some of the full-bodied dark cherry liquid.

"You see here where it says Bendigo?" Stewart asked, having picked up on my curiosity about the bottle that *he* chose especially for me.

Completely under Stewart's spell, I cast my eyes to the label, and exclaimed, "That's in Australia!"

Delivering the first part of his punch line, Stewart proclaimed with great pride, "Well, this fellow, Stuart Anderson, his ancestors, are from right here in Balgownie!"

"That's amazing!" I blurted, dying to get my hand on that tempting glass of gorgeous Cab, cleverly kept just out of my reach.

Stewart choreographed his presentation with perfect aplomb and delivered the closer. "He's a legendary winemaker now, Stuart Anderson is. Started planting his vineyard back in 1969 and called it Balgownie Estate!"

The Monarch of The Marcliffe clearly delighted in romancing his exceptional wine selection, while at the same time, making me feel oh-so-special. Then he performed with utmost composure, that delightful part of the European fine dining custom and took us to our table in the Conservatory Restaurant.

Kevin, who had not yet become a red wine drinker, was also seduced by the story and said, "Maybe I'll have some too!"

"That would be wonderful, sweetheart," I coaxed him. "I'm already thinking of having beef as my main course, but you know, this wine will also go well with sticky toffee pudding!"

That's when Kevin clued Stewart in. "We're on a sticky toffee pudding tour while we're in

Scotland, so I sure hope you have it on the dessert menu?"

"Not only do we have it on the menu, we also sell a lot of it," Stewart beamed, while reaching for a small pad of paper in his pocket.

"We call it S-T. Our pastry department knows exactly what S-T is." He demonstrated exactly how he writes it: 'S.T. + Ice Cream & or Cream'.

And boy do they know! It was right up there as an easy 9 on our 1 — 10 scale. We still felt like we had to hold out until the end of the tour before we bestowed a 10 on any contender.

Oh, and the beef was superb too, and made even better by the outstanding cabernet that Kevin enjoyed nearly as much as me. Maybe I'll turn him into a red wine drinker yet.

Nairn

Part 1 — Clubhouse Experience

What could be better than playing golf at Nairn? How about watching Andy Murray play Wimbledon? It's just gone 2:05 pm and we were supposed to tee off at 10:50 am but it was lashing rain. We figure since we have the option to play tomorrow with a much better forecast, we'll power up our computers, get some work done here in the clubhouse, have a bit of lunch and settle in for the afternoon. Besides, the Scottish Open at Castle Stuart will come on at half past two.

We are watching the Scottish, Glasgow-born hopeful, No. 2 ranked player in the world, Andy Murray. He's playing against Milos Raonic, a Canadian of Serb heritage, ranked No. 10. Milos holds his first serve of the match. Murray quickly goes to 40 — 15. Finishes with a service winner and they are immediately one all.

Raonic is strong. I don't even know who he is, other than he beat Federer in the semifinal. That's a bit tragic. Haven't followed tennis much since I took up golf.

A guy pops his head into our lounge and says, "Somebody died? It's very quiet." His pal informs him, "They're all watching the tennis."

Nairn Golf Course and Clubhouse, beside the Moray Firth.

We are, after all, in a golf club. But since golf isn't on yet, a couple of dozen eyes are glued to the telly, watching the Wimbledon final.

The last time I watched Andy Murray in the Wimbledon final, we were in the clubhouse at Walton Heath, about twenty miles south of London, and he won. Everyone in the room was cheering. I don't even remember who he defeated. Didn't matter. He won was all that mattered.

Raonic wins his next serve. It's 2 to 1. Murray's up. There's so much power in Andy's serve. He launches himself far off the ground and fires a missile. Goes to 30-love. Now 40-love, Raonic capitalizes on Murray's second serve and drills one down the forehand line. Big forehand return on the next second serve. But Murray blasts an ace and it's 2 games all.

"Only a few minutes before the Scottish

Open comes on," someone in the back of the room announces. "Will we switch?"

No one replies.

In the meantime, the lounge fills up with hungry golfers who braved the rain. One group is a foursome who I met earlier while they were having tea in the other restaurant with no TV.

Raonic went 3 — 2. Murray sits in his chair on the switchover; a bundle of nervous energy. Right leg quivering. Camera pans to the Duke and Duchess of Cambridge and various celebrities in their boxes.

Murray to serve. Wins first point off his blistering ace. Goes 40-love. Seconds later, that's it. Three games all. Match time is 21 minutes.

Raonic winds up. Big serve. Wins first point, but it goes to 15 all. Then 15 — 30. Murray takes it to 15 — 40 and has his first break point. A chance to win the game, but he blows a forehand past the baseline. *C'mon Andy!* Okay, he breaks Raonic. Crowd goes crazy.

The foursome take a table in front of a second TV in the now crowded lounge. The first man

Nairn salmon storage hut.

who chats with me is John Van Bork. He says, "I'm from Amsterdam and I'm a member here." He looks very dapper in his pale blue wool sweater. To his left is a Dutch friend, Reynoud Van Doorne. At first, I didn't notice what he's wearing, he's so handsome. Dark hair and did I say *handsome?* Actually, he's wearing his handsomeness with an understated light gray sweater. To his left is Rüdiger (omlaud or omlaut over the u) Klahr, in a smart black, gray and red argyle sweater. And the fourth is a slender Scot, Alasdair Finlayson, who said when they played golf here yesterday, he was "soaked to my underwear." Then he revealed, "I'm still not dry yet!"

Murray is up 5 games to 3 and 15 — 30 on Raonic's serve. Service winner for Raonic to go 30 — all. Big ace down the middle: 40 — 30. Wins his serve so now it's Murray 5, Raonic 4. *Andy, keep it together!*

John says, "Have you played Nairn?"

"No, not yet" I reply. "We were supposed to go off at 10:50 am, but I think we'll play tomorrow instead with the better forecast."

"Well, it's the best course in Scotland," he avows.

I gather he's played a lot here and we launch into a discussion about the fact that Scotland *is* the Home of Golf.

I tell the lads, "'It absolutely is the place where golf—the game that we play,' quoting Malcolm Campbell, 'was created—the defining factor being that our target is a hole in the ground.'"

The Dutch gents had to agree, saying, "Yes, we played a game on ice, but it's not the same."

All the history books about golf, including *Golf in the Making* by Ian T. Henderson and David I. Stirk, trace the evolution of numerous stick and ball games like paganica played in Roman times, to jeu de mail played in Italy and then taken up in France, right up to games played in Holland. Some of the games resembling golf were played in Dutch city streets before edicts against such rowdy games forced the players farther afield. Paintings from the 16th and 17th century show people playing a game they called colf on ice wherever lakes and rivers froze over. Many historians believe that sometime during the Middle Ages, the colf craze traveled across the North Sea from the Netherlands to Scotland, where it was adapted and played on linksland at St Andrews and other places along the coast from Musselburgh near Edinburgh to Dornoch in the Highlands.

Murray takes the first set 6 to 4. A cheer goes up in our lounge, "Andy! Andy! Andy!" Good to see that it is sunny at Wimbledon. The players' shadows are strong. Murray goes 15

Nairn in winter.

love on Raonic's serve but it goes to 15 all when Murray dumps one into the net. It only takes a few seconds for Murray to win the next point, and another few seconds to go 30 all.

"I'm a bit of a geek," I tell the lads, after learning that Alasdair was born in Skye, lives in Glasgow and is a member of Troon. "I've just published a new book about golf in Scotland, and in a story called *Thin Red Line,* which I wrote while staying at Castle Stuart, I talked about how the guide at Culloden Visitor Centre, said, 'The Battle of Culloden was the last battle fought on English soil.'"

I figured that Alasdair, having Highlander ancestry and being intimately familiar with Castle Stuart and the geography of the Inverness area, might find it a bit ironic that I had such a keen interest in this part of the world. And I hoped he'd find me somewhat of a kindred spirit.

The first game of the second set goes to Raonic. The camera pans the Royal Box. All the men are in coat and tie. The women; fancy dresses. No hats, please! It will obscure the view of those seated behind.

Murray makes short work going to 40 love. Drops a shot to go 40 — 15. *Oh Andy!* Now 40 — 30. *You're going the wrong way!* Oh, thank goodness, he pulls it out. It's 1 game all. Raonic wins his serve and goes 2 to 1.

Nearly every seat is taken up now in the 'spike-friendly' bar lounge. Golfers stripping off their waterproofs as they come through the door.

Murray advances to 15 love. Next serve is long. Now 40 love with a forehand that Raonic pushes wide. Raonic wins a point, and it's 2 games all.

I tell the lads, "We know that history is always written by the victors, but this was never English soil! I say in my book, 'this is the Highlands, Nairn is there, Inverness is there, and it was never English soil.'"

I think I've won their hearts, especially Alasdair's, who is the true Scot of the group.

Alasdair quips, "You know, when Scotland has its second referendum and we become independent, Scotland will make all the new rules for golf all over the world. The US will have no say."

He was pulling my leg, but only just a little.

Murray goes 15 love, but Raonic slams a backhand down the the line and takes it to 15 all.

"Have you heard of *To the Linksland?*" Alasdair asks me.

"Oh yes. Love that book. Bamberger" I exclaim, "Michael Bamberger is the author."

"Well, I knew the guy in Crieff who he

wrote about," Alasdair declares. "He was the inspiration for the book."

Oh my. That is fascinating. More kindred spirit synergy. It's 3 games all. Crowd erupts, "Go Andy!"

"How long are you in Scotland?" John asks.

"We started in Turnberry and played the renovated Ailsa course," I respond. "Then we went to The Marcliffe. Have you ever been there?"

They all say no.

"The story in my book called *Monarch of the Marcliffe* is all about the owner, Stewart Spence. He's a mad keen golfer, member of Royal Aberdeen and Cruden Bay. I have a copy of the book to give to Fraser Cromarty, he's the CEO here. It's already signed to him, but here, have a look. I pull the book out of a bag and hand it to John.

Murray! He's on fire. Gets the ad point on Raonic's serve. Murray's advantage is lost with a backhand into the net. Deuce. Service ace for Raonic. Now it's his ad. First serve. Raonic wins next point off his second serve. An, "Ooooh!" resonates from the crowd.

Room is heating up. Gotta take off a layer. Murray up 40 — 15. Raonic rushes the net. Deft drop shot. Murray has no chance. *Oh-oh!* Four games all now.

Raonic's serve sets up a huge smash to go 15 love. Serve and volley forces another error from Murray. Murray gets a point and then another to go 30 all. Everybody's forgotten about the Scottish Open.

Murray has a break point but slams one into the net. Screams above the roar of the crowd.

Murray goes back to his ad and loses it just as quickly. Raonic sends his ad court serve wide. Wins the point and the next one to bring the set to 5 — 4.

Still pouring rain outside. We're glad to be inside where it's warm and dry.

"Where can I buy your book?" John asks. "I always like to buy books when I've met the author."

I wink at John, slip outside, get a book out of the boot of the car, and come back upstairs.

I write an inscription to John and he kindly hands me a tenner.

Murray goes 40 — 15 on his serve. "Andy! Andy!" *Boom. Boom.* Five games all.

Alasdair and I pick up our thread and I say, "I'm a member of Machrihanish, but we also plan to play Shiskine on the way there and then Machrie."

Alasdair cautions, "Machrie is a mess right now."

"We'll go anyway," I shrug. "Then we're going to Troon for The Open. It's sort of funny, people are always surprised when I say I live at Troon in Scottsdale. It's called that because Tom Weiskopf and Jay Morrish designed the course at Troon Country Club some thirty years ago, and they named it as a tribute to Tom's win at Royal Troon in 1973."

Murray holds serve to go 6 all, and Raonic serves first in the tiebreak. Raonic loses that point. Murray serves. The players are both grunting now. Raonic loses the next point. Murray goes 3 — 0 just like that. Raonic to serve again. Gets a point on the board. It's now 3 — 1. Murray steals one back. The Royal box claps vigorously. Murray goes up 5 — 1 with a backhand winner.

Raonic gets to 3 but Murray with 6 points is serving for the set. *C'mon Andy!* Raonic's return doesn't clear the net. *Whew!* That's Murray's second set.

"We were wanting to get to Askernish this year, but it's too complicated," I tell the lads.

"That's the old James Braid course that was lost," Alasdair says.

"It's thought to be an Old Tom Morris design," I say, but it sort of falls on deaf ears.

Raonic is serving but Murray takes the first point, and when Raonic rushes, he drops one into the net to go 15 all.

"We are planning to go to the Open at Troon," I say to Alasdair.

Alasdair replies, "My friend is the archivist at Troon, and I might be able to arrange for you to go in the clubhouse."

My eyes lit up. That would be quite unheard

of while Troon is hosting the Open, as only R&A officials, their VIP guests and players would have access to the clubhouse. "There would be one thing he wants though in return." Alasdair flashes a conspiratorial smile. "You know how hard it is to get on Augusta?"

"I do," I nod.

"Well, he wants a ball marker from Augusta."

"It's 2 games all in the third set."

"Do you mean a fancy ball marker?" I ask.

"No, just an ordinary one that you push into the ground."

"I think I have one of those," I reflect.

Now Alasdair's eyes lit up.

"Let me go see if I have one. If I find it, will you give it to him for me?"

As I stand up to leave the lounge, Alasdair announces, "I'm going down to Kerry for a couple of weeks."

"Don't tell me you'll be going to Lahinch when we're over here in Scotland?" I say, taken

"My friend is the archivist at Troon, and I might be able to arrange for you to go in the clubhouse."

aback. "Have you played Lahinch? That's Kevin's home course!"

He replies wistfully, "No, I've not played Ballybunion or Lahinch."

Kevin picks up on Alasdair's piqued interest and asks, "When will you be there? I could arrange for you to play with another member."

"Oh no, don't…" Alasdair demurs.

Murray blasts a backhand down the line past Raonic to take the ad, and then the game!

"…I don't want you to go to any trouble."

With it now only raining lightly, I go back to the car and dig into my golf bag. I fish around in the plastic Ziploc bag where I keep my tees and ballmarkers. I find the small Augusta National ballmarker, and although it's no longer pristine, I bring it up to the lounge with me.

"Pick a hand," I say to Alasdair. He taps my right hand, I pop it open, and there it is! "You rascal," he says with a big smile.

"I know it's not in the best shape," I admit, "but will you give it to him for me." "Aye," says Alasdair with an ear-to-ear grin.

I don't know if that'll get me into the Troon clubhouse during The Open, but I hand him the mini bribe anyway.

"Don't lose it," I plead. "It's my only one!"

Andy Murray now leads 5 to 4 in the third set after a hard-fought service game.

The gladiators sit for a minute, then Raonic goes to` the baseline to serve. Tough rally with Raonic taking the first and second point fast to go 30 love. *Oh-oh!* Service ace. He holds to extend the set to five games all. When I say his serve is strong, I mean *strong*. It's been clocked as high as 147 mph!

It's now 5:45 pm. Murray goes up 30 love. 40 love. Game.

Umpire requests a ball change during the break while the players rest in their chairs.

Murray with his jittery knees hops up to get back on the court.

Raonic serving now, down 5 to 6.

"I hope Murray wins it in three sets so we can watch the golf," Kevin groans.

"Me too, sweetie," I proclaimed, "I'll be ready to switch to the golf as soon as Murray is holding the bloody trophy!"

Raonic's massive ace clocked at 124 mph earns him 30 love, but then he pushes a backhand wide. Still, he wins the game to get into a third set tiebreaker.

Murray takes the first two points. Now 3 — 0.

"It's lookin' good," Kevin bellows, crossing his fingers.

Murray smells victory and goes to 4 — 0. Now 5 — 0. Crowd on its feet.

When I saw Andy Murray win Wimbledon the first time, we were at Walton Heath in England. The topper would be to see him win while in Scotland!

It's championship point. Murray leads 6 — 1. Net first serve.

Stay focused Andy!

Net second serve. *Ooooooh noooooo!* Raonic

takes another point, 6 — 2. Murray serves wide—Raonic's return finds net.

A monstrous roar goes up on the telly and in our lounge too! We're all on our feet, shouting and clapping until our hands hurt. Scots and Brits everywhere must be euphoric.

Murray: Relief. Smile. Throws his hat into the crowd. Sits. Covers his face with a towel.

Shoulders heave. He's crying tears of joy. Raonic: Stoic. Changes his shirt.

Murray got the job done for his second Wimbledon title. He's overcome with emotion.

Crowd yells. He sobs some more.

Trophy presentation swiftly follows.

Andy is a gracious winner: "Great, great match. Praise to Raonic and his whole team."

The commentator says, "You were so emotional back in 2013. Do you think you're going to enjoy this one a little more?"

"Yeah, I'll make sure I do," Andy declares with exquisite conviction.

And did we have dinner there in the clubhouse? Yes, we did. And did we top it off with sticky toffee pudding? Yes, we did. And how did we rank it? We gave it a 9.5 for presentation…with exquisite conviction!

Nairn

Part 2 — The Course

Although Kevin and I thought we might have a chance to play Castle Stuart the day after the Scottish Open, we used the day instead to play Nairn. We did drop in with *Stroll* books for Stuart & Elaine McColm and Mark & Dede Parsinen, since I had written the story *Thin Red Line* primarily about the Battle of Culloden, while we were staying in the recently remodeled Farmhouse on the Castle Stuart property.

Yet knowing where Nairn was on the map and driving into the town and then getting onto the grounds of Nairn Golf Club, was a whole different matter. For instance, I didn't even know that besides the 18-hole championship course, there is also the 9-hole Cameron Course.

Nairn was founded in 1887 and has an impeccable pedigree. The driving force in the early days was Robert Finlay, born in Edinburgh. His time as a local MP, then a Viscount, and three years as Britain's Lord Chancellor, positioned him perfectly to persuade his London pals to join as members with the initial course design done by Archie Simpson.

Later, Old Tom Morris revised the course and extended it. Twenty years later, five times

Open Champion James Braid put his hand to altering tees and bunkers and creating new greens. Other improvements were undertaken by Ben Sayer and C.K. Cotton, but it is largely considered a Braid course.

A tip: Before you head out to the first tee, one of the best things you can do is pop into the pro shop and pick up, along with a 'Strokesaver', a booklet titled *A Guide to the Wildlife of Nairn Golf Club*, by Alistair Young, Captain (1997 — 1999) with the support of James Asher.

You'll be apprised in the Foreword: "When our golf goes wrong, as it usually does, it is a constant source of delight to be consoled by the natural surroundings of Nairn Golf Club. The essence of the game of golf which we all love is in the resonance of that perfectly struck 3-wood to the 13th, in the fun & fellowship of Saturday's fourball but also in the coconut scent of the gorse or the moment we startled a roe deer at the 17th tee. The three-foot putt just missed never seems to matter when you cast your eyes out to the Firth and are lucky enough to glimpse the dolphins at play."

"When our golf goes wrong, as it usually does, it is a constant source of delight to be consoled by the natural surroundings of Nairn Golf Club."

As the wildlife advisor to the club, Mr Young knows his birds, and describes them in detail. Another lovely passage from the Introduction reads: "We cannot all enjoy the luxury of a handicap of less than five but we can add to the pleasure of our game by knowing a little more about the wildlife we are helping to protect."

He then enlightens us with:

"Nature is never constant and throughout the year the character and feeling of the course changes with the seasons. It is easy for instance to curse the thorns of the ubiquitous gorse bushes but we would never wish to miss the amazing heralding of summer that greets the golfer when it bursts into flower and the

View from the course across the Moray Firth.

fairways are bathed in sunshine yellow."

If for no other reason, you should visit Nairn just to get your own copy of this booklet.

But there are plenty of other incentives to go there!

Having never played there before, I relied heavily on the course guide. Unless you already know the holes, you'll be unaware of the challenges or dangers that lurk hundreds of yards out. Before you tee up however, take a look at the starters hut, where all sorts of fascinating information are posted, such as this hilarious framed sign:

"When primitive man screamed and

beat the ground with sticks, they called it — WITCHCRAFT. When modern man does the same thing, they call it — GOLF."

The first hole looks rather flat, but at the same time, wide and inviting. The first seven holes run out with the Moray Firth on your right. If you slice the ball, you're in trouble. Luckily, that's not my problem...today at least.

Although it is called *The Guide to the Wildlife of Nairn Golf Club*, it is chock-full of information on a variety of grasses, shrubs and low growing plants like Daisy, Dog Violet and Clover, that create a carpet of color along the fairways.

The booklet imparts this knowledge: "Along the burn on the second hole, clumps of Meadowsweet, covered in downy cream colored flowerhead in summer, grow alongside the beautiful and delicate Cuckooflower which in Summer encourages the stunning Orange Tip butterfly." You'll generally be playing into the prevailing westerly wind on the outward seven, where you'll have an ideal opportunity

View across the 17th and 1st greens to the Moray Firth.

Approaching the green at Kopjes — the long Par 3 14th Hole.

to see birds such as Oystercatchers, Curlew and Redshank throughout the year.

On the eighth you reverse direction and have the wind helping; only somehow it didn't help me! The ninth takes you right back into the wind and leads to a modest white house called a bothy.

An oval-shaped bronze plaque hanging above a bench informs that it was originally built in 1877 along with an icehouse for storing salmon. It makes a charming, if modest, halfway house where you can purchase some snacks to fortify you for the returning nine. The plaque discloses:

The fishermen would go out in their Cobble Boats to fish the tide twice daily, once on Saturday, but never on the Sabbath. A Season's catch would be up to 5000 Salmon.

If you think this seaside links course is in any way a pushover, guess again. It's a good test of golf skills, having been the venue for the 1999 Walker Cup, the 2004 Jacques Leglise Trophy, the 2012 Curtis Cup, and many other prestigious tournaments. The humps, hollows and challenging greens will test you too.

I was happy to be heading back toward the clubhouse on the tenth, which borders the farmland of Delnies. The booklet informs it is here the Lapwings are often heard calling. Here, too, the exceptionally bright head of the Yellowhammer can be seen as he sings from the top of the gorse.

Now on the inward nine, with the wind behind me, I picked up several yards off the tee. I even managed to par the hole, which was a 466 yard par 5 for me, and 496 from the members' tees.

A 141 yard par 3 followed, and did me in, like most of the other par 3s. They were all quite long and the 14th hole, called Kopjes, meaning 'small hill' and being the highest point on the course, measured 177 yards from my tee box. That one was a complete disaster, facing the Moray Firth with a strong wind. There was a huge tanker cruising by, out on the firth beyond the green, which I found captivating so my triple bogey six was easily forgotten.

As unkind as the 14th was to me, the 15th hole was a short 223 yard par 4, measuring 306 yards from the members' tees, so I felt like I had a chance. It was a tight driving hole straight into the wind, but when I managed another par I found renewed energy to face the finishing holes.

The final holes start from the shelter of pine trees. Alas, I didn't fare too well; in part due to the wind and the dip in temperature. But my disappointment abated when I shifted my attention to the beautiful bronze sculpture of the magnificent Roe stag nestled down into a lovely hedge behind the 18th green. It was visible earlier from inside the clubhouse, but now, close up from the fairway, it was a particularly magical sight.

And how did Kevin fare? He shot a ho-hum 74; being one of those people who enjoys the luxury of a handicap of less than five.

Thankfully for me, it's not all about score. I'll be back some day to see the Great Spotted Woodpecker or maybe a Velvet Scoter. With a bit of luck, the gorse will be in bloom too and not gobble up too many of my balls.

Eden Mansion and the Old Course

St Andrews

Once upon a time there was a princess who lived in a great big mansion on the outskirts of St Andrews. That was me for two days and nights; and it was a life-altering experience.

It wasn't just that our room, the Royal Eden Suite, was so impressive, it was over the top. Owned now by an enterprising couple, it was once the principal family home of the Haig whisky dynasty.

I had learned a long time ago when I started to spend a lot of time with Kevin in Dublin that when we played golf at Portmarnock, it was on land that was once the private golf course of the Jameson family. It turns out, John Jameson, who hailed from the village of Alloa in Scotland, married Margaret Haig, John Haig's eldest daughter. The couple moved to Dublin where the Jameson Irish Whiskey company was founded. That connects a few interesting dots but doesn't explain why the Irish spell it whiskey instead of whisky. Another mystery to be solved one day!

You might think there are sensors in the driveway when your car approaches the front door of the grand Victorian house-now-hotel,

The dramatic entrance to Eden Mansion.

when an impeccably groomed young man, dressed in tuxedo-like formal attire, appears before you've rolled to a stop.

We asked if we could check in early and were told that if we could wait about ten minutes, our room would be ready. Oh yes, please, we'll happily wait and wander around. The manager of the property, Calum Cruickshank, suggested, "Why don't you have a look at the Gatsby Bar."

Great idea, I agreed, and I headed in that direction straightaway. It was an intimate little room and indeed, it did have a handsome wood bar.

Every square inch of wall was covered in

patterned gold art deco wallpaper and the entire effect was sheer glamour, right down to the vintage Victrola Phonograph with an ornate big horn. I noted that the bar was well stocked with Eden Mill Gin. I had every intention of taking the tour at the distillery the next time I found myself in St Andrews, and that was before I noticed that we could see the building from the window of our suite.

I had discovered the range of Eden Mill gins at the PGA Show back in January, held in Orlando every year. They had set up a table for sampling within the Visit Scotland tourism stand, so naturally I had to have a taste of the one called Love. Well, I had more like three samples over as many days, but who's counting? I really loved this gorgeous pink gin, made with hibiscus and rose petals, so they said. I think, perhaps, I was born in the wrong age, not to have known the pleasures of pink gin. Well, I can make up for it now because I believe it will become available in the US in due time, if it isn't already.

Once we were shown to our room, I knew for sure that I was born into the wrong age. Starting with the very dramatic and luxurious canopy over our bed. There was a wall sconce mounted on top of the cascading drapery with attractive pulls on each side of the bed that were shaped into delicate balls of woven silk.

All the window treatments were crafted with magnificent, scalloped valances in sage green silk damask, featuring swags and beautiful bunting in a soft rose and sage green plaid. I could go on and on. And I will.

The bathroom was perhaps the most opulent one I have ever seen. If the attention to detail of the design was mind-boggling, the expert execution exceeded it. Well, no wonder,

I learned much later that this salle de bains extraordinaire was a Clive Christian creation.

Every inch of wall, including the ceiling, was covered in sophisticated patterned wallpaper. Exquisite carpentry, finished in a sage green color, adorned the entire space. The intricate crown molding even surrounded the inset white porcelain tub where the walls were mirrored instead of papered and tasteful embroidered pillows were placed in the corners for an extra visual treat.

Other elements adding to the aesthetic appeal were handsome carved ornaments in the shape of beautiful bows and mini medallions in rose gold, perfectly matching the rosette candle cups of the attractive chandelier. The shower was a standalone semicircular glass affair of generous proportions. Opposite it were sage green cabinets with extra toiletries and shelves showcasing beautiful porcelain and gold pieces made in Italy. Yes, I picked one up and checked.

Capodimonte no less. It was first made in Naples, Italy, from 1743 to 1759. Apparently, the factory moved to a location near Madrid, Spain for a while and then the Ginori family of Doccia, Italy acquired the molds and is using the crown and N mark that is visible on the bottom. Well, no wonder I am enamored by these eye-catching porcelain pieces—my own kitchen cabinets are full of Ginori dinnerware (although mine are predominantly white because I prefer to eat off a pristine white plate).

We needed to rush away to meet some friends in town and we also had managed to get a tee time on the Old Course around noon. Our plan was to be at least a half-hour early to check in with the starter. When we did, we weren't prepared for what happened next. With a brusque, ex-cop manner, he actually asked us to produce proof of our handicaps. Neither of us had a printed copy of a handicap index card. He glared at us and growled, "Can't you get it on your phones?"

Well, no. We thought he wasn't going to let us play, but catching a glance of the many prestigious private club bag tags gracing our

Portmarnock and Troon golf bags, he relented and gave us the go ahead. My suggestion for anyone planning to play the Old Course, be prepared to produce an up-to-date handicap; and keep in mind the maximum is 36 for both men and women.

It's not uncommon to get a case of the jitters when you walk onto the first tee of this most hallowed ground. In my case, it certainly didn't help to be feeling like such an idiot over the handicap cock-up. Kevin and I certainly knew the requirement for proof of handicap, but we somehow both had amnesia about this small, important detail.

"If there is ever a time you want to have a good start, it's on the Old Course, when there are always dozens of people crowding around the fences."

If there is ever a time you want to have a good start, it's on the Old Course, when there are always dozens of people crowding around the fences, and it seems as if all eyes are on you. Whether you are teeing off on the first or holing out on the eighteenth, you are on view for scores of golfing pilgrims and sightseers, who all act like they are impressed with your booming drives or collectively groan when your ball lips out of the final hole.

In Kevin's case, he bombed his tee shot to position A. The Canadian father and son duo that we were paired with both hit gorgeous tee shots as well. I hit a weak drive but at least it was in the right direction. We were off. Kevin had three birdies and one eagle in his round of 74 and finished very strongly.

On the 18th green, playing to the crowd, Kevin announced, "I have this putt to win the Open Championship!"

One guy in the crowd took the bait and bellowed back, "I have 100 pounds riding on you!" When Kevin holed his final putt for a birdie, a big cheer went up and the guy shouted,

"You've just won me 100 pounds!" Chest puffed out; Kevin took a bow.

The thing I remember most vividly from my own round is my birdie on the ninth when I nearly drove the green. Wind helping. The yardage from my tee was 261 yards and from only 30 yards out, I putted the ball to within 6 inches of the hole. Everyone in my foursome yelled, "That's good!" There's nothing like scooping up your ball and strutting off the green to savor the moment.

Riding the wave of confidence, I started the back nine going 5, 5, 5 and thought I might have a stellar finish. My streak did not continue, but I enjoyed the experience on the Old Lady all the same. It wasn't so much of a stroll, though, like in the feature story of my second book, *A Stroll on the Old Lady* — it was probably more of a do-si-do.

On the tee of the par 4 12th hole known as Heathery, we had the Eden Estuary on our right and the tide was out. The 13th hole makes a turn toward the town, and we had the wind behind us once again. This is where you find the famous group of bunkers known as Coffins. Be advised, steer clear of them. There is plenty more danger lurking on this hole, playing as a par 5 for me. The friendly looking grass to your right might be tempting, but that is the Eden Course!

In fact, the Eden, Strathtyrum and Balgove Courses are all on this side of the Old Course, but they were built much later. Most golf historians agree that golf was played on the linksland of the Old Course for at least six centuries, but at least one historian, Sir Guy Campbell, believed that some primitive holes existed as far back as the 1100s.

You could make a case for it, given the fact that King David I of Scotland granted the linksland to the people of St Andrews in 1123. Since that time, the citizens of the town have had the right to use the links for recreation, with golf evolving as the favorite pastime.

Golf was so popular in Scotland that it was banned in 1457 by King James II, essentially to punish the men who were not practising archery, which was far more important to the defense of the realm. This edict became the first written reference to golf, and therefore we can surmise the game has been played since the early 1400s for it to have become so popular.

Although the iconic clubhouse of the Royal and Ancient Golf Club of St Andrews sits behind the first tee, it's just one of many clubs that have playing privileges on the Old Course, along with the public. And since the course is closed on Sunday, except for the playing of the Open Championship or a tournament like the Alfred Dunhill Links Championship, the public literally wanders all over the course, like they would any common land — especially an inviting expanse of green grass near the West Sands beach.

"the public literally wanders all over the course, like they would any common land."

And when you get to the 18th tee, there are so many tourists around, who seem oblivious to the golfers, you might think it's a picnic Sunday, no matter what day it is. Group after group of visitors are clamoring to get their picture taken on the Swilcan Bridge that's only about 100 yards in front of the 18th tee. Consequently, it can feel like an interminable wait to hit your tee shot, as it did for us.

At last, it was time to launch the final drive, with the line being the clock on the R&A clubhouse. There appears to be plenty of fairway, and there is, but that's because you are really aiming for the first fairway, and chances are good that a group will have just teed off and they are walking right into your line of fire!

And so it goes, the finishing hole can be equally bewildering and exhilarating, with golfers going in both directions, people of all nationalities and descriptions wandering hither and thither over the links, and even cars streaking across Granny Clark's Wynd — all at the same time!

Score on the last hole and score for the complete round are only one way to define the feeling of finishing this most famous course in the world, where millions of commoners, professionals and royalty have walked the glorified ground.

In a word, I think it's accurate to say, the four of us were elated.

After handshakes all around, we cleared the green, with Kevin and me joining friends for dinner at the New Golf Club of St Andrews, which overlooks the 18th fairway of the Old Course. New is all relative here, though. The New Club was founded in 1902 and took its name mainly to distinguish itself from the very old club, that being the Royal and Ancient Golf Club formed in 1754, and originally called the Society of St Andrews Golfers. Yet the R&A, as it is commonly known, didn't even lay a foundation stone for their own clubhouse until July 1853!

However, at the time of the New Club's formation in 1902, there was a considerable amount of discussion about the name of the club. Apparently, the majority of early supporters were Thistle Club members who wanted to retain that name. On the New Club's website, it says:

"A proposal was made for the Tom Morris Golf Club, which the great man himself modestly insisted against."

To have drinks in the lounge, dinner in the restaurant, and walk in the footsteps of so many of golf's historical figures, including Old Tom Morris, was certainly a treat. Even if, sadly, it is here where Old Tom, the most famous man of golf and the father of modern greenkeeping, met his death in 1908 when he fell down a flight of stairs.

Born in 1820 in St Andrews, and apprenticed to Allan Robertson at age 14, Morris learned the skills to be a club and ball maker, back in the day when the feathery ball was at its height of popularity. Robertson, considered to be the world's first professional golfer and the best golfer of his day, often partnered with Morris in challenge matches and legend has it the team was never defeated.

When the new gutta-percha (nicknamed guttie) ball first came into use around 1848 as a cheaper and more reliable alternative to the feathery, Morris and Robertson had a falling out. As the story goes, Morris was seen playing a guttie ball (loaned to him when his own feathery fell apart mid round) and Robertson, who felt betrayed, believing his profitable ball making business was threatened, fired Morris on the spot.

As fate would have it, in 1851 Prestwick Golf Club on the Ayrshire coast was just starting up, and Morris was hired to design and maintain the course. At Prestwick, Morris ran his own golf equipment business, selling gutties and making clubs. This was a momentous year for Morris, as Tom Morris Jr was born in 1851. Young Tom, along with his revered father, became one of the greatest golfers of this age.

When the Open Championship was created in 1860, the competition was held at Prestwick. It came about in large part because of the sudden death of Allan Robertson after an attack of jaundice at the age of 44 in 1859, to establish who was now the best golfer in the world.

It was Tom Morris whose drive was the first shot of the event. Although he did not win the competition that year (Willie Park Sr beat him by two strokes), Morris went on to win the Open four times, as did Young Tom, who started playing in what was now an annual tournament, at the age of fourteen. To this day, Young Tom is still the youngest competitor. Not only that, he also won the event four times in a row, and is the only person to hold that distinction. It is almost unimaginable what he might have accomplished if Young Tom had not passed away at the tender age of 24, on Christmas Day 1875. Most thought he died of a broken heart after his wife had died in childbirth in September that year, but the official cause of death was pulmonary hemorrhage causing apnea.

The senior Morris, who became known simply as 'Old Tom', returned with his family to St Andrews in 1865, and assumed the position as the professional golfer and greenkeeper for the Old Course. Along with raising the condition of the course to a very high standard, he was sought out to design other courses in Scotland and Ireland.

It was Old Tom who built two new greens,

the first and eighteenth on the Old Course, which later led to the 18th hole being named Tom Morris. Along with all his other accolades, Old Tom still holds the record of the oldest winner of The Open Championship at age 46.

All this history, the sense of drama that has taken place in this theater of grass, made our entire day on the Old Course much more special. To some first-time golfers on the Old Course, it may seem flat and featureless. But to a student of the game like me, it's enchanting to have played a round on a golf course that has been around for six centuries.

For entirely different reasons, we were looking forward to our dinner at Eden Mansion the next night, following golf at Kingsbarns. Displeasure about any errant balls or less than gratifying scores immediately dissolved upon returning to the sumptuous environment there.

Indeed, once we were back, Calum Cruickshank seated us in the lounge so we could order drinks and have a look at the menu. It's *so* civilized the way they do it. You never feel rushed. If the attention lavished upon you when you arrive is exemplary, the staff ratchets up a notch at dinner, providing literally white-glove service.

We ordered a bottle of Sauvignon Blanc, Eradus Estate, New Zealand, 2014 while we sat in the luxuriously appointed lounge. We were waited on by men in tailored black dress tailcoats. Again, from another time — a Downton Abbey era. Along with several sips of wine, we'd studied the menu, and our dinner order was taken. Calum appeared at our table to say, "We'll take you through now."

In the dining room, wherever you cast your eye, there was ornate crown molding with beautiful beige swag valences trimmed with black beads, and clear crystal hanging from elaborately decorated pole brackets. Outstanding pieces of period furniture, sculptures, paintings, mirrors, porcelain figurines and other stunning enamel and Meissen pieces were tucked into every nook and cranny. And in case you're wondering, the meal, served on silver trays, equaled its surroundings.

For appetizers, Kevin ordered the Eden Oak Gin Cured Salmon and I had the Golden Cross Goats Cheese served with beetroot, pears and truffle. For our main courses, I had the Roast Fillet of Cod served with brown shrimp, wilted spinach, chives and confit garlic mash. Kevin was much more adventurous, having the Loin of Highland Venison served with thyme fondant, soft herbs, baked carrot, and roasted turnip. He devoured every morsel on his plate and could still find space for a few bites of my scrumptious meal.

And the sticky toffee pudding? None on the menu that night. We had to settle for the Ginger and Orange Cake, served with Eden Ale Sorbet and Haig Whisky-Soaked Sultanas. One serving, two spoons please. It was awesome.

On warm summer nights, even if you've already walked the Old Course, I suggest a stroll in the grounds of the Victorian walled garden. There you'll find graceful figurative weathered stone sculptures, flowering plants of every color and description, and one other most unusual feature — some very tall trees that the gardener told me were called 'monkey' trees. A pair of them, looming at least one hundred feet tall, stood like two sentinels at the garden gate.

It was their bark that first caught my attention. It looked like thousands of old-fashioned rounded, wooden abacus beads, but all jumbled up. This bumpy, higgledy-piggledy, disorderly surface is probably why the tree (indigenous to Argentina) is also nicknamed monkey *puzzle*.

It only took quick online research to learn that the Victorians became enamored with these trees and planted them everywhere in both Britain and Ireland. Apparently, sometime around 1800, Archibald Menzies, a mad keen Scottish botanist and tree collector, germinated seeds on a sea voyage from South America back to Britain and presented five young trees to Kew Gardens. And that's how the craze started.

Eden Mansion is truly a must-see grand historic residence. It's the way a great golf course is supposed to leave you feeling — like you can't wait to come back.

Kingsbarns Course and Clubhouse.

Kingsbarns

A new course at the home of golf

I could say this is where it all started for visionary golf club developer Mark Parsinen, but that would not be entirely true. His actual first foray into golf was at Granite Bay with the golf architect Kyle Phillips. And it was Kyle who he brought to this, his first project in Scotland. To be asked to design a course in Scotland — the Home of Golf, well that's a feather in one's cap.

Although many of our golf travel clients are keen to make the pilgrimage to play the Old Course at St Andrews, the overwhelming majority come away saying their favorite course in the Kingdom of Fife was Kingsbarns. It's that good.

People often mispronounce the name, calling it Kingbarns, but it is Kingsbarns. Several years ago, while standing next to him on the fifth tee, my caddie on that day pointed to somewhere yonder and said, "This is where the King's barns used to be." An online search confirmed that the barns used to hold grain that was later transported to the royal Falkland Palace.

It should be noted that Kingsbarns is also the name of a village, with several historic buildings. Former notable residents include the famous philosopher Robert Adamson (1852–1902) and Alexander Peebles (1856–1934), who became a prospector and mine owner in New Zealand. Both men were born in Kingsbarns, located just 6.5 miles southeast of St Andrews.

The official golf story, as told by late Scottish golf historian David Malcolm, goes: "In the eighth decade of the 18th Century, at the same time as the Thirteen States were declaring their independence and the Constitution of the United States was scripted, the Merchants and Lairds of Kingsbarns drafted articles to form the Kingsbarns Golfing Society.

Golf has been enjoyed over the links land of Kingsbarns beginning in 1793. Attired in their blue coats, the Kingsbarns men met for their Spring and Autumn Meetings to challenge for the Society's medals on the links and to enjoy the conviviality of friends over dinner in the Golfers Hall. The Society continued to wager, wine, and dine for decades until the Cambo Estate tenant farmer ploughed up the links in 1850 in order to add to his farmable area. Farmland in that period was more valuable than land set aside for golf.

Prompted and inspired by Lady Erskine of Cambo, the old Kingsbarns Golfing Society was re-established and founded as Kingsbarns Golf Club in 1922 and Willie Auchterlonie laid out a nine-hole course on the links about Kingsbarns Bay. This course served the golfing needs of the locals and holidaymakers until the onset of World War II when the Links was mined in the national security defense effort, and it quickly reverted to rough pasture.

Golf was resurrected on Kingsbarns Links at the dawning of the 21st century as the only Scottish course to be built on links land in over 70 years. With its seaside setting, Kingsbarns joined the great old courses of nearby St Andrews and Carnoustie, bringing with it a new dimension to the traditional Scottish game."

We were paired with two lads who were up from London. One of them hailed originally from Sweden. He certainly had the Swedish look about him in both dress and mannerisms.

Think of Henrik Stenson, who went on to win the Open Championship at Royal Troon, and you have the picture. The other lad was equally stylish. They both played off about 8 or 9 handicaps and were a joy to spend time with.

Part of the reason this course is so beautiful, and fun, relates to the routing. It takes you through linksy terrain, then through a bit of a forest, and finishes with a links feel again. There's a wonderful variety of holes and rhythm to your round that is utterly unique.

The first hole starts out in a northerly direction, but by the time you have finished all eighteen, you've covered every point on the compass. With five sets of tees, the course measures between 5257 yards to 7224 yards from the championship tees, so there's plenty of challenge for players of all skill levels.

Majestic views are afforded everywhere on the course, but the dogleg left par 5 twelfth is a real gem. It hugs the curving coastline of the North Sea and stretches to 606 yards from the back tees. At 442 yards for lady me, it's still plenty long, yet

Kingsbarns 15th Hole.

I can't wait to stand on the forward tee even though it sits far below the other four elevated ones. It really gets my adrenaline going as I relish the chance to get on the peninsula-like green in three. The name of the hole, Orrdeal, suggests that it will, in fact, be an ordeal. But it actually takes its name from the former landowners of the green site, the Orr family.

Another favorite hole is the par 3 fifteenth. Although it's relatively short, ranging from 110 to 212 yards, with trees left and a rocky coastline to your right, it can be treacherous, especially if the tide is in and the waves are crashing onto the rocks. I'll never forget the first time I played here in 2003. Although my playing partner and I started as a twosome, we came to a halt on the par 3 second hole, where a Japanese couple were waiting to tee off. We wound up joining them for the rest of the round.

"with trees left and a rocky coastline to your right, it can be treacherous, especially if the tide is in and the waves are crashing onto the rocks."

It was a special golf experience. I'd never played with anybody who did not speak a word of English. Husband and wife, both had caddies who had to lug around heavy leather pro-golfer size bags, weighing probably 50+ pounds, stuffed with balls, gloves, umbrella, rain gear and a full complement of 14 clubs.

I felt bad for the lady's caddie, who was always on the tee box with both of us, but other than pointing in the general direction of the tee shot, he was relegated to being a mute Scottish sherpa. I wasn't a seasoned player back then, but I did know enough about golf etiquette not to sponge off her caddie, asking him for pointers.

When we got to the 15th hole, my lady companion hit a weak shot into the rocks on the right. My own shot found grass, but I'd pushed it out to the right, and it trickled a couple of yards down a slope. With the tall, over-hanging branches of the trees on the left, you had to flight your ball as straight as an arrow. While the caddie made a cursory attempt to find the other lady's ball, he quickly determined it was irretrievable and she had to take a drop.

With it being somewhat cold and windy, with rain threatening, I wasn't inclined to stand around much longer. I chipped up near the flag

Kingsbarns 18th Green

and managed to hole-out for a par. The caddie, having had to restrict himself to just pointing this way and that and waving his arms around, bellowed in his strong East Neuk brogue, "My goodness lass, you're up and down faster than a bride's nightie!" We both had a good laugh.

Back to the round of today. As usual, when the temperature dropped toward the end of the round, I struggled a bit more. Irish Kevin is always making fun of me and saying, "You're not going to die of hypo *termia*." That's exactly how it sounds when he says it. Hypo *termia* has become a running joke with us, as I'm often dressed in four or five layers. Meanwhile, the Scots and Irish are almost always wearing just a golf shirt and shorts.

Kingsbarns 18th Green at sunrise.

The two guys paired with us were part of a larger group and several of their *fans* were waiting by the eighteenth green to cheer them on. The final hole is very challenging to say the least, beginning with a blind tee shot over a prominent hill. The approach shot is an intense test of nerves and concentration to reach a smallish green on the other side of a deep ravine. There is a burn at the very bottom that was uncovered during construction of the course.

The complete story is artfully told in *Scottish Golf Links* with Photography by Iain Macfarlane Lowe, Historical Commentary by David Joy, and Architectural Observations by Kyle Phillips.

An excerpt: "It was decided early in construction, that the final hole at Kingsbarns would benefit from having a stream protecting the front edge of the green. To this end, a search began, near to the present 10th tee, for the source of the outflow further down the course. Just below the surface solid stone slabs were found and, under these, a beautifully constructed dry-stone walled river. This feature was excavated as it made its rather erratic way towards the 18th green.

With a final twist, the burn, now nine feet under the natural site level, turned directly along the front of the green. To the amazement of all, a bridge was also uncovered and, after some minor repair, it is now once again in use. The green was slightly lowered, but still towers above the water hazard, and the fairway was lowered to gently slope down to the burn. Research discovered that the river was constructed during the first decade of the 1800s as part of a program of draining land, it was routed to tie in with the bridge constructed at a much earlier time."

Fascinating as the story may be, the burn is a card-wrecking water hazard to be avoided at all costs.

The guys all had a stellar finish. Me, not so much, but I do keep my scorecard from the last time I played there to remind me of my best round on that course.

I had a terrific young English caddie who was a student at the University of Aberdeen, founded in 1495, highly regarded but lesser known than St Andrews University, established about 80 years earlier. He was a perfect caddie for me that day. His judgement in club selection kept me out of hazards. His sharp eyesight led to a 96, which could easily have been a 95 or 94 if I hadn't had a couple of lip-outs on the greens.

I sometimes wonder where he is now. If only he could be my caddie for life, whenever I play golf anywhere in the world. Now I have my darling Kevin, whose eyesight is just as sharp, more than keen to keep me out of the hazards, and there to celebrate my ecstatic moments at all the faraway places we are blessed to go!

The spectacular beauty of Shiskine, Isle of Arran.

Shiskine

A Dream Come True

I have wanted to play Shiskine for the longest time—ever since I first heard of it more than ten years ago. I was always intrigued about a course out on an island that's just 12 holes. It sounded so idyllic, and so it turned out to be.

The closest I got to it before now was in 2013, on our way from the Ayrshire coast to Machrihanish. Kevin and I wanted to test the ferry system that provided an alternative to going north around Glasgow and skirting the Firth of Clyde, a three-hour drive. Don't get me wrong, it's a beautiful trip worth taking, but I've done it 30 or 40 times, so I was excited about exploring a new route.

The first time, our ferry landed in Brodick and it was all we could manage to traverse the slow, winding road to Lochranza to catch the next ferry that would take us to the Mull of Kintyre. It was the last boat out, so we had no choice but to take on the challenge, Stirling Moss style, stressful as it was at the time. We made it without a single minute to spare.

From the Grand Prix History website, I learned that after Stirling's parents tried to steer him into various professions, for which he proved to be a total misfit, it became clear that Stirling had no aptitude for anything but racing. Eventually his father relented and allowed Stirling to borrow his BMW sports car that he had recently purchased. It was in this BMW that Moss would start to compete in local speed trials. Ironically, Kevin has driven nothing but BMWs since he bought his first car a year after finishing college.

This time we could plan properly, with a hotel booked for two nights and our golf set up for 11:20 am on Tuesday the 19th of July. At last, I would have my chance to play Shiskine!

The Course Guide, of what is now called the Shiskine Golf & Tennis Club, states that the club was formed in 1896. Willie Fernie of Troon designed the original 9-hole course, but only the 5th and 9th holes survive intact.

The booklet goes on to inform:

"In September 1912, agreement was reached to extend the course to 18 holes. The existing 9-hole layout was scrapped, and new holes were created, two on the now Crow's Nest shelf. Six of the holes were on Drumadoon Hill, but during the 1914-1918 war they reverted to their natural state and were later deemed not to be of an acceptable standard. They were seldom played and gradually fell out of use."

We changed our tee time to 1:20 pm to give us a more leisurely breakfast at Auchrannie Resort. It's quite a sprawling place with lodges, a spa, and a few different restaurants. Some were fancier than others, but the entire resort has a rustic feel. Going across the String Road, one of only two roads that go east to west on the island, we reached the course early enough to have a brief chat with the Head Professional, Dougie Bell (pronounced like Doogie). A more amiable fellow you're never likely to meet.

At 12:20 pm Dougie said, "I don't want to rush you, but if you want to go off at 12:25, there is an opening."

"Oh yes," Kevin and I said in unison.

"We don't usually warm up anyway," I went on to explain. Not wise maybe, but true. We rushed to the car to get our shoes and load my golf clubs on my motorized trolley.

Five minutes later we were on the first tee with our scorecards and a yardage book that turned out to be quite helpful.

Dougie made sure to tell us, "On the third hole, aim for the black and white marker, don't aim for the big yellow signal flag!" (Once out on the course, a sign tells you to remove the signal flag when you reach the green and replace it when you are leaving.) He further mentioned, "There are members playing behind you, so if you get confused, you can call them through and then you can follow them."

He chuckled, then delivered the oft-heard advice, "There are some blind shots, but they're only blind the first time."

The reason this is so hilarious is, a blind shot is always blind. You cannot see the target on a par 3 (yes, there are blind par 3s like the exhilarating Himalayas at Prestwick, the Old Tom Morris-designed Dell at Lahinch, and the eccentric fifteenth at Cruden Bay) or the landing area of the longer holes. That never changes. What Dougie meant is, the second time onward you'll see the entire shot in your mind's eye (i.e. your imagination). You must *exercise* your imagination on this course like no other.

All I can tell you is that this is the most fun I've *ever* had playing golf. Anybody who doesn't have fun playing this course should give up the game altogether. For those of you who are not eager to play 18 holes, the 12 at Shiskine make a perfect magical round. Especially if you embrace the idea of being creative while playing, rather than being fixated on the numbers printed on the scorecard.

For me, it was the closest I have come to the childlike feeling of being *at play*. As adults, all too often, we have lost touch with our early memories of having playful outdoor experiences, where we interact with other children (or maybe our imaginary friends) and encounter the wonders of our world. The wonders can be as simple as cool grass under our bare feet or being on a natural path through enchanting woods hearing the birdsong. From my childhood, I have vivid memories of standing on a smooth creek bed, the mud oozing between my toes, where I could catch tadpoles and see the luminous iridescent wings of the dragonflies, and the glow of fireflies at sundown. It is this delightful wondrous feeling that playing Shiskine conjured up in my mind.

There's another unique thing about this course. Kevin and I both played off the same yellow tees! The other tees, red and white, are reserved for competitions. Dougie had said, "Everybody plays off the yellow tees for a bounce game."

"What's a bounce game?" I asked him, unfamiliar with the phrase. "That's when you're just going out for fun, and it is not a medal round."

Whatever it takes for you to get to the Isle of Arran, I encourage you to do it. There are seven golf courses on this island, but based on its glorious reputation, I was determined to play just this one. Later we met a young lad who proudly informed us, "After playing Shiskine I've now completed five of the seven courses on the island." That was so precious to me, as many of our clients are on a quest to play the Top 100 in the world, but from his expression, I could tell his more modest quest was just as enthralling for him.

Without a doubt, for breathtaking beauty, my favorite hole was The Shelf. The tiny tee box is perched on an extremely elevated bit of turf that snuggles up to the sheer rock face of the dramatic Drumadoon Cliff. From this exhilarating height you have a panoramic view over the Kilbrannan Sound, the western arm of the Firth of Clyde. Further north along the coast is the intriguing King's Cave, described as having a treasure trove of Norse carvings and Ogham inscriptions.

In his book, *The Guide to Mysterious Arran,*

Geoff Holder tells us: "A pair of legendary stories are attached to the cave. The first is that it was once home to Fingal, here represented not just as a hero but as a giant. "The most persistent current legend, however, is that Robert the Bruce took refuge in the cave on his way from Rathlin Island to the Scottish mainland, and it was here that he encountered the resilient spider whose persistence inspired him to never give up his quest for the crown. A quest which eventually led to the famous victory over the English at Bannockburn."

To celebrate our round at Shiskine, we indulged in refreshing mint chocolate chip ice cream in the airy clubhouse cafe, then set out for the standing stones at the Machrie Moor. Kevin wasn't particularly interested in making the 2.5 mile round trip, but I was especially keen, having read in the Holder book that Machrie Moor is one of the best stone circle sites in the UK.

From the car park, I went through a gate up a narrow dirt road, really just a farm track with grass growing in the middle. On each side, dozens of sheep were grazing. Unconstrained

Machrie Moor standing stone

by typical fences, the flock could wander willy-nilly, chomping on the lush green grass. Some were shorn already, others wooly as could be, and on this particular day, deemed a 'heat wave' in Scotland, seemed to be bleating, "Hey, you there, can you give me a haircut?"

I have seen a lot of sheep in my time, but on this walk, one was kneeling with her front legs tucked under her. Kneeling! Her wooly butt up in the air, she looked straight at me as if to say, "What's the matter, haven't you ever seen a sheep do yoga? It's like Downward Facing Dog, but it's the Ruminant Dandelion Pose!"

Sheep doing yoga.

The road led to fields full of Foxglove, a delicate tubular flower, magnificent magenta in color. I was soon to be rewarded a good half mile out when I encountered the first stone circle, believed to be a Bronze Age cairn, marking the burial site of a rather important person.

Measuring about 75 feet in diameter, dating back to 4000 BC, it was once surrounded by a complete circle of stones. But many had been removed over the ages, leaving only seven upright stones with five more strewn about.

I met two guys, one tall and one short, who were on the return and I asked them, "How much farther to the standing stones?"

The tall one replied, "About fifteen more minutes."

"Is it worth it?" I pressed.

"Oh, aye," they said, both being Scottish. "But I don't know how spiritual it is," the short one volunteered with a smile.

"You're a golfer," tall guy said, noticing my Masters visor, which I'd kept on after our round of golf.

"Yes, I am. I came over with my sweetheart to play Shiskine," I tossed a thumb over my shoulder, "he's back in the car reading a book." We all had a laugh about that.

They returned to the car park, and I continued along the path through the meadows. The mountains in front of me were stunning, and as I climbed higher, when I glanced backward, the sea down below was equally beautiful. Dougie was spot-on when he said, "It's well worth it. The views are spectacular."

I passed some smaller standing stones, and finally got to the most majestic one I've ever seen outside Stonehenge.

The solitary stone was possibly twenty feet high. Reddish in color, it had to be sandstone.

The very top was etched into an elegant wavy pattern. With verdant fields in all directions and framed by the stately mountains, it was an ethereal place.

On the walk back, I met people from Scandinavia and San Diego. But most of the time I had the path to myself. My thoughts drifted to the cultures existing long before us and their mystical ways in these ancient moorlands.

I had picked up *The Guide to Mysterious Arran* on the ferry and became intrigued with the prospect of learning about folklore, fairies, and stone circles.

I read a fascinating tidbit in the introduction: The island is considered to be Hebridean and is both Highlands and Lowlands. The Highland Boundary Geological Fault Line runs midway through the island, so essentially you have all of Scotland in a microcosm.

"The island is considered to be Hebridean and is both Highlands and Lowlands."

When I bought the book in the eclectic shop on the Cal Mac ferry, I carried it back to where Kevin and I were sitting. But I only got as far as the first paragraph when I decided to return to the lady who sold me the book to ask her a burning question.

"Excuse me," I said, "when I see the word gaelic, I'm not sure how to pronounce it.

Do you say gay-lick or gall-ick?"

She smiled ear-to-ear. "Where I'm from we pronounce it gay-lick, but I don't speak it myself."

Her badge told me she was named Tricia. She had lovely strawberry blonde hair, pulled back into a ponytail, and was wearing a simple white blouse and black pants.

"Where are you from, yourself?" I queried.

There was a framed hand drawn map of Scotland, showing all the Hebridean Islands on the wall behind her. Tricia pointed to a tiny peninsula to the west of Fort Williams, jutting out into the Sound of Sleat, facing the little island called Eigg. "Here's where I live."

"Oh my. You live way up there? How in the world do you get there?" I blurted, shocked at the distance she would have to travel to get to Ardrossan where we caught the ferry on the Ayrshire coast.

"I have to go up here, through here, over here, around this way..." Tricia said, tracing a circuitous northern route with her finger. Anticipating my next question, she volunteered, "It's not too bad, I work two weeks on, two weeks off."

Since the shop was quiet except for a young girl buying a small tub of ice cream, Tricia expanded a bit more, "See all these places like Arisaig? Well, anything ending in 'aig' is a Viking word."

"Oh wow. That's interesting," I said, my eyes roaming over the map in search of other aig names.

She seemed so open and I ventured to ask, "What's it like living someplace so remote?" "It's pretty quiet," Tricia said matter-of-factly. "We don't have electricity. We're off the grid."

Off the grid, indeed!

I was dumbfounded, having never met anybody who lived without electricity in the year 2016. It took me a few moments to process her stark reality. "How do you manage?"

"We have a gas generator," she said with a note of exasperation.

I voiced my concern. "What would it take to get electricity to where you live?"

"Well, the last vote we had about twenty years ago, and we were told it would take about £300,000 to get a line down there."

With that, we heard the rumble and felt the shudder of the ferry, reversing engines to slow down and dock in the terminal. Tricia immediately flew into action, closed the shop, and we said our goodbyes.

As we got ready to disembark onto a small island that was a borderland, I too, felt like I was reversing my engine in so many different ways. Geologically. Politically. And even supernaturally.

As the cover promised, the Holder book had numerous stories about fairies and spirits in Arran and there's even a place called Fairy Dell, rumored to be a gateway to the land of the fairies. Myths and legends are legion. Many stories in the *Mysterious Arran* book are excerpted from a much more massive book known as *The Book of Arran*.

The first date of publication was 1910 and edited by J. A. Balfour. But the story I'm about to share is from Chapter XII on Folk Lore, in the second volume by W. M. Mackenzie.

The text I accessed online says the original of this book is in the Cornell University Library. That seems to have a tinge of strangeness to it too, doesn't it? Here it is.

The Hunchbacked Weaver

"Ages long ago there was a hunchbacked weaver dwelling in Loch Ranza. One day as he was going to the hill to cut brackens, he suddenly came upon a band of fairies as they were actively engaged at dancing in a green, sunny, secluded hollow. Full of curiosity he lay down at the back of a turf dyke to observe their antics. Active and nimble were they at the dancing, and the tune they had was 'Monday Tuesday, Monday Tuesday.' He soon got tired of this short tune, and he jumped to his feet, and shouted out 'and Wednesday.'

On seeing a man near them, the little folk started, but that did not put a stop to their diversion. They continued dancing to the tune 'Monday Tuesday and Wednesday,' and conceived that the tune was the better of the turn the weaver put in it. To show him their gratitude, they took the hump off his back and placed it on the top of the turf dyke. The weaver went home rejoicing, light as a feather and straight as a ramrod.

It happened that another diminutive hunchbacked weaver resided at Loch Ranza at the very same time, and on hearing how his neighbor got rid of his hump, he determined that he would try the same plan in order to get rid of his own hump. Up he goes to the hill where the fairies were, and he found them there dancing as lively as ever. He listened for a short time, and then shouted out, 'Monday Tuesday Wednesday Thursday Friday Saturday' but instead of improving on the tune, he spoiled it out and out. The little folk were so displeased at him for spoiling the tune, that they lifted the other man's hump off the dyke and placed a second hump on the top of the other and sent him home twice as hunched as he was before."

So maybe when you are waiting for the ferry at Lochranza, you could indulge in replaying your round at Shiskine in your own mind, and refrain from composing any new verses for the fairies you might see dancing in a glen.

Machrihanish

Mull of Royalty

It's always a thrill to visit Machrihanish and this time was no different. My love affair started with my first romp around the course in 2003, which convinced me on the spot to join the club. Luckily, I was playing with a member who was willing to propose me to the deciding committee.

Getting to this remote part of Scotland certainly requires planning. That is, unless you have a private helicopter. Thankfully, all we had to do was catch a ferry from Lochranza on Arran over to Kintyre. We knew not to take the wee road down the east coast of the peninsula, rather to cross over to the bigger A83 on the west coast.

In fact, we pick up the A83 near Kennacraig, where we'll be catching the ferry over to Islay in a couple days' time. We zipped along, with views of the Paps of Jura and then Islay off to our right while we sped toward Campbeltown and then Machrihanish.

When we reached the Ugadale Hotel (built in 1898 and masterfully restored to a very high standard by Southworth Development for the 2012 reopening), a parking space right in front was waiting for us. We were ecstatic to be shown

The historic Old Tom Morris links, set in natural dunes, overlooking Machrihanish Bay.

to the luxurious Duchess of Argyll Suite — the same room we had last time. Our stay right here in 2013 led to 'Knock the Spots Off', the final story of my book, *A Stroll on the Old Lady*. 'Old Lady' of course being the Old Course at St Andrews.

We didn't waste any time making a reservation at the Old Clubhouse Pub and lucked out with a perfect cozy table in the corner of the bar. We started our meal with a refreshing bottle of Panul, a Chilean Sauvignon Blanc. And ended our meal, like every other one on our Scottish Golf Odyssey, with sticky toffee pudding for dessert. As the self-appointed sticky toffee authorities, we were obligated to taste as many as we could.

The old stone building served as the original clubhouse of the Machrihanish Golf Club back in the days of Old Tom Morris, who was hired in 1879 to expand the then 12-hole course to 18. It was Old Tom who moved the first hole to its current position, and it is now recognized as one of the best opening holes in all of golf. Some would argue that it is *the* best, as you must

Sign on the first tee.

drive over a crescent-shaped inlet of the Atlantic Ocean to reach the fairway. It is beautiful and daunting, especially at high tide.

I have written about Machrihanish a lot, yet I never get tired of describing it or playing it.

It's one of those experiences that fills you with anticipation hours or even days before you get there and comes back to you again and again in reverie.

Before playing the historic Machrihanish Golf Club course, we built in an extra day to experience the new Machrihanish Dunes course. We played it when it first opened and had trouble finding our way around. Not this time. Peter, the genial starter, came to the first tee with us to give some pointers. Also, there was better signage on each tee box, providing an aerial drawing of each hole and small signs on the greens showing us which direction to go for the next tee. It's an enormous time saver to know where to park your trolley when you get up near each green.

Because the course was built on an SSSI (Site of Special Scientific Interest), the architect, David McLay Kidd, was not permitted to move much land. Mach Dunes, as many call it, is very proud of the fact that of 259 acres, only seven were disturbed during the construction of the course.

"that this remote part of Kintyre boasts the most famous Scottish lady golfer, Isabella (Belle) Robertson, was reason enough for me to go there."

I saw the land back in 2003 long before it became a golf course and enjoyed taking snapshots of numerous sheep grazing all over the dunes. As the world's first lawn mowers they did an excellent job keeping the turf low yet springy. It's positively marvelous to see the linksland go from the domain of the sheep and rusty, abandoned farm equipment to what it is now. Our collective opinion: The course is a far better experience, and it has matured quite nicely.

We finished up in time to take a drive down the Mull of Kintyre to a spot called Southend. It is, as the name implies, the very southernmost tip of the peninsula. Next stop is Northern Ireland, which on a clear day you can see from the Mull.

Our goal was to find Dunaverty Golf Club, even though we didn't have enough time to play it. The fact that this remote part of Kintyre

The Machrihanish Clubhouse, which replaced the original, destroyed by fire.

boasts the most famous Scottish lady golfer, Isabella (Belle) Robertson, was reason enough for me to go there. Born in 1936 on a nearby farm, Belle learned to play golf at Dunaverty, then went on to win the British Ladies Amateur in 1981, and seemingly just about every other competition she entered over several decades.

Her illustrious career included representing Great Britain and Ireland in the Curtis Cup nine times, twice as a non-playing captain. In 1986, in her ninth appearance, Belle was victorious, beating the US team 13-5 at the Prairie Dunes Country Club in Kansas. When we popped into the modest clubhouse, the first thing that struck me was the framed photograph of a smiling Belle, wearing a blazer with an SLGA badge. Belle Robertson MBE became an Honorary Vice President to the Scottish Ladies Golfing Association for her services to golf and was presented with her badge in 2007.

Perhaps if you asked her today how she feels about becoming one of the first honorary female members of the Royal & Ancient Golf Club, she might respond like Annika Sorenstam and say it is a "super honor". In 2015, Belle, who still plays off a 2 handicap, was invited to join the R&A along with Annika, Louise Suggs, Renee Powell, Laura Davies, Lally Segard, also known as Vicomtesse de Saint Sauveur, and Princess Anne. (It should be noted, that since that announcement, other women, such as Lady Bonallack, have also been admitted as members.)

Below Belle's photograph was a list as long as your arm of other accomplishments in her stellar golfing career. Some of the highlights include Dumbarton and Argyll Ladies Champion ten times, New Zealand Match Play Champion 1971, West of Scotland Ladies Champion four times, Babe Zaharias Trophy 1964-1971. Scottish Ladies Amateur Champion six times, Scottish Sports Woman of the year four times, Daks Woman Golfer of the Year twice, and numerous international team triumphs. Belle is, without a doubt, golf royalty in this part of the world, or anywhere else, for that matter.

On our way out of the clubhouse I picked up a scorecard as a memento of my visit and found these unique Local Rules:

1. SUNKEN LIES: A ball plugged on the fairway, or lying in a rabbit scrape/rabbit hole, or scrape, hoofmark, tractor road/tractor run, anywhere on the course, may be dropped immediately behind without penalty.

2. When a ball lies in or touching dung, or if the dung interferes with the player's stroke or stance, the ball may be lifted and dropped immediately behind without penalty. The ball may be cleaned.

3. FENCE ROUND GREEN & TEES: When a ball lies near or under a fence round a green the Player must elect to have the wire held by his fellow competitor to enable him to play the shot, or he may use his equipment, or he may take the ball two club-lengths away from the fence, not nearer the hole, without penalty. Should a ball strike a fence near a green to which the Player is playing it may be replayed without penalty.

4. OVERHEAD WIRES: If a ball strikes any of the overhead wires, or poles supporting them, it must be replayed without penalty.

Dunaverty Golf Club was founded in 1889, ten years after Old Tom Morris extended Machrihanish to eighteen holes. The Dunaverty course, sited on ground around the dramatic Dunaverty Rock, was laid out from the very beginning as 18 holes and was completely remodeled and extended before World War II.

But long before then, the rocky headland was the site of Dunaverty Castle. The bulbous promontory, which is visible from the car park of the golf club, was a natural stronghold, with sea on three sides and the castle was only approachable by a narrow path.

"The village, located beside Dunaverty Bay is thought to be the place where Saint Columba first set foot in Scotland."

Going back to the 13th century, Dunaverty Castle was taken by or surrendered to various Kings of England, Norway and Scotland. Over the centuries, the conflicts between warring Scottish clans eventually resulted in the devastation of Dunaverty Castle, with little remaining.

From the Mull of Kintyre website, I learned that one must go back many more centuries to understand that this very place is (drum roll please) ... the ancient cradle of Scotland, for it is here in the 5th century AD that Fergus Mór Mac Eirc and the Scoti from Ireland came to establish the kingdom of Dál Riata (Dalriada) and to give our country its name — Scotland."

OK. I'm officially blown away. Naturally, I must delve below the surface of that statement.

Wikipedia describes the area of Southend as a village and surrounding land, with a population of about 500 souls. The village, located beside Dunaverty Bay is thought to be the place where Saint Columba first set foot in Scotland, traveling over in an ancient curragh, made of wood covered in leather. Kevin and I still see people out on the bay in curraghs when we are in residence at the house in Liscannor, Ireland, where we are based during summertime. The Irish spell it 'currach' and nowadays you might even see one of these versatile vessels out on Liscannor Bay being propelled by an outboard motor.

It's here, near the village where two human footprints are carved into the rock. Known as Columba's Footprints, legend has it that he first preached on Scottish soil until a tribal feud back in Ireland forced him into exile.

According to the Columba Heritage Trail website: "Columba was born in Gartan in Donegal, probably in 520 AD. His extended family, the Cenél Conaill, were powerful local aristocrats, some of whom became kings of Tara — the most powerful office in Ireland."

Still in sight of Ireland (on a clear day), from which he'd been banished, Columba moved farther north and eventually settled on the island of Iona. Some accounts say it was his kinsman Conall mac Comgaill, King of Dál Riata, who invited him to Scotland in the first place.

Columba, credited as a poet and a writer, was considered a holy man, energetic in founding a monastery on Iona. While it's a tiny island in the Inner Hebrides, just 1.5 miles wide by 3 miles long, it holds a monumental place in the history of Celtic Christianity.

Columba died on Iona and was buried in 597 by his monks in the abbey he created. The Viking raids between 794 and 802 laid waste to the settlement, and the monks of that age, who were working on what is now known as the *Book of Kells,* fled to Ireland.

The extraordinary illuminated manuscripts, sometimes referred to as the *Book of Columba,* and believed to have been finished in Kells, County Meath, are now housed in the Library of Trinity College, Dublin. However, many scribes worked on it over many centuries and this masterwork of calligraphy is now regarded as Ireland's finest national treasure.

I never could have anticipated that stepping foot on this southernmost promontory of the Mull of Kintyre could lead to such a revelatory history lesson for me.

Here I've come over from Ireland on a grand golfing adventure, and like Columba, I will be going to the Hebrides. Then, like the great literary work, widely known now as the *Book of Kells,* my circular journey will bring me back to Ireland.

We'll have to return another day to play the Dunaverty Golf Club and explore the castle ruins, but there is something else looming off in the distance that has also piqued my curiosity. High up on a hill, a giant white monstrosity is tucked into a wall of lush green trees.

This stark white modern oddity is so incongruent — juxtaposed with the historic golf course wending its way around an ancient landscape — it sticks out like a sore thumb.

Once able to do some research, I discovered that this behemoth, standing five stories tall, was originally built as a hotel. The Art Deco structure was attributed to the architect James Austin Laird and the original owner, who is believed to have been Captain James Taylor, named it Keil Hotel.

The word 'Keil' is a derivative of Cill or Kil, a Gaelic word meaning sanctified. The hotel surely took its name from Keil Hill, the site where it was built, and would've had commanding views over Dunaverty Bay and beyond.

As fate had it, the new hotel was requisitioned in 1939 by the Royal Navy for use as a hospital. It was returned to the owner in 1947 and eventually reopened as a hotel. However, it changed hands several times during the next few decades and by 1990 the business came to a complete close. It was reported that the proprietors ripped out the plumbing and electrics and sold them off leaving gaping holes in the walls and ceilings, causing the building to deteriorate.

Sadly, what is now just a skeleton of a building, seems on the verge of collapse, and has been on the Building at Risk register for many years. It's hard to imagine a white knight coming to the rescue of this distressed Art Deco artifact, so I wonder if I will still find it standing the next time I return.

When we headed back up the road toward Machrihanish, passing through beautiful farmland, gazing out our windows at patches of primroses, bluebells and thrift, we suddenly came to a screeching halt.

"Are you in a hurry?" An old man, standing firmly in the middle of the road, said tersely to Kevin, as he rolled down the window.

The gent was wearing a blue sweater, baggy brown pants, and a grey wool cap. Although I was strapped into my seat and could not see his face, I could tell by his accent and perhaps more so by his manner, that he was a descendant of a Southend Clan. The road was narrow and the old boy had parked his own car up against the dense trees to our right, pretty much making it impossible to pass.

"No, not particularly," Kevin answered nonchalantly.

"Well, you need to wait right here," blue sweater stated, standing his ground. Kevin, a little irritated by now, calmly asked, "Why is that?"

"The cows are on their way," he declared.

And sure enough, after a few interminable minutes, a herd of massive Holsteins came ambling down the road. The boss cow, her swollen udder bulging, knew the way and made the turn up a side road right in front of us without much cajoling from blue sweater.

A few of the younger cows following behind her were straining to chomp on the lower hanging juicy green leaves. Another man with a faded black baseball cap and a dark blue denim jean jacket, brought up the rear.

Without too much urging, the huge cows lumbered up the slight incline of the dirt road, and blue sweater, with a tip of his hat, let us go on our way.

On we went, back to the comfort of the Ugadale, where through our window we could see the Paps of Jura disappearing in the magical blue haze of a calm Atlantic Ocean. Hopefully, it would stay that way for our ferry crossing tomorrow.

In the meantime, I'll dream about returning to see the footprints of Columba and the castle ruin.

We will also play Dunaverty and walk in the footsteps of Belle Robertson, who brings a gentler kind of royalty to the land of Southend, once the scene of many bloody battles, that is now carpeted with wildflowers, and where the songs of skylarks fill the air.

The Machrie

Terroir Revelation

In 2005, Prince Andrew arrived at Campbeltown Airport in his RAF helicopter after playing golf at Machrie on Islay. Ever since that day, I've dreamed of playing there myself. I'd just come off the course at Machrihanish and raced over to the new 'Tiger Tee' on the first hole, to witness HRH hit a few drives to inaugurate the new teeing ground.

I even wrote a story about it back then called *Keeper of the Royal Ball*. It could be considered my first golf story. And, in case you are wondering, I am the keeper!

Although we were not, like royalty, going by helicopter, Kevin and I were going all the same!

It should be stated, Islay (pronounced eye-la) is certainly better known for its whisky production than it is for golf. As I mentioned in the story about Machrihanish (from *A Stroll on the Old Lady*), Islay, visible from Machrihanish, has eight distilleries.

When we had dinner at the Bridgend Hotel on our first night, I asked for a copy of their menu of whiskies, so I'd have the most current and complete list of the Islay distilleries. They are Ardbeg, Bowmore, Bruichladdich,

Machrie, the 9th hole.

Bunnahabhain, Caol Ila, Kilchoman Machir Bay, Laphroig, and Lagavulin. Jura whisky made the roster, but the distillery is on a nearby island.

We were told that a new distillery had applied for a license, meaning there could now be nine on Islay as you are reading this. There were 23 distilleries at one time, so obviously the number fluctuates.

Bowmore is considered the oldest registered distillery on Islay, dating back to 1779. We stopped by, but it was Sunday, and they didn't offer any tours. We had a tasting (after our round at Machrie) and bought a rather nice bottle of their single malt to take home.

On weekdays they offer a Craftman's Tour (by prior appointment for £55 per person); you go from the malt barns to the maturation warehouse and even a visit to the No. 1 vaults. That has a nice ring to it, doesn't it? Then there is the Master Distiller's Tour (for £225 per person) that includes a walk to their water source, peat cutting, distillery tour, two course whisky paired lunch and naturally the visit to the legendary No. 1 vaults. So, all you whisky lovers might want to plan ahead — and bring your wellies!

When we disembarked from the ferry in Askaig, road signs pointed to Caol Ila and Bunnahabhain, farther north on the island. Our immediate concern was to find our accommodation, Skerrols House about 5 miles from the ferry terminal, set back on a single-track road.

Our genial host, Thomas, showed us to our room and I must confess, I was surprised and delighted that it was so luxurious. Every modern convenience you could want, including unbelievably fine bed linens and a very spacious bathroom. Although they did not serve dinner, the continental buffet choices were beautifully presented, and the made-to-order breakfast was cooked to perfection and positively delicious.

Everything about Skerrols House oozes serenity. Just outside our window a herd of cows grazed in the green pastures that seemed to stretch endlessly, on this, the southernmost island of the Inner Hebrides of Scotland. Known as 'The Queen of the Hebrides', it's 25 miles north of the Irish coast. Perhaps that's why some historians believe distillation reached Scotland *from* Ireland, via Islay in the 13th century, when the Lord of the Isles married the daughter of an Ulster baron.

We had a little spare time on the day we arrived, and did some reconnaissance, exploring the road down to The Machrie. David Russell had informed us that there was some work being done on the course but encouraged us to come anyway. Russell, who played on both the European Tour and European Senior Tour, has partnered with Ian Woosnam (winner of the 1991 Masters, a winner on the European Tour, and victorious captain of the Ryder Cup in 2006 at The K Club) to form RAW Golf Design. This was one of their current projects.

Upon our approach to the course, we discovered a large, derelict hotel on the property. The new owners were committed to a major refurbishment over the next couple of years, but in the meantime, the pro shop was rather makeshift, operating out of a modest dilapidated cottage. We circled around and left, with a good idea of the time required to get there and play our round the following day.

"Known as 'The Queen of the Hebrides', it's 25 miles north of the Irish coast."

Our route, back and forth, took us through Bowmore, the island's capital. That made it easy to drop by the distillery, otherwise, we might not have visited a single one, which would have been an absolute shame. When I had asked the cheerful cashier in the gift shop onboard the Cal Mac ferry how many distilleries there were on Islay, by way of an answer, he gave me a sheet showing the location of the few roads and all the distilleries. That placemat sized map proved to be invaluable.

I did not know that Islay was historically a strong Gaelic-speaking area. I could guess now, after my lesson on the ferry to Arran about the words ending in 'aig' being Viking words, that Islay had been under the control of Scandinavian settlers of Norse origin several centuries ago.

But when it comes to golf, The Machrie takes its name from the Gaelic word *machair*, meaning 'links'. The course was originally constructed in 1891 by Willie Campbell, born in Musselburgh in 1862. A renowned matchplay competitor, who lost the 26th Open Championship at Musselburgh in 1886 by two strokes to David Brown, after leading in the final round until he took a seven on the 5th hole. The prize money was a mere £8 to the winner.

I mention the prize money because in 1901, to attract publicity for the golf course, the Islay Open competition was cleverly conceived. It had the highest prize of any Open competition at that time — £100! The mission was accomplished when The Great Triumvirate of Harry Vardon, John Henry Taylor and James Braid, who were all at the peak of their games, took up the challenge. Between 1894 and 1914, these three men collectively won the Open Championship sixteen times, with Vardon capturing a record six of those victories. At The Machrie, it was J. H. Taylor who narrowly nabbed the title.

"Between 1894 and 1914, these three men collectively won the Open Championship sixteen times."

To shed more light on the importance of Willie Campbell during this era, his prowess as a matchplay competitor developed from playing big money matches and going head-to-head against the best golfers of the day, including Willie Park Jr, Jamie Anderson and Willie Dunn. Campbell was known to be fearless, and his numerous high-risk shots delivered many a drubbing to the world's best golfers.

From the Largs Golf Club website (a course Campbell laid out in 1891, the same year as The Machrie): "Despite all his success his most famous golfing moment was a failure. In the 1887 Open Championship at Prestwick, where Campbell was an assistant professional, Willie was coming home the sure winner when he heeled his drive at the 16th and found a deep bunker (later dubbed Campbell's grave).

The gallery tried to convince him to play backward, unfortunately he ignored their advice and took eight instead of four. Willie Park Jr won the title by a stroke.

Horace Hutchinson told the sad story of coming into Charlie Hunter's shop after Campbell had thrown away the Championship. On either side of the shop were upturned buckets. On one sat Willie Campbell and on the other his caddie, both weeping bitterly.

After the disappointment, Campbell challenged the champion to a match over 72 holes. He defeated Park 18 up with 17 to play. The year before he had finished second in the Open to Davie Brown at Musselburgh. Again, he issued a challenge; ultimately defeating Brown 13 and 12. He had similar one-sided victories over Bob Martin and Willie Fernie. His match against Archie Simpson may have been the most publicized as it was held over Carnoustie, St Andrews, Prestwick, and Musselburgh in front of huge crowds. The battle ended at Musselburgh with Campbell 16 up.

Campbell was engaged as professional at Prestwick (1887-1888), Ranfurly Castle (1889-1891) and North Berwick (1892-1894). His first architectural involvement appears to be at Ranfurly Castle in 1889, where he designed their nine-hole course. In 1891 he laid out the wild links at Machrie on Islay, considered a cult classic today. That same year he designed Largs, Cowal, Rothesay and Kilmacolm in western Scotland, and in 1893 the first nine at Seascale.

Although not as prolific as some, he was without a doubt one of the most important early golf architects, especially in America. Unfortunately, his place in American golf architecture history has been largely ignored."

In 1894, at the age of 32, Campbell was lured to America where he became the professional at The Country Club, Brookline, MA. The golf course at the time was just six holes and Campbell altered and expanded it to nine. Years later, in 1913, Brookline became famous as the US Open site where the young amateur, Francis Quimet, won the championship, beating Harry Vardon and Ted Ray in an 18-hole playoff.

In 1895, Campbell played in the first official US Open at Newport Country Club, coming in sixth, and in 1896, Campbell took up the position as the professional at Myopia Hunt Club. Sadly, Willie Campbell's life was cut short when he succumbed to cancer in 1900 when he was only 38.

On the day we played, the golf gods favored us with dry weather. It was truly an adventure. If Shiskine is the most fun I've had playing golf, Machrie is a close second. Shiskine was unique in so many ways, not the least of which required Kevin and me to play off the same tees. Then at Machrie, I was surprised to discover it had no bunkers! Fun, quirky, memorable and plenty of challenges, but not so punitive. It occurred to me that, if they haven't already, contemporary golf architects would profit from visiting these places (long before the days of bulldozers) to round off their education.

When we checked in before our round at the cottage-cum-pro shop, we were given an ordinary sheet of paper listing the 18 holes and their yardages, which served as our scorecard. We weren't even sure where the first tee was, but once found, we were giddy with excitement.

From our first drives to the last putts, we were enthralled to be on the course. In all the years I knew of Machrie, I never even bothered to look for a website; maybe wanting to preserve the element of surprise. I had nothing to go on except the knowledge that the course existed for more than a century, and I'd be experiencing golf the way it was meant to be played, without any preconceived notions.

There were no yardage markers other than a 150 yard stake on each hole. I think Kevin relished the challenge as much as I did, to just feel our way around. We practically had the

6th hole, The Machrie.

course to ourselves and with the absence of any pressure whatsoever, I had one of my best rounds of the summer, finding pars and almost-par bogies. I felt emboldened by the terrain, the atmosphere, the layout, the lot.

The entire magical experience led me to a whole new awareness, that of the *Terroir of Golf*. I'm coining the phrase right here and now.

It was only a few years ago, while watching a documentary on an airplane, that I first heard the word terroir (pronounced tear-wahr) and learned that, with wine, all the elements — climate, soil, topography, and the hand of man in making of the wine, combine to create the finished product.

Besides the environmental factors, there is also the impossible-to-define passion and poetry of the visionary, and in the case of a golf course, the architect — the heart and soul that person or group brings to the project. When you factor in the history and tradition of a club and/or a course, you have the ingredients to create a great *golf experience.*

To be sure, I will be making my plans to go back when the work is finished on the course and the hotel has been restored. There's plenty more to explore on this beautiful island, besides another distillery or two. On the west side of Islay there are the Rocks of the Rhinns, where interesting geological features were formed millions of years ago when Islay was part of a very early supercontinent known as Rodinia.

And then there is The Oa. That's not a typo. It is, simply, The Oa. Here, on the Mull of Oa, you will find the American Monument. Built in the shape of a lighthouse by the American Red Cross in 1910, it stands high on a cliff overlooking the spot where the Tuscania sank to the bottom of the Irish Sea.

The Tuscania, originally a luxury passenger liner, was refitted and pressed into military service in 1918. While on its way from New Jersey to the coast of France, with 2,013 American soldiers and a crew of more than 300, the ship joined a convoy in Nova Scotia and entered the icy cold British waters between Islay and Northern Ireland.

On the morning of 5 February 1918, a German UB-77 submarine followed the convoy and under cover of darkness at 6:40 pm, fired two torpedoes. One found its target which resulted in heavy damage to the Tuscania and the deaths of 230 men.

Eight months later, on 6 October 6 1918, during a heavy storm, HMS Otranto, carrying troops from New York to Glasgow, collided with the steamship HMS Kashmir. Both British crews and US servicemen, totaling over 400, met their deaths, a short distance from the site of the Tuscania catastrophe.

In sum, Islay abounds in a wealth of geographical and historical sites and sensations. So along with your golf shoes and your wellies, bring your hiking boots and be prepared to be enriched in body, mind and soul.

Murmurs abound that a new golf course on Jura is in the making. So, we will definitely have to plan another pilgrimage to the Hebrides.

Lochgreen House

Tour Conclusion

How do you finish up an amazing golf odyssey such as this? In grand style, is how.

Kevin, wanting to position us on the Ayrshire Coast where we'd be catching our final ferry, booked us into Lochgreen House in Troon for our final night in Scotland. We'd driven by it a few times while we were attending the Open Championship at Royal Troon, a little over a week ago.

Kevin knew it well from having stayed there before, but I could only try to catch a glimpse of it on our way to the tournament. Kevin had built it up quite a bit, and when I stepped foot on the property, I was not disappointed in the least. Our well-appointed room was incredibly spacious, as was the stylish bathroom. It featured a large, footed white porcelain enamel tub, and along one wall a bank of electric heating rails for the towels.

Having made the long journey via a road from Kennacraig on the Kintyre coast, around Loch Fyne, through Rest and Be Thankful and then past Loch Lomond (remember the Paul McCartney ballad, *The Long and Winding Road*? Well, this is it), before negotiating the

Lochgreen House in Troon

motorways running through Glasgow, we were more than happy to avail ourselves of all the luxury our room and the hotel had to offer.

It wasn't until we were checking out that I learned Lochgreen House is the flagship property that's part of Costley & Costley Hoteliers Ltd. That's when I asked, "Why are there so many paintings of chickens and roosters?" There were even life-size ceramic roosters perched jauntily in the main dining room!

I was told the owner, Mr William Costley, is fond of chickens and that he had trained as a chef in France, becoming a Master Chef at the age of 21. And since the cockerel is the gastronomic symbol of cuisine in France, he adopted it as the emblem of the hotel group.

The whole enterprise is a family affair. Mr Costley is the chairman of the company and Catherine Costley is a director of the company. She is the visionary behind the sumptuous interiors. Their son, Andrew Costley, is also a director and having followed in his father's footsteps, he's also the Executive Chef. He oversees nearly eighty chefs within ten kitchens throughout the company.

So, *cock-a-doodle-doo*. Now all the pieces fit together nicely.

On our way to our last dinner in Scotland, we entered the charming lobby and headed straight for the Lochgreen Malt Room. It was a marvelous semi-circular space with a white domed ceiling. Six floor-to-ceiling shelves held bottles too numerous to count. Framed by a perfectly placed narrow window sat the pièce de resistance — a spectacular cockerel statue of prodigious proportions.

Now that we had experienced a true feast for the eyes, it was time to progress to the restaurant for the final feast of our incredible journey.

We were seated in comfortable, moss-colored upholstered chairs at a white skirted table.

The nicely proportioned, light-filled dining room was decorated with original works of art. A charming side-view portrait of a young women in soft pastel colors was mounted above a fireplace at the opposite end of the room. A large, brightly colored still life in a handsome gold leaf molding was suspended from the dark-stained wooden frame around a large mirror.

My chapeau is off to Andrew, who created an incredibly sophisticated menu. Dinner began with bottle of perfectly chilled New Zealand Sauvignon Blanc and an Amuse Bouche.

For Starters we both had the Half Lobster Salad and Bisque with Croutons Rouille and Parmesan.

For Mains, I chose Seared Orkney Scallops with Dressed Crab Cake, Oriental Mango Salad, Cucumber and Wasabi Butter Sauce.

Kevin chose: Tournedos of Beef Fillet Rossini with Chateau Potatoes, Truffled Spinach and Madeira Sauce.

If you're a foodie and wondering if I took photos, you bet I did.

And for dessert? You know darn well — our last sticky toffee pudding in Scotland. So how did the Sticky Toffee Pudding Judges rank the entries?

Best overall: A tie between Marcliffe Hotel in Aberdeen and Auchrannie Resort on the Isle of Arran. Both got a perfect 10.

Best presentation: Nairn. A 9.99 score.

However, the biggest win of all, I personally bestow upon Kevin, who brilliantly masterminded the entire golf odyssey, which truly was the trip of a lifetime. While we strive to create this kind of experience for our clients, for once it was splendid to do it strictly for ourselves. Other than having our own private helicopter, it could not have been better.

The Claret Jug

A Singular trophy

Nobody, it seems, gives a thought as to why the trophy awarded at the Open Championship is a jug. Its proper name is The Golf Champion Trophy, but it's commonly known as the Claret Jug.

Now, a jug may not sound like much of a prize, unless, as in this case, it is made of sterling silver. Additionally, the main body is decorated with a gentleman golfer expertly embossed. The elegant spout was created from a sterling silver casting.

The singular trophy, presented to the winner of the Open Championship since 1873, is mounted on a pedestal, and as the years progressed, more stepped bands were added to accommodate the Open Championship winners' names.

Like other Victorian sterling silver claret jugs made in the 1870s, this one appears to be in the Cellini style, adopting a shape made popular by the famous 16th century Florentine silversmith Benvenuto Cellini.

Before the jug came into existence, the winner of the world's first 'major', was bestowed the honor of wearing the Championship Belt for

an entire year, provided he could guarantee its safekeeping along with a promise to surrender it for the next year's competition. The belt was made of red Moroccan leather with a giant, elaborately embellished silver buckle, depicting a golf scene with four figures — most likely two golfers and their caddies. This belt, created by Edinburgh silversmiths James & Walter Marshall, was purchased by the members of Prestwick Golf Club, where the first twelve Open Championships were held from 1860 to 1872.

Young Tom Morris won the belt three years in a row, and according to the rules, this gave him the right to permanently retain this magnificent prize.

Young Tom's golfing exploits and numerous victories catapulted him to rock-star status, especially in the town of St Andrews. For his formal portrait, Tom wore the sensational trophy, but he didn't just *possess* the belt, he *adorned* himself with it. Posing in the studio of Thomas Rodger, considered to be the first professional photographer in St Andrews, Young Tom stood proudly, if not impatiently for the full minute it would take to expose a calotype image.

With his finely filigreed silver buckled belt perched on his athletic frame, riding just below his stylishly tailored double-breasted waistcoat, Tom exuded a dashing handsomeness that would make even the most reserved of the landed classes sit up and take notice. From his lustrous locks and the body of an action hero to the arrogant attitude, Young Tom embodied the cockiness of the sports celebrity he clearly was.

When the Open Championship was to be played in 1871, it was realized too late that there was no trophy to present. And as ridiculous as it sounds, the tournament was cancelled.

"When the exquisite silver jug was hallmarked and ready to present, the first winner to receive it was Tom Kidd in 1873"

By 1872, three clubs decided on a rotation to host The Open and contributed £10 each toward the creation of a new trophy. The clubs, Prestwick, The Honourable Company of Edinburgh Golfers (today usually called Muirfield where the club moved in 1891), and The Royal and Ancient Golf Club of St Andrews proposed a silver claret jug as the winner's prize. The decision was not unanimously agreed upon until 11 September 1872, so the winner of the 1872 Open (Young Tom for the 4th time in a row!) was awarded a Gold Medal inscribed with "The Golf Champion Trophy", a tradition which continues to this day.

If the three clubs moved slowly, at least they chose wisely. The firm they selected was formed by James Mackay and David Cunningham and was established sometime before 1824 in Edinburgh. By 1873, Mackay Cunningham & Co were known as the 'Goldsmiths to the Queen, HRH Prince of Wales, watchmakers, and manufacturers and designers of Scottish jewellery'.

When the exquisite silver jug was hallmarked and ready to present, the first winner to receive it was Tom Kidd in 1873. Although Kidd triumphed that year and claimed the shiny new prize, the 1872 winner, Tom Morris Junior, was the first name engraved on the body of the trophy, and rightly so. For those folks who are fascinated by this kind of detail, on the spout of the jug, the first Champion engraved is Jack Burns at St Andrews 1888, and the last that of James Braid at Muirfield 1901.

The importance of Young Tom being the only person to ever win The Open four times in succession cannot be overstated. Furthermore, he accomplished this feat by the age of twenty-one. Consider this: Young Tom won the Open Championship in 1868, 1869, 1870, (1871 was cancelled) and then 1872. That's four *consecutive* Open titles. So whatever victories the young guns are racking up today, no modern-day golfer has duplicated this remarkable achievement.

Old Tom Morris, Young Tom Morris, around 1870-1875

As the golf world's first major tournament continued to evolve, all responsibility for The Open Championship was entrusted to The Royal and Ancient Golf Club in 1920. After the 1927 Open, won by Bobby Jones at St Andrews, the Championship Committee decided to retain the original Claret Jug in future years, and present the winner with a replica.

Anyone who thinks the Winner's Replica (which the Champion Golfer holds for a year until the following Open) is somehow inferior to the original would be mistaken. It's the same size and an exact duplicate of the prize that now never leaves the clubhouse of the Royal and Ancient. However, it should be noted that the winner is also presented with a slightly smaller replica Claret Jug that he gets to keep forever.

In 1928, Walter Hagen won the third of his four Open titles and was given a replica Claret Jug, having already been presented with the original in 1922 and 1924, which he had to hand over before the start of the following Open. Nowadays, a replica Claret Jug is treated as the priceless treasure it is, and the ceremonial return of the trophy has become a major press event.

Over the 54 years in which the original Claret Jug was awarded, twenty-eight different players held it aloft, including Harry Vardon on a record six occasions.

What is the rest of the story? How did this iconic trophy come about? And why a jug?

Why not a footed cup or a chalice?

Take the Wanamaker Trophy for instance. Now there's an award of mammoth proportions. Its fire hydrant size dwarfs the Claret Jug *and* the Ryder Cup. Yet which, I ask you, is more coveted?

Not this, the biggest hunk of hardware of them all. It's named after Rodman Wanamaker (1863-1928), a driving force behind the creation of the PGA of America. The Wanamaker Trophy is 28 inches high and weighs 27 pounds. That is hefty. The winner might even need a spotter when he hoists it over his head for the adoring crowd to see. It is the prize for what is now considered the *fourth* major in golf. So, is it a big deal? Sure, of course it is. But it's still the diminutive decanter the guys all want to get their hands on.

Long before the golf clubs of Scotland had clubhouses of their own, the members usually met in a local tavern. For instance, when Prestwick Golf Club was founded on 2 July 1851 by a group of 57 golfers, they met at the Red Lion Inn in the town of Prestwick. In those days, an inn would have been a tavern that had a license to put up guests as lodgers and was an establishment that served wine, beer and ale. That is, a perfect post-match drinking house where the gentlemen would remove their hats and coats, have a full meal and settle their bets. In other words, it was the sport of golf's original 19th hole.

We must go back in time even further to follow the movement of the Muirfield members, who originally played their golf over Leith Links, just five holes at the time, each stretching over 400 yards long. In 1744, a committee of members, then known as the Gentlemen Golfers of Edinburgh, drafted the original 13 Rules of Play, before a competition to be held on Leith Links. These rules became the basis for the modern game. The sole signatory on this document was an Edinburgh surgeon and Muirfield member, John Rattray.

Eleven players participated in this 1744 competition, and *coincidentally* John Rattray won the event. His prize was a silver golf club, thought to be inspired by the silver arrow awarded to the winner of the Royal Company of Archers commencing in 1709.

Later, in 1768, the Gentlemen Golfers, who had been meeting in a tavern called Luckie Clephane's Inn on the ancient narrow thoroughfare known as Kirkgate, ponied up the money and built themselves a private clubhouse. It was sold in 1833, eventually demolished, and the Leith Academy Secondary School was built on the site in 1931.

And where did the Society of St Andrews Golfers meet before they had a clubhouse of their own? Having formed their club in 1754, ten years after the Gentlemen Golfers established the Honourable Company of Edinburgh Golfers, the St Andrews guys used to regularly dine (and imbibe) after their round in Bailie Glass's Inn. They didn't build their own clubhouse for over 100 years after the founding of their club. And for two decades before that, they regularly used a building called the Union Parlour on Golf Place, that they shared with other residents and visiting golfers. It was situated where the Grand Hotel (now Hamilton Grand) was later built.

"They didn't build their own clubhouse for over 100 years after the founding of their club."

Following a spirited match, what did

these clubs and societies do in their makeshift clubhouses, which evolved from tavernous origins? They'd eat a hearty supper and drink, then drink and drink some more! Copious amounts of alcoholic beverages were consumed. Whisky, one might presume. After all, Scotch whisky distillation was coming into its own.

No. They drank wine. What kind of wine? French, of course. Red, for sure. Claret, to be exact. Claret is a dry red wine produced in the winemaking region of Bordeaux. So, the trophy was fashioned in the style of the silver jugs customarily used to serve claret in the 19th century, at the same time the Open Championship came into existence.

Is there more to the story of the Claret Jug? There is!

To delve far enough into the past, we practically need a time machine to take us back to the century when Eleanor of Aquitaine (1122 — 1204), who became Queen of France, married King Henry II of England in 1154.

At the time, *clairet,* as Bordeaux reds were called in French, was a difficult word for the English to pronounce. They simplified it to 'claret' which in French means 'clear' and in those days the Bordeaux reds were fairly light in color compared to their current hue. By the 17th century the Bordeaux reds had gone through a gradation to a darker shade as winemaking techniques changed, and vintners discovered that wine aged in oak barrels took on properties that improved the taste.

Due to the British trade, 'claret' became the generic reference to Bordeaux wines. As wine production increased and storage techniques improved, the ensuing ease of transport between the countries enhanced the popularity of Bordeaux wines in England.

But let's not get too far ahead of ourselves.

The marriages, regicide, and wars of England and France are more complex than even the biggest and most full-bodied red wines. In a nutshell, or in a wine barrel, when the export of Bordeaux wine was interrupted by the outbreak of the Hundred Years War between France and

England (apparently round-numbered by the historians since it actually lasted 116 years from 1337 to 1453), the Auld Alliance, an accord between the kingdoms of Scotland and France, took on more significance.

By the end of the conflict, France had repossessed the province of Aquitaine, thus taking over control of the wine production in the region that had come under English control back when Eleanor married Henry.

So how is it that the Scots came up with the Claret Jug as their trophy?

As the red wine darkens and the plot thickens with the many convoluted conflicts between all these countries, it turns out that the Scottish merchants were granted a privileged position in the trade of claret by the French.

So much so, that even when the Protestant kingdoms of England and Scotland, both ruled by the same Stuart king, were trying militarily to aid the Huguenot rebels in their fight against Catholic France in La Rochelle, Scottish trading vessels were not only permitted access to the Gironde (a major waterway and location of the Bordeaux wine region), they were escorted safely to the port of Bordeaux by the French navy for their own protection from Huguenot privateers!

In their wisdom, the sagacious Scots, in creating the Claret Jug trophy, added a very interesting decorative feature, which is more than just an adornment. On the handle of the jug, precisely at the thumb point, the head of a bearded man was soldered into place.

I very much enjoyed this chapter, found it entertaining and it accurately gives the background to the Claret Jug's origin. Taba cleverly tied in the relationship of the 'Auld Alliance' between Scotland and France and the advent of claret's place in Scottish golfing society. This is a welcomed new wrinkle in the history of this great game of golf.

Dr Tony Parker, retired Historian at The World Golf Hall of Fame

Who is this mystery man?

None other than Dionysus, the Greek God of Wine, also known as Bacchus to the Romans.

Leave it to the clever Scots, who not only invented the game of golf, but found an ingenious way of giving a subtle nod to the Romans, who planted the first vines in France.

So ultimately, we should give Julius Caesar and the subsequent Roman emperors a nod of thanks for the Claret Jug!

Zenith Vineyards outside Salem, Oregon

Terroir of Golf:

What is Terroir?

When I first heard the word 'terroir' I was watching a fascinating documentary on an airplane about winemaking in France. I learned that due to the wide variety of soils in any region, one wine coming from a particular vineyard can taste completely different from one that's only 100 yards away.

All the winemakers featured in the documentary had very different personalities, but in common they shared an indisputable love for their land. They also shared a philosophy of minimal intervention with the vines to let nature do her work, so that the wine can best express the 'terroir'.

In the summer of 2016, I was playing golf at The Machrie on Islay — an island off the west coast of Scotland that is part of the Inner Hebrides — and I had an epiphany. On a magical course spread out over pure linksland, I realized there's a relationship between grapes and golf, since with both, everything begins with the ground.

And, as with grape *vines* and golf *courses,* the end result is a *living* work of art. The other parallel is how much the winemakers and course designers respect the land and its nature as well as Mother Nature herself.

How do these passionate artists employ a subtle alchemy to create their wines and golf courses?

I asked some winemakers and golf course designers to give their views about terroir and what it means to them. So, whether they are part of the wine culture in Saint-Emilion where the Romans planted the first vines in the 2nd century, or modern-day architects who fly all over the world to craft their courses, here are their thoughts, in their own words.

Winemakers Talk Terroir

The dramatic driveway entrance, Ocean Eight.

Mike Aylward, Winemaker

Ocean Eight Wines

Mornington Peninsula, Victoria, Australia.

Australia has 65 recognised wine regions, with about a third of those in the state of Victoria. Probably the most recently established is the Mornington Peninsula region which began commercial production in the 1980s. It now has over 60 wineries, plus breweries and distilleries, and is well serviced with restaurants, golf courses and holiday resorts.

In 1996, the Aylward family planted vines which symbolised a new wave of investment in the region, and at their Kooyong and Ocean Eight properties have championed the production of high-quality pinot gris, pinot noir and chardonnay varieties. Manager, Mike Aylward, was introduced to winemaking and golf by his father whose entrepreneurial flair created one of Mornington Peninsula's great successes.

Conversation with Graeme Ryan

Graeme: How and where did you get into golf?

Mike: At about the age of 12, I did a few clinics at Royal Melbourne Golf Club where my father was a member. Then later, a few lessons, more clinics, and many rounds at various municipal courses in suburban Melbourne.

We had a holiday house on the Mornington Peninsula where we spent most weekends. We loved it and played golf at Cape Schanck and The National Golf Club where my father became a member.

At the time, the region was growing rapidly. The National built two new courses while others were being put in by property developers. It is now a golfer's Mecca.

Graeme: How did you get into wine?

Mike: My parents found an attractive property which had three acres of vines. Although they had no previous interest in winemaking, they became curious and hired a consultant who was unimpressed with the site. Undaunted, they looked elsewhere and found *Kooyong* nearby which was considered most suitable for pinot noir. That's how we got into wine.

At that time, I was a teenager at school, then later did a Bachelor of Science degree at Melbourne University. During vacations and at weekends, I worked in the vineyards and wineries at *Kooyong* with the team there. They gave me the necessary education and helped me get established here.

Mike Aylward at work.

Graeme: How did *Ocean Eight* come about?

Mike: My father bought this property and installed me as manager. The name derives from the demanding 8th hole of the Ocean course at The National. Although that course has lately been modified by Tom Doak, and named Gunnamatta, the 8th hole remains with only minor changes. It is a challenging par 4 of 452 yards and beautifully bunkered.

Graeme: The National is unique in Australian golf since membership is obtained by the purchase of shares. That is not uncommon overseas, yet relatively rare here.

Mike: The value of the shares has gone up and down over the years, yet The National is a great success story. It now owns four brilliant courses, with three of those in the top 20 in Australia. Also, the Mornington Peninsula boasts five in the top 20 and fourteen in the top 100 according to the latest ranking by *Australian Golf Digest*.

Graeme: Do you supply The National with your wines?

Mike: We do, along with several other golf clubs down here. Also, for years, my father's wine from *Kooyong* has been going into many of the best restaurants in Australia and we have benefitted from that.

Graeme: Tell me Mike, what is your understanding of terroir in general, in this grape growing region, and your vineyard in particular.

Mike: Terroir is a word used in the wine world where a particular site is allowed to express its own unique character in the wine. This is determined through soil profile and environmental influences on each site. I feel the less manipulation in the winery enables the terroir from the vineyard to shine through.

I believe the Mornington Peninsula wine producers are finding out what their terroir is, and there is still a lot of prospecting going on to find the most suitable sites, particularly for pinot noir.

Ocean Eight's vineyard gives great perfume and red fruit characters in our pinot. We mostly produce very elegant wines over rich and tannic wines. That is what our terroir brings each harvest.

Graeme: So, life is good for you, your wife Hollie and four children.

Mike: Yes, it is. Hollie does a lot on social media together with promotion, sales, distribution, and deliveries. She is a great asset to me and the business which allows me to get on with the tasks of growing grapes and making wine. Also, I'm doing less on the management side, as I have a very good team around me.

The children are healthy and happy, and I play golf at least once a week.

Vista through the Eucalypts.

Scenes from Chateau de Pitray

Jean de Boigne

Owner, Chateau de Pitray, Cotes de Bordeaux Castillon, France

Taba: Was your vineyard in your family for centuries? How did you establish your vineyards here? What is it about St Emilion?

Jean: My family established here before America was discovered. Pitray is the oldest family property in Bordeaux. I'm twenty-sixth generation. And I'm quite lucky they established here, because in 1450, they had no idea of terroir.

Taba: You were indeed lucky, as you say, they didn't establish the vineyard in a cow pasture!

Jean: Yeah, the terroir is very important – for me, the terroir is underground. What makes the quality of the wine is the soil, climate, the grape, and the man who makes the wine. The importance of terroir is that the vine, the roots of the vine, go very deep and take some nutriments from thirty meters deep.

Taba: Thirty meters deep? I had no idea.

Jean: Yeah, it goes very deep. That's the terroir! (Pointing to the tree outside). You know this tree? This big oak? The roots go as deep as the tree that you see. You have exactly the same below the ground as what is above the ground. There is a big difference between up the hill where we are and down the hill. If you plant vines down there, it's going to be very different.

Taba: Why is that?

Jean: Because below the ground up here, we have what we call the 'limestone tongue'. It goes through St Emilion to this plateau where we are — just about six kilometers east. If you are above the limestone, the roots will grow on the limestone and that will bring minerality to your wines. If you are down the hill the soil is more sandy—on the bottom part of the appellation—that will bring you very fruity wines, but not wines with the same base structure. If you have limestone and clay, you'll have more structure like we do up here on this plateau. The tongue of limestone that goes through St Emilion and ends here means high quality for the terroir.

Taba: How fortunate that your vineyard is in such a special place.

Jean: Here is half Gironde and half Dordogne — two states. In the middle we used to have the Demarcation Line. The Freedom Line. Here was free, over there was German. And, here in Castillon is where the Hundred Years War ended. This area is so full of history!

Taba: Your own family was a part of many wars and battles. The Pitray Chateau is full of portraits of men in military uniform. One of the most prominent portraits I noted was the one of General de Boigne, after the battle of Patan, 1790. Tell me more about him.

Jean: I come from a family of big fighters. That was a battle in India. On my father's side, my ancestor, General de Boigne, conquered, at the beginning of the nineteenth century, all north of

India for an Indian Prince, a Maharaja. He was in charge of all the military and army securing this part of India. My mother's family history is longer because the oldest papers we have are from the thirteenth century when my ancestors arrived here.

One of the most important things was during the American Independence War (1775–1783), my ancestor, Admiral de Suffren, was one of the allies of Lafayette. They went to the US to help you against the British.

General Washington, after the war, to put all the officers together, created with my ancestor, Pierre Andrew de Suffren, the Society of the Cincinnati (founded 1783). In this society, all the members are descendants of officers who fought during the American War of Independence. My father is a member. My eldest brother is a member. Only the eldest male of each generation can be a member.

Taba: That is fascinating. I've come here to speak to you about terroir and I'm learning so much more. No wonder it says in the Chateau de Pitray pamphlet, "Each bottle contains 600 years of history written by the same family."

Jean: It's a long time, for sure.

Taba: I feel so lucky, to see the new Tom Doak course at Saint-Emilionnais Golf Club, and meet you as well. This is such a special place.

Jean: It's true. There is even a dolmen on the Pitray estate, which is proof that this is a very specific place in prehistoric time. I used to come here a long time ago, for hunting and picking mushrooms, long before the golf course. What they did is amazing!

Taba: Have you met the architect, Tom Doak? I asked him the other day, "What makes you the happiest after somebody plays a course you designed? Is it that they had fun?" Tom said,

"The most important thing is they want to play it again."

Jean: It's exactly the same for me. When somebody drinks my wine, they want to have more!

Taba: I'm so blessed to have the opportunity to come here, to one of the greatest wine regions in the world. What else would you compare to this?

Jean: Well, it's certainly one of the oldest. You cannot compare. You have good terroir everywhere. In many countries, you have fantastic terroir.

Every soil needs a kind of grape. Every grape needs a kind of soil to express all the aromas.

That's the magic of wine!

Bartho Eksteen

Winemaker Director, Bartho Eksteen Winery, Hemel-en-Aarde Valley, Hermanus South Africa

Over a huge part of his career, Bartho has focused on three specific wine styles: Methode Cap Classique, Sauvignon Blanc, Rhône-style blends.

Although passionate and proud of his wines, awards, and trophies, these are not the only points of pride and passion in his life. Bartho's focus is also on his family dynamic, which he believes forms an integral part of the brand. His wife, Suné, has become the principal of the culinary side of the brand (under the brand new Maná Restaurant name), whilst his son Pieter-Willem and Mendocenean wife, Sol, are both well on their way to becoming acclaimed winemakers in their own right. His daughter, Shani, is headed toward her dream of being an educator, using the farm premises to mold the minds of the future and becoming a Meester in her own right.

Excerpts from our conversation.

Taba: I am very curious about your name, which is very exotic sounding to me. Where do you hail from? And what is the origin of your name?

Bartho: My mother tongue is Afrikaans, and my full name is Bartholomeus. In English it would be Bartholomew, so I am named after one of the apostles in the Bible. It's a name that runs in our family from both my father's and my mother's side. In the US I most probably would be called just Bart.

Taba: Where did you grow up?

Bartho: Franschhoek in the Western Cape. It's a small town about fifty miles from Cape Town. This is the Dutch spelling for 'French Corner'. It's one of the oldest towns in the Republic of South Africa.

Taba: What path led you to the world of wine?

Bartho: I have to go back a few centuries to answer this question. Our German born ancestor, Heinrich Oostwald Eckstein (changed to Eksteen due to Dutch influence), settled in the Cape in 1702. Ever since, the Eksteens have been involved in wine farming. They set down roots in Bergvliet, then Constantia and Loevenstein (now Welgemoed) and later Franschhoek. The family has always had a passion for vines and wines.

It was in Franschhoek that my grandfather first tried his hand at winemaking on our farm, La Bri. From there, I inherited the winemaking passion and nose for a vintage.

"The family has always had a passion for vines and wines."

Taba: Goodness, that's quite a lineage. How many years have you been working in the wine industry?

Bartho: A total of thirty-three years.

Taba: I came across a terrific story online about you by Malu Lambert in Wines of South Africa. Could you recount for my readers some more of your early childhood?

Bartho: While my grandfather was making wine back at La Bri, I lived with my parents in a second house on the property. My bedroom was next to the wine cellar. I was a real boerseuntjie (farm boy). I would lie in bed and wait to crow back at the roosters in the morning.

Then I went to a boarding school called Boland Landbouskool. We worked the farm most of the week, but on Sundays we could relax and read the newspapers. I came across an advert for a winemaker in *The Rapport* and that's when I thought, "I can do this."

Taba: Where did you go from there?

Bartho: My first job was at Rooiberg, where I learned to classify the grapes into quality categories. The big shift for me was when I went to Romans Rivier (now Mountain Ridge). I was mentored by winemaker Olla Oliver, who handed the red wine production over to me, as well as the wooded white.

Bartho Eksteen

Taba: How did you continue to follow your dream?

Bartho: Well, first I met my wife, Suné. Then I found out about an opening for a winemaker at Wildekrans. I had five great years there. After consulting gigs at Sumaridge and Raka, I established Hermanuspietersfontein (known as HPF), and was both winemaker and director.

Taba: You are so well versed in the whole history of wine growing in South Africa.

Could you please enlighten me?

Bartho: Following the devastation from the phylloxera epidemic in the late 19th century, many vineyards were replanted with high yielding grape varieties, such as Cinsaut. By the early 1900s there was a large glut of wine, creating a wine lake effect which led some producers to pour their unsaleable wine into local rivers and streams. The depressed prices caused by this out of balance supply and demand dynamic prompted the South African government to fund the formation of the Koöperatieve Wijnbouwers Vereniging van Zuid-Afrika Bpkt (KWV) in 1918.

Initially started as a co-operative, the KWV

soon grew in power and prominence, setting policies and prices for the entire South African wine industry. To deal with the wine glut the KWV restricted yields and set minimum prices, encouraging the production of brandy and fortified wines. The KWV put a quota system in place, which forced all farmers not to exceed the quota issued to them. This was a very effective system, but the negative side of it was that it bounded entrepreneurs to explore new areas. It was only after the quota system was lifted in 1992 that new areas started to emerge.

Taba: How did this affect you?

Bartho: Although I grew up in Franschhoek, and was also offered a winemaking position in Stellenbosch, I decided to explore the new, cool climate sites along the Atlantic coastline. Then, in 1996, I established myself as a winemaker in Bot River.

Taba: When David Frost introduced me to you, I had no idea of the depth of your knowledge. Now I know why he picked you (having been a fourth-generation winemaker himself) to be the perfect person to be profiled for this book. Where is your business based now?

Bartho: Our farm is in the Hemel-en-Aarde Valley, about 2.5 miles from the Atlantic Ocean. We're near the beautiful coastal town of Hermanus in what is now known as the Walker Bay Wine District.

Taba: How does this land influence your wines?

Bartho: The benefit of this area is that the cool climate is extremely beneficial for wine production. Gentle southeastern breezes from across the bay make for longer, cooler ripening seasons than is generally experienced in most other South African wine regions. Grapes ripen to their full potential without the dangers of heat waves experienced inland. This results in wines with a high fruit profile, soft and refined tannins, and an extremely elegant, long finish.

Taba: I read that you've been hailed as the 'Sage of Sauvignon'. Please tell me how you earned that esteemed moniker.

Bartho: Well, Vloekskoot ('Lucky Shot'), this Sauvignon Blanc is really my baby.

After years of trials with different terroir, barrels from different coopers, wood from different forests, barrel sizes, roasting intensities, grain and age of the barrels, and time spent in barrel, my first wooded Sauvignon Blanc was released in 2008. I exchanged 225 liters for 500-liter barrels, and new wood for older wood. The right barrel age, roasting intensity and time in barrel, produced a very satisfactory final result: a Diners Club Winemaker of the Year Award, a Platter's 5 star, '93 from Tim Atkin (MW, UK), '92 Lauren Buzzeo (Wine Enthusiast, USA), '94 Christian Eedes (RSA), and '96 Miguel Chan (RSA)."

Taba: And that's just one of your outstanding wines!

Bartho: Our Flagship Range includes Houtskool ('Charcoal'), which is made exactly in the same style as Vloekskoot, but differs slightly due to a small percentage of wooded Semillon that was blended in. The grapes were handpicked, after which it underwent a whole bunch, long and gentle pressing cycle. No settling took place and the juice went straight to an older 500-liter French oak barrel for natural fermentation, where it matured on lees for ten months, with minimum interference prior to bottling.

Taba: You do make some reds as well?

Bartho: We do indeed. One of my favorites is Groepsdruk ('Peer Pressure'). We are very proud to have won the prestigious General Smuts Trophy one year for this one. My son, Pieter-Willem, and I selected the best barrel of red wine in the cellar for this release. It's so great to be able to work with both my son and my wife, Suné, in the business.

Taba: Could you tell me more about your personal philosophy regarding winemaking?

Bartho: I'm a strong believer that as a winemaker, I should spend as much time as possible in the vineyard during harvest, so I can see the challenges of every vintage. It certainly keeps me humble and on my knees. I believe unreservedly in the terroir of Hermanus and its surroundings. It is known as one of the most extreme areas in South Africa.

Taba: Will you please describe what terroir is to you?

Bartho: Terroir is a French term used for the relationship of soil, climate, topography and all other factors that influence the vine and the ultimate character of a wine.

Terroir is everything to me. There are big wine countries who define a great wine in the amount of oak it received. I call them 'man-made' wines. A winemaker's job is to read a vintage and just to guide nature's 'hand of cards' dealt to you.

Taba: Do you grow different grapes on different parcels or blocks of land?

Bartho: I define it even more. A winemaker should at least be on a farm for six years to enable him to learn every aspect of his vineyards. It so often happens that the best wine comes from a small part of a block. You must spend time in the vineyard, especially during harvest.

Taba: Being a winemaker is just one passion. Teaching other people about wine has grown into a school. Please elaborate.

Bartho: We have created a two-tier business model: Bartho Eksteen Wines and Wijnskool (Wine School in English). Bartho Eksteen Wines is focused on crafting wines of distinction, while Wijnskool became a wine academy for young, up-and-coming winemakers.

Suné and I are the founders of the academy. It's a unique concept where we endeavor to impart our knowledge and passion for all things pertaining to wine — from the art of winemaking, the wine industry, its challenges and responsibilities and production.

Our ambition is to enable future generations of winemakers through the academy and grow their passion from high school and onwards. We also decided to use the elements of a school in the christening of all our wines.

Taba: So that certainly illuminates the name of the wine called Professore?

Bartho: Ah, yes, the Professore. I wanted to create a wine in honour of two of the greatest pioneers in South African viticultural history: Professor Abraham Izak Perold and Professor Christiaan Johannes Orffer.

I am quite sure this unique style of wine has never been made in the world. This is a true Cape-blend, consisting of Pinotage, Nouvelle and Roobernet. Pinotage is a red cultivar, a cross between Pinot Noir and Cinsaut created by Professor Perold. Nouvelle is a white variety created by Professor Orffer by crossing Ugni Blanc and Crouchen Blanc. Roobernet is a red variety also created by Professor Orffer by crossing Alicante Bouschet and Cabernet Sauvignon. It's extremely limited and only 34 six bottle cases go on auction.

Taba: It's been so illuminating for me to learn about winemaking in your region of South Africa. It certainly gives me a deeper perspective of David Frost's wine heritage. But now I think David's been having too much fun on the Champion's Tour these days, so it's a good thing the winemaking for his brand is in your hands!

Andrew Keenleyside

Winemaker Akarua Wines, Central Otago NZ

Excerpts from our conversation.

Taba: I am so happy to be introduced to you through Brendan Allen, General Manager of The Hills Golf Club. This is a whole new world for me. And your wineries would be considered New World as well, am I right?

Andrew: Yes, that's correct, we are New World.

Taba: I am curious about your surname. What is the origin, or where do you hail from?

Andrew: Keenleyside comes from Northumberland, England, just south of Hadrian's Wall near Hexham.

Taba: Well, you are a long way from your English roots! Where did your path to the world of wine begin?

Andrew: I developed a taste for wine while at university. I was studying General Science and as part of those studies took a Wine Science paper. That's when I decided I wanted to be a winemaker. Using my degree and horticultural background — I grew up on kiwi fruit orchards — and became a vineyard manager. After three years I decided it was time to move into the winery, so I got a winery job in Napa. In 2003 I came to Central Otago just to do a vintage, and haven't left.

Taba: Would you be considered one of the early pioneers of your industry?

Akarua vineyards with wind turbine

Andrew: Not me personally, but Akarua's founder, Sir Clifford Skeggs, certainly is.

Akarua was established in 1996. I joined in 2009.

Taba: How and where did he get started?

Andrew: He started with the 125-acre 'Home Block' in Cairnmuir Road at the Eastern end of Bannockburn.

Taba: Is Sir Clifford still involved?

Andrew: It is currently run by the second generation with his son, David Skeggs, as our Managing Director.

Taba: From the Akarua website I learned that your vineyards are at forty-five degrees south, and you are the southernmost grape growing region in the world. (For my readers, I should establish the fact that the Otago region is in the South Island of New Zealand.)

Andrew: Correct, Central Otago is in the lower South Island.

Taba: I was curious where Bordeaux in France would be, and it's forty-five degrees north, rather amazing, it is the complete opposite!

Andrew: Yes, several renowned Pinot Noir regions sit on latitude forty-five, Burgundy, Oregon, and Central Otago. It is considered a factor in making great Pinot.

Taba: It is also fascinating that your vineyards at 200 — 400 meters above sea level are also the highest in New Zealand. That's high for New Zealand, but what is the average worldwide?

Andrew: Not sure what the worldwide average altitude is, but I know there are vineyards in California at about 700 meters above sea level and in Argentina at 1000 meters above sea level. So, while we aren't the highest, our altitude certainly has an impact.

Taba: I love that the Akarua logo features the alpine daisy — Celmisia Semicordata, and it symbolizes that beauty is still achievable even in harsh climates like Central Otago. Why is it so harsh?

Andrew: Central Otago is an alpine region, so subject to unpredictable changes in weather. In Bannockburn, where the winery is based, we are officially a semi-arid desert. We typically have very low rainfall and high temperatures in summer with large shifts from day to night. For example, we can have thirty-eight degrees C in the vineyard during the day dropping to eight degrees C at night. The winters can also be very cold and hard. Some winters we can regularly hit minus five at night and have highs of zero during the day.

Taba: What is the story of the Akarua name? It sounds so exotic to me.

Andrew: Aka is the Maori word for the grape vine and rua is the number two, so Akarua translates to 'two vines'. When Sir Cliff planted the original block in Bannockburn, it was only planted in Pinot Noir and Chardonnay, hence two vines.

Taba: There are seven geographical sub-regions in Central Otago, is Bannockburn, where you are, one of them?

Andrew: Yes, Bannockburn is the best-known and highly regarded sub-region in Central Otago. We are very fortunate to have over half of our vineyard area here.

Taba: It appears you have several vineyards. At least five, is that right?

Andrew: We currently have six vineyards. Two in Bannockburn and four in the Pisa sub-region.

Taba: What is unique about the Pisa sub-region?

Andrew: Pisa has the same dry, warm climate as Bannockburn. Very hot days are followed by much colder nights. However, it is only protected on one side, as opposed to three, meaning it can often have more dramatic changes in temperature and wind. This extends the growing season and contributes to the development of rich fruit flavors and acidity in the grapes. The acidity is the key attribute of this sub-region for me. It has real energy and life to it.

Taba: Some parcels are quite small, like the vineyard called 25 Steps is about twenty-two acres and it is terraced. This must be an extra challenge to plant and harvest?

Andrew: Yes, everything is slightly more difficult on this block. The tractor drivers require maps, because if they enter the block on the wrong terrace, they have a long and tricky reverse out. So 'challenging' is a good word for it. Here's how we describe it. The 25 Steps vineyard site in Pisa is a dramatic, terraced vineyard planted entirely to Pinot Noir. It is highly undulating and exposed with a multitude of natural microclimates. The flavours from this vineyard are wonderfully complex and utterly unique in Central Otago.

Taba: In the Felton Road Vineyard you have three blocks of mostly Pinot Noir, Pinot Gris

Springtime at Akarua.

and even Riesling. Why is this land, this terroir, good for all three?

Andrew: The soils here are alluvial. They are a magic rumble-jumble of fractured schist, river gravels, and wind-blown loess, making them very complex. Bannockburn is a north facing crescent surrounded on three sides by mountain ranges. With the Felton vineyard being at the western end of Bannockburn, this is the first vineyard to see the sun in the morning. When we reach the hottest part of the day, which for us is around 5 or 6 pm in summer, the surrounding mountains are starting to shade this vineyard. So, it doesn't get too hot, and we get larger and quicker shifts (drops) in temperature here. This drives flavor development. At this same time, our other vineyard at the eastern end of Bannockburn is in full sun, so it is hotter for longer. This gives us a much different tannin and flavor profile, particularly in the thin-skinned temperature sensitive Pinot Noir.

Taba: Can you speak 'terroir' to me. Winemakers certainly have their own language

Andrew: Bannockburn has one of the warmest, driest climates in Central Otago.

Warm summers are followed by long autumns. The harvest here can come almost a month earlier than in the cooler sub-regions, for example, Gibbston. This warmer climate leads to ripe fruit flavors in the grapes, and Bannockburn Pinot Noir is often heavier and more tannic than wines from other parts of Central Otago. The schist-based soils also bring wonderful brown cooking spices to the wines. Clove, cinnamon, fennel, anis.

Taba: Even though I'm not fluent in the language, I get the gist, or the schist, of it. I've read that the Kawarau Vineyard is the first to hold an organically managed block, growing Chardonnay, Sauvignon Blanc, which is a big favorite of mine, and the star of the show, Pinot Noir. That is very exciting. What do you do differently there?

Andrew: Truthfully, not a great deal. Under-vine cultivation is the main difference and some extra canopy management to keep things open and reduce the risk of disease. We have less options on this block to deal with disease, so extra monitoring is also conducted.

Taba: How would you sum up the company philosophy?

Andrew: We grow all our own grapes, and we don't lease vineyards or purchase fruit. This gives us control over quality and certainty of supply. To meet increasing demand, we have purchased several vineyards over the last five years.

Taba: Now that I have saved up a million and a half reward points, I know exactly where Kevin and I are going when we get to the South Island of New Zealand. Between The Hills and Akarua Winery, like Andrew, I may never leave!

First day of Autumn at Rutherford Hill Winery.

Bryan Parker

Winemaker, General Manager Terlato Wine Group
Rutherford Hill Winery, California USA

EXCERPTS FROM OUR CONVERSATION.

Taba: Where did your path to the world of wine begin?

Bryan: I grew up in New Jersey and attended Rutgers University to study chemistry. I had a great high school chemistry teacher who inspired me. After graduating from Rutgers, I went on to earn my PhD in chemistry from the University of Illinois at Urbana-Champaign.

Taba: How did you wind up in California?

Bryan: After doing postdoctoral studies at Northwestern University, I moved to California in the mid-1990s to study enology and viticulture at UC Davis. This was really to apply my chemistry knowledge in a different field of study. After working a harvest in 1996, I was hooked.

Taba: This sounds like the beginning of a perfect convergence.

Bryan: I continued with classes at Davis for a couple more quarters, worked a second harvest, then started full-time at Beringer Vineyards in 1998.

Taba: That must have been an ideal place to start.

Bryan: It was. Then after working two years at Pine Ridge Winery, I joined the Terlato Wine Group and I've been with them for more than sixteen years.

Taba: Now that you've been in the industry for two decades, how would you define terroir?

Bryan: Terroir is the combination of the climate, soil, and terrain for a particular vineyard. It also includes the grape variety to some extent, and potentially the microbiological makeup of the vineyard. But I'd say it does not include the human inputs such as the trellis system used, irrigation, cluster thinning, or winemaking itself.

Taba: How does the terroir at Rutherford Hill influence the wines you produce?

Bryan: All the wines I make are blends from several different vineyard sources for each wine. The resulting wines exhibit regional styles, but I will say they are not necessarily terroir driven. I do not make any single-vineyard wines which may show more terroir aspects.

Taba: Why is that?

Bryan: In California, I just don't think we have as much experience with terroir as compared to other areas.

Taba: How would you describe the Rutherford AVA?

Bryan: The Rutherford AVA is a moderately warm region with some fog penetration, definitely this morning, and late afternoon cooling breezes. The eastern portion of the AVA has more volcanic soils that are deep and fertile. The western portion has more gravelly, sandy, alluvial soils with moderate fertility.

Taba: This is fascinating, please go on.

Bryan: We can actually go even deeper. The Rutherford AVA has a distinct terroir driven note of dust, known as the famous Rutherford Dust, which gives a fine tannin profile not seen in the AVAs to the north or south. The great winemaker Andre Tchelistcheff said, "It takes Rutherford dust to grow great Cabernet."

Taba: So, the dust is your not-so-secret ingredient. Is it addictive?

Bryan: Ha-ha. Not really, but it does make Rutherford unique.

Taba: Would you call making wine an art or a science?

Bryan: Winemaking is both an art and a science. The science comes with knowing the risks and rewards of the different decisions that are required. The art comes with the sensory aspects of tasting and smelling wines, blending to make the best wines possible, knowing which barrels to use and what percentages of new oak, when to press the wine off its skins, and when to pick the grapes. It really is artful.

Taba: The process seems very complex.

Bryan: Wine is not a simple recipe since each vintage gives you different raw materials to work with. So, some amount of artistry is required to craft wines that appeal to your current and future fans.

Taba: It certainly appears that you have found a way to utilize all your knowledge and passion.

Bryan: As I mentioned, I was drawn to winemaking after my postdoc work. I wanted to stay in an area where I could still use my science background but potentially use it in both an indoor and outdoor setting.

Taba: I think you've got the best of both worlds.

Bryan: That's for sure. I used to make home-brewed beer for several years during graduate school and postdoc, and I'm still fascinated with fermentation. And now I make a lot of fermented products as home — yogurt, kim chee…

Taba: Seriously, kim chee? I only had it once when I was in South Korea. That is certainly an acquired taste, is it not?

Bryan: Probably, yes. Well, I also make pickles, olives, giardiniera, and even sauerkraut!

I think an appropriate title for Bryan would be 'Gourmet Scientist'. I'm wondering if I could persuade him to make me some high-protein breakfast cookies, not pickled, thank you.

Alcsútdoboz, Pannónia Golf & Country-Club, Máriavölgy, Magyarország

Jan Bel Jan, ASGCA

Principal, Jan Bel Jan Golf Course Design

EXCERPTS FROM OUR CONVERSATION.

Taba: You're a Certified Arborist. What inspired that seed to sprout in your early years? Perhaps you were a tomboy like me, and you loved to climb trees?

Jan: Yes, I was a tomboy of sorts. There were acres of fields and forests around the club property where my father designed the golf course, but tree climbing usually revolved around apple picking. I learned about plants from my father when we gardened and took walks through the woods. As soon as we were old enough, each of us children had to plant a garden with at least one vegetable for family meals, and one flower to enjoy the beauty. My Dad showed me how to shape shrubs like roses and azaleas. He also taught me about trees, and why pruning was necessary to reduce limb breakage from heavy, wet snow or ice storms.

Taba: You just reminded me of why I moved from Washington, DC to Scottsdale, Arizona! You certainly were immersed in nature and developed a special appreciation of trees.

Jan: Nature was part of life for us. For firewood, my father would fell trees that were leaning or broken. So, I became familiar with trees in a way that most youngsters could not imagine as being interesting.

Taba: I read that at age 12 you were already working. What compelled you to be so industrious beyond all your gardening and other chores?

Jan: The club was comprised of three farms and 435 acres. I ran the riding stable at the club from when I was 12 to 14. I took care of 8 — 28 horses. I watered, fed, mucked stalls, baled hay, kept the barn and tack clean, and cleared and kept clear the riding trails. I rode English and Western, showed Percheron draft horses at halter, and drove a three-horse hitch hay wagon.

Taba: Given your amazing upbringing, I suppose I shouldn't be so surprised that you were already running an entire equestrian operation when the rest of us are still in sixth grade, starting to learn about algebra and how to use ratios. What came next?

Jan: After three years, the owner of the club sold the horses. Then I started working on the golf course and in the golf shop at age 15.

Taba: Was this the course that your father designed, outside Pittsburgh. Is that where you grew up?

Jan: Yes, with my four brothers and two sisters. I was raised three miles from the closest town. Our nearest neighbors were a quarter mile away. We were about 35 miles from Pittsburgh on the property where my dad designed and supervised the construction of the golf course, and then became the pro-superintendent. We lived 8 miles as the crow flies from Latrobe Country Club where Deacon Palmer, Arnold's father, was the superintendent. He was my dad's mentor.

Taba: With your father, George, being a golf professional and a superintendent, it could be said that golf course design is in your DNA.

Jan: My father was one of six brothers who all grew up caddying at Highland Country Club in the north side of Pittsburgh. The five oldest brothers, Joe, Carl, Eddie, Andy and George, were all in different branches of the military at the same time during World War II. Willie, the youngest, saw Korea up close and personal. I'm proud of their service to our country.

Taba: You had enviable exposure to strong family bonding and gained so many life lessons that you absorbed in a profound way. The Beljan history book sounds like it would have to be several volumes.

Jan: My dad and uncles all came home safely and returned to what they knew best: golf. Eddie and George didn't like the Pittsburgh winters, so they headed south to Miami to caddy during the cold months. Back then it was a three-day drive on US 1. I can remember them telling stories about those days. One of the most memorable was when my dad caddied at La Gorce Country Club for a member who hosted Babe Zaharias in his foursome. Dad said he was awestruck by her power, tactical mind and gamesmanship.

"My dad and uncles all came home safely and returned to what they knew best: golf."

Taba: My goodness. You already knew about this incredible female athlete when you were that young? What are some other stories you remember from that time?

Jan: My uncle Carl often played in pro-ams with Arnold Palmer. Carl was the pro, Arnold was the amateur. Carl was 10 years Arnold's senior. They would frequent the driving range my father operated on US 22 in Murraysville and competed in 'pop-up' long-drive contests. Carl was the pro at the William Flynn-designed Sunnehanna Country Club near Johnstown (PA) from 1946-1949 and my dad was the caddie master. Carl went on to Churchill Valley CC in Pittsburgh, and finished his career at a Donald Ross course, Tippecanoe CC, near Youngstown (Ohio).

Taba: I am bowled over by the pedigree of the Beljan dynasty and how all this family lore stuck with you. If you haven't started writing your memoirs, you better get going!

Jan: Well, we have barely scratched the surface. Here's another remarkable tale. My uncle Andy was the teaching pro from 1951 to 1956 at the Seth Raynor-designed Fishers Island Club (NY) and then he was promoted to head pro until 1975 — in the summers.

Taba: I have been to Fishers Island. It's magical. I have goose bumps. Go on.

Jan: In the winters until 1965, Uncle Andy was the pro at several courses on the east coast of Florida, including Lost Tree (in North Palm Beach), and Ormond Beach GC. During his two winters at Ormond Beach, Andy played golf several times a week with Moe Norman. Moe, and everyone else, liked Andy because he was low-key and genuine.

Taba: I am blown away. A few years ago, I read *The Legend of Moe Norman*. He was a phenomenal golfer. A misunderstood genius. And here he figures into the Beljan biography.

Jan: Well then, you'll love this last bit about Andy. I worked on several projects in Naples for Tom Fazio some years ago and I was able to spend time with Andy. Weekly, he lunched and played golf with Gene Sarazen. In his 1982 book, *Following Through*, Herbert Warren Wind writes of one of those days in the chapter titled 'An Old Master'. Mr Sarazen was 80 at the time. When Uncle Andy passed, I inherited the letters Gene Sarazen wrote to him through the years, Mrs Sarazen's handwritten recipe for her apple pie, as well as a framed print of Augusta National's 12th green from Hord Hardin. He was the Chairman of the Masters Tournament from 1980 to 1991.

Taba: I was already a little nervous before this conversation, knowing I am talking to the current President of the American Society of Golf Course Architects. Now I have crossed into the realm of sheer amazement by this narrative, and we haven't even started on how your own career began. With all your inherent knowledge, why did you even bother with college?

Jan: I realized that Landscape Architecture would allow me to convey ideas graphically as well as verbally, and that I could capitalize on what I had learned about plants and turf. My intent was to attend Penn State. But as I finished high school, my father took a pro-superintendent job 25 miles south of the Mason-Dixon Line in West Virginia. So, I applied to West Virginia University and was rewarded with an academic scholarship.

Taba: What did you do with your degree?

Jan: After I earned my degree, I was hired as a sales rep and technician for the Davey Tree Expert Company's Lawn Care Division in Pittsburgh. One of my clients, Jack Mahaffey, recognized the Beljan name on the business card I had left and asked to meet me. The Beljan name was well-known in western Pennsylvania golf circles and Mr Mahaffey was surprised it was a niece, not a Beljan nephew or son who greeted him.

Taba: Why was this such an auspicious meeting?

Jan: Mr Mahaffey was a long-time member of Oakmont CC, a superb amateur golfer, president of the Pennsylvania Golf Association and a USGA Executive Committee member. He had played in tournaments with my uncles and at their clubs. He was so gracious to have an interest in my career and me and arranged for me to meet a friend who was looking for someone to work in a golf course design office in Jupiter, Florida. It was Tom Fazio.

Taba: Then what happened?

"Then he offered me a job with George Fazio of Tom Fazio Golf Course Designers Inc. How incredible is that?"

Jan: My first interview with Tom was on the veranda of Oakmont's clubhouse. Tom was interested enough to ask me to come to Florida for a second interview. Then he offered me a job with George Fazio of Tom Fazio Golf Course Designers Inc. How incredible is that?

Taba: Wow. This had to be a dream job, right?

Jan: I didn't know what a dream job it would be — to learn from someone as savvy and astute as Tom Fazio, who had learned from his uncle, George Fazio (a contemporary of Ben Hogan) and at a time when golf was on the verge of a rapid increase.

Taba: Nothing like starting at the top, Jan. What sorts of projects where you involved with?

Jan: One of the first was PGA National. I did the plans and construction documents for the original three courses there: The Squire (a tribute to Gene Sarazen), The Haig (Walter Hagen) and The Champion, which was designed to host the 1983 Ryder Cup.

Taba: Did you even use computers at that time?

Jan: These were the days of manual hard-line drawing, using ink on mylar. A change on one plan meant re-drafting on all the plans in the set and reprinting with an ammonia print machine. The IBM Selectric typewriter was high-tech and push-button phones were trending.

This was pre-computer aided design (CAD). To estimate volumes of dirt to be moved, contour lines on plans were manually measured and recorded. Then a series of mathematical formulas were used to arrive at the volume. Adding machine tape was used so we could double-check our input for accuracy.

Taba: I feel like I have struck gold, Jan. To be able to tap into your rich vein of knowledge is nothing short of mind-boggling. Can you tell me a few more courses you worked on with Fazio?

Jan: Sure. The Vintage Club in Indian Wells (CA). Wade Hampton in Cashiers (NC), Ventana Canyon (Tucson, AZ), and Lake Nona in Orlando (FL), to name just a few on which I did the plans only. I started field design at Pelican's Nest (Bonita Springs, FL) and worked on-site at The Farm (Dalton, GA), St Ives (Atlanta, GA), World Woods (Brooksville, FL) and many others.

Taba: So, not only were you doing courses all over the country, they were on different types of terrain, or terroir.

Jan: Right. Each of these courses was designed on a very different land. Sandy soils, coupled with wetlands on some, deserts with flash floods in barrancas from the surrounding mountainous watersheds, Smoky Mountain granite rock and clay with a topsoil layer. It's not just the soil type, but the orientation to the sun, the amount of rain annually, as well as the kind of slope and vegetation that helps determine how any course may be designed.

Taba: Now that you've been running your own firm for the last ten years, and you are at the top of your profession, do you find time for a glass of wine?

Jan: Yes, indeed! My favorite is Shiraz. I was introduced to Australian Shiraz, specifically, Penfolds Bin 128 Coonawara Shiraz when I stayed at Greywalls in Gullane, Scotland. This memory takes me back to when my grandfather grew grapes in Pittsburgh and made his own wine. He used to have big crocks in his basement, in fact, it was a cellar. It wasn't until I was in France many years later, that I understood why he used a small water glass for his wine. It was how families in Europe drank wine at home or in small restaurants. No fancy glasses there.

Taba: I'm in the habit of doing that myself when I'm home too.

Jan: Well Taba, someday soon, I would enjoy sharing wine with you in paper-thin crystal glasses with beautiful tones that make you happy when you toast 'good health!'

Bill Coore, ASGCA

Principal, Coore & Crenshaw

Excerpts from our conversation.

Taba: How did you first get interested in golf course design?

Bill: In a nutshell, I grew up in North Carolina and my closest neighbor lived down a dirt road. In a county. Not even in a town. He liked to play golf and I'd caddie for him. He gave me some old clubs. He's the one who introduced me to golf. He'd take me with him once in a while and even took me a couple of times to Pinehurst. Some of us would hit balls out in a cornfield, just making up holes and play from here to there to there.

Then I played some very inexpensive courses in the area. I realized the great thing about golf is that it's something you could do by yourself.

I wound up going to college. But not on a golf scholarship. I became a member of the golf team.

Taba: Where did you go to college?

Bill: Wake Forest. I was so far down the bench. Technically I was on the team for a couple of years though. But I got a chance to play golf at Old Town Club in Winston-Salem. It's an old Perry Maxwell course. Extraordinary course. Immediately adjacent to the campus at Wake Forest.

If you were a student at Wake Forest, they

charged you a dollar. One of the best in America. He (Maxwell) designed it right after working at Augusta National in the 1930s.

I had the opportunity to experience Pinehurst #2 and Old Town.

In those days, all of us who played golf were focused on our games. There came a time that you wondered, "Why do I like this course?" Little by little, what seeped into my thick skull was, I could play an assortment of shots to get to the green as opposed to modern courses where you would play shots in the air.

It was just sort of a hobby. I had no intention of getting into this business and thought I was going to be a university professor and play some amateur golf.

Taba: Then what happened?

Bill: Uncle Sam decided I should do some other things. I spent time in the military. Just as I was getting out of the army, I saw a course that Pete Dye was doing. Very few people had heard of him. He was doing things like Harbour Town — not in vogue at the time.

Bill Coor and Ben Crenshaw at Brambles California

I found it interesting and wondered, "How did he do this?"

I was thinking of going to graduate school at Duke, but didn't.

I thought maybe I could see how you actually build a golf course and literally badgered Pete Dye until he finally agreed to let me work for him as a laborer. One thing led to another, and another.

Pete sent me to east Texas. I inherited the job as a superintendent and had no idea what to do.

I went there to work in construction. I had no training yet had played enough golf to know what a course should look like. But how do you get it from that?

People who were very well-versed, wrote out notes for me: "This is what you're doing the first two weeks. This is what you're going to do the next month." It led to several years of being a superintendent.

I learned how to take care of a golf course and how to get it into condition to play golf.

Not something I planned to do. Evolutionary process. One of the very best things that I could do to prepare me.

Taba: A neighbor who I walk with says, "Providence works in mysterious ways." It seems like you were sort of being guided.

Bill: I'd like to say I had this plan. You played golf at Tom's (Tom Doak) course in France. I've known him since he was right out of Cornell University. He's the most brilliant to practise golf architecture. Very analytical. Very structured. Very mathematical.

Tom has pursued this career since he was a young kid. Very systematic to get to where he is.

Mine has been like a wood chip pitched into a creek. Water flows down. I bump into a rock. I'd like to say it's been forethought. It's been accidental more than planned.

Taba: It sounds like an organic evolution.

Bill: You have to be prepared to observe and be aware of what is happening around you.

Some good things that happened to me are things I never planned. "Oh, this could be pretty good. I'll try to make something of this." It's a combination.

Taba: So back to how things went when you became a superintendent.

Bill: I was introduced to some people building a nine-hole course on the gulf of Texas. They had parted ways with the designer. They were desperate. They had equipment working out there in the field and were asking, "What are we doing?"

The project manager took me down there and said, "I know you'd like to be in the golf design business. These people might need your help. Why don't you finish these nine holes?

Here's the budget. Can't spend one dollar more."

I was thrown into the deep end of the pool. The nine holes turned out reasonably well. People liked it. Then they asked me to design the second nine.

The course got a reasonable amount of acclaim.

That set the stage of moving me forward into becoming a full-time designer.

Taba: Another main question. Do you have a special affinity for a certain type of land or terrain or soil? If somebody said, "You pick anywhere in the world." Where would you want to design a course?

Bill: Every architect will say, "Land along the ocean." It's the birthplace of golf.

"Every architect will say, "Land along the ocean." It's the birthplace of golf."

Sand is the link throughout the history of golf and golf architecture. Because of where the game was born — in those windswept dune features. Sandy ground generally has huge character.

It's the easiest ground to work with, the most appealing and attractive, and has the greatest potential of yielding a beautiful golf course.

That's what everyone would seek. Now, beyond that, look for sites that are naturally gifted for golf. Sites that require minimal alteration to make them suitable for golf. Sites that have an individual character.

Like you said in your introduction, Taba, "Soil types give birth to different types of wine."

They give character and individuality to wine. Same with golf.

Individual sites, if they have a strong individual character and are readily adaptable for golf, should yield interesting, high-quality courses. The best courses complement their landscapes.

Taba: I agree with that.

Bill: Back to your point. Individual ground should yield an individualistic golf course with its own characteristics. With Mike Keiser, we have got this amazing site in Scotland, Coul Links, going through the approval process now.

Taba: I've been reading about Coul Links for a few years. I love that part of Scotland.

I'll be up there this summer. I'll be at Dornoch.

Bill: That's Mike's favorite course and the inspiration for him to do all these courses.

Taba: What project, anywhere in the world, would you say has been the most challenging?

Bill: Might give you two. Opposite ends of the spectrum. One would be the Sand Hills in Nebraska. Considered a great course. The reason it was challenging, physically challenging, was all the sand dunes. The wind blows quite consistently and strongly.

The biggest challenge was living up to its potential. We knew when we, with Bill and Ben Crenshaw, saw that site if we didn't create one of the world's truly outstanding golf courses, we'd have failed.

The potential is way up here (holding one hand very high). In the end, it could be up here, it could be extremely good even if was here (holding his other hand lower). But it wouldn't be what it could have been.

The mirror image of that is here in Scottsdale, Arizona, at Talking Stick. If you said the Sand Hills, zero to ten, where did you start. Probably already a nine.

Talking Stick. What was the potential for the site to produce interesting golf? Probably point two-five. Less than one. Almost zero. The challenge there was how to make something interesting and enjoyable.

They were fascinating things. Happened in close proximity.

Sand Hills opened in 1995. Talking Stick, both courses, opened in 1997. People asked us, "Why would you go there?"

We get kidded all the time with, "You guys get the best sites." There's a lot of truth to that.

But Talking Stick, we had just come off working on one of the best sites in the world. Maybe we should go work on a site with no potential and see if people find it enjoyable?

People ask, "What's the best course?" How do you define the best?

Is the best defined by the world's critics? Or is the best course one that had no potential?

Yet the parking lot is full and has been all these years. People play them over and over again.

Maybe that is the best thing we have done.

Taba: If I could be born again, I'd want to be a golf architect. I wish I had taken up the game at an early age. Now I'm getting worse because I don't have time to play. I took a lesson at Talking Stick with Christine Reese. She's with Vision 54.

Bill: They do a fabulous job.

Taba: I would take a lesson with her every week for the rest of my life if I needed it or not. For me, golf is a reward. I must do my work first.

We-Ko-Pa Golf Club in Fountain Hills, Arizona.

Bill: But you're enjoying seeing the courses and seeing other people enjoying the courses. All these lists and rankings — it comes down to: Are there people enjoying playing these courses?

Mike Keiser said it best with, "The definition of a great course is one where you walk off the 18th green and want to go immediately to the first tee and do it again." Sums it up.

Tom Doak

Principal, Renaissance Golf Design

Excerpted from our conversation.

Author's note: All words in [square brackets] are asides by Tom Doak, and all words in (parentheses) are my asides.

Taba: I learned from reading in your book, Anatomy of a Golf Course, that your mother, Betty, grew up on a farm in Missouri and you believe she imparted her love of the land. Where did you grow up?

Tom: Actually, both of my parents grew up on farms in central Missouri. But my dad wound up being in charge of commodities buying for Lever Brothers in New York City, so I was born there. We moved to the suburbs when I was three, and I grew up in Stamford, Connecticut.

Taba: Your mother was also a big influence on you in other ways. You said it was she who taught you to write. So, you were doubly blessed with such an incredible mother. Please elaborate a little.

Tom: Mom was a journalism major at the University of Missouri. After graduating she worked for the extension offices at the University of Delaware, and then at Cornell where she met my dad when he was pursuing

Cape Kidnappers 15, 16, 17th Holes.

his PhD after the war. Her job was to take the advice of the professors and edit it so that the farmers could understand it clearly.

She wasn't able to have children, but when she was 41, her doctor told her there was a new operation which could change that. I was born the next year, and my brother arrived two years later. We were always encouraged to pursue our interests, whatever they might be.

Taba: You wrote that your dad let you tag along

on his golf trips when you were 10 or 11, and you had exposure to some really outstanding courses. Can you describe how you became fascinated with how different they were to the course where you learned the game?

Tom: My parents were not country club types and I would never have become interested in golf except for two things. First, when I was ten years old, the City of Stamford opened a new public course a mile from my house, at Sterling Farms. As kids, we could play after 3:00 pm for one dollar per round. So that was my access to golf.

My dad didn't play all that much. But once a year, he went to a convention to meet the people he did business with on the phone all year. It was in August, so that was our big family vacation every summer. When we were young, they'd hold it in cool cities [Denver, Montreal, Seattle] and just have a one-day golf outing at a club. But as it got bigger, they decided to take it to golf resorts. As a result, I saw Harbour Town when I was 11, Pinehurst at age 12, and Pebble Beach when I was 13 [and every other year after that!]. Those courses were so different from Sterling Farms, that I got fascinated about why that was.

The other lucky break for me was that Harbour Town had a little yardage book of sorts. Although nobody played by yardages then, it had diagrams of every hole and two sentences about how to play them. It was written by Charles Price (historian and author), who was friends with Pete Dye (golf architect genius and mentor to many) and lived on Hilton Head while the course was being built. I'll give you an example, "Second hole. This par 5 is reachable in two shots, but to get home you will want to drive near the fairway bunker on the left, so that you can avoid the tree short of the green on your second shot." It was the perfect primer on golf course architecture for a kid who was interested in the subject.

Taba: Let's fast forward to how you found your way to Cornell University.

Tom: I was a really good student, especially in math and science, and I was admitted as a freshman at MIT. For the first time, I was surrounded by thousands of other students who were just as good as me at all that stuff, and I just wasn't excited by the thought of a career in engineering, or anything indoors, to be honest.

I was reading The World Atlas of Golf, and any other golf book I could get my hands on. So, I wrote to a handful of golf course architects, asked for advice, and got two responses. One from Pete Dye, who said he didn't have any work for me but didn't discourage me. And one from Geoffrey Cornish [the designer of Sterling Farms], who wrote back, "There is always room in the business for someone with real talent."

Geoffrey recommended landscape architecture as the best major for me. Of course, MIT didn't offer that, but one of the two schools in the northeast that did was Cornell, which helped alleviate any doubts my parents might have had about the change of venue.

Taba: And then your path took an amazing turn when a Cornell alumnus endowed a scholarship that allowed you to spend a year studying the great golf courses of the British Isles. There is so much serendipity here. How great is it when a gifted person receives such a great endowment?

Tom: Ezra Cornell's mission was to "found an institution where any person can find instruction in any study", so my department was entirely accepting that I had a very specialized career I wanted to pursue, even though my first two years of landscape architecture classes were pretty much the same as everyone else. Also, it didn't hurt that Robert Trent Jones Sr (considered the father of modern golf course architecture whose career spanned nearly 70 years) had studied there for two years before embarking on the same career. They let me take some courses in agronomy and turf management on the side, too. Landscape Architecture is part of the School of Agriculture.

But by far the best aspect of the department, which I didn't know when I started there, was that there is an endowed scholarship left by a gentleman named William Frederick Dreer (an innovative seed dealer and florist from Philadelphia), specifically set aside for overseas study for a graduating student who isn't able to study exactly what they wanted at Cornell. As soon as I read it, I thought that it was written for me. But I also wondered how I would ever convince a group of professors to send me to Britain and Ireland, essentially, to play golf. So, I rounded up letters of recommendation from all the people in golf I had been corresponding with while in college. This included Pete Dye, Deane Beman (professional golfer and PGA Tour commissioner), Herbert Warren Wind (prolific golf writer who coined the phrase 'Amen Corner'), and Ben Crenshaw (two-time Masters winner). I got the scholarship and during the summer of 1982-1983, walked and studied 170 courses throughout Britain and Ireland, including a two-month stint living in St Andrews and caddying on The Old Course.

Taba: The second book in my library after Michael Murphy's *Golf in the Kingdom*, is your book, The Confidential Guide. My copy was published in 1996. (Ha-ha, it's worth a few bob now.) This is where I learned that you are a true renegade. I found so much of your commentary to be irreverent. I loved it. You hooked me on golf architecture. So, it's all your fault that I've followed the breadcrumbs down this path!

Tom: The original version of that book was written strictly for all the people who had helped me get started in golf. Everyone knew how much I had traveled at that point, and people would call asking if it was worth it to go see Shoreacres or Cruden Bay or wherever. So, I figured I would just write it all down for them. I printed 40 copies and gave them away at Christmas, in 1988. And since the book was for friends, I didn't worry at all about offending anyone. If I didn't have something good to say about a course, I'd write something funny and irreverent, or skewer it.

I was pretty surprised at how much everyone enjoyed my reviews, but I had done some writing for Golf Magazine by then, I actually started while I was still in college, and I understood that you never saw anything negative in the

Stone Eagle Golf Club, 19th Hole.

magazines. This was because magazines don't want to risk offending a potential advertiser. So, every course they write about is even better than the last, no matter how good or bad they really are. I just didn't think I could write about what was good, without making the contrast with what was not so good.

Taba: In your years of studies, I guess you read all the great literature about the game of golf — and now you've become a prolific writer, too.

And, since I've been an art dealer for 40 years, it was music to my ears (or to my eyes, since we are talking about reading) to see that you wrote, "Remember, too, that like any other fine art, all golf architecture is a matter of opinion." How or when did it occur to you that golf architecture is an art form?

Tom: I suppose I knew it for sure the first time I saw Cypress Point, when I was 15. Cypress Point is not just a golf course, it's an incredibly beautiful place, and the sequence of holes gives you a guided tour of that beauty.

After college, I spent four years working for Pete Dye, who approached golf course architecture much like sculpture. Pete would laugh at that and describe what he was doing as, "playing around in the dirt," yet he certainly had the artistic temperament. He had no fear of changing his design on the fly when an inspiration came his way.

Sometime during that first summer when I worked for him, Pete said to me that not just golf architecture, everything in golf was a matter of opinion. There was no right way to build a golf hole, like there was no right way to swing a golf club, or to grow grass. I've always been an independent thinker, and that was when I stopped worrying about what others might think about my designs. [If I ever got to do one . . . I was twenty at the time!]

Taba: Since I sense you are a kindred spirit in this regard, I will risk going off on a tangent. Perhaps it is esoteric. I have been saying for years that golf course architects are Rembrandts and Beethovens of their domain. It is not a mistake that I chose Beethoven, a composer, and not Michelangelo or da Vinci, to make my point. In your own heart and mind, do you feel that you are an artist, whose canvas is the largest in the world — the planet Earth — yet also a composer? You are composing an experience, are you not?

Tom: One of my former associates used to say that when he was running a golf course construction project, he was like the conductor of a symphony, telling the shapers [musicians] how wild they could go in their solos, but keeping the whole team on the same page. He was leaving the 'composer' role to me [until he decided he could do that part, too].

I have played golf over the years with a couple of famous musicians. A lot of them are avid golfers, because they work evenings. When I've asked how they write a song, it sounds a lot like how I route a golf course. Sometimes, it all comes together in a matter of a few hours, and other times, you'll have a lyric [or a golf hole] sitting around in your head for years, until suddenly you find the right place for it.

Taba: Well, Tom, I'm glad I went out on a limb and dangled out there with Beethoven! Please go on.

Tom: The order of the holes is an important part of the experience. Many architects have a way they prefer it to unfold. The cliché is that you build to a crescendo at the end, but not all great songs are like that, and great golf courses have their own different rhythms, too.

Another cliché of golf design is that the opening holes should provide 'a gentle handshake', but it depends on the terrain and on how you want people to feel. Personally, I think most great courses have you under their spell by the third hole, so it's no coincidence that Pacific Dunes works its way to the oceanfront at the third green.

Golf is a much more emotional experience than most people give it credit for. And I like to highlight those aspects in my designs — the thrill of driving from a high tee, or getting over a big bunker [or out of one!], or threading your ball through a narrow space.

One of my most treasured reviews is by one of the players from the US Public Links Tournament at Pacific Dunes. She said that when she came around the corner to the fourth tee for the first time, she cried because it was so beautiful. I probably wouldn't cry, but it still gives me goosebumps.

Taba: Because this is a book about terroir, I am most curious about your view of just what is terroir, or what kind of land or ground is your favorite, or intrigues you the most?

Tom: The answer, not to your surprise, would be sand or sandy loam soils, which have been a lot of the key to my success, I think.

Building a modern golf course can require replicating your work in all kinds of layers — the base, gravel layer, and sand mix for a USGA green, or drainage, liner material, and bunker sand in a bunker. Building in sand eliminates all those extra steps. What you see when you shape the ground is the finished product. You can stand in a bunker and decide if it ought to be deeper or shallower. You can move the edges of a green farther out, or in tighter, just by painting a new line, and without having to worry about whether or not the contractor will get all the tie — ins right after all the other layers go on. It's just so much easier. It's akin to the revolution in desktop publishing, where what you see on the computer screen is exactly what you will see on the finished page.

Sand also allows you to create different landforms from what you could on heavier soils. You can make an area of short grass steer balls down onto a green or into a bunker, and drain down into them, without worrying about the mix or the bunker sand getting contaminated with silt. Or, whether a little pocket in the fairway will drain after a big rain.

Last, but not least, construction delays are minimized by the superior natural drainage, so it makes my job much easier. I can plan on visiting New Zealand for six days and not worry what will happen if it rains hard and we can't work that week. Believe me, it was not so easy in Houston this year!

Ironically, though, I have found that my preferred design style of using the natural contours is actually the most valuable on severe terrain and heavier soils, where every change you make is far more expensive. Courses like Stone Eagle in California and Rock Creek in Montana are not my usual fare. But we managed to make them feel like they are natural terrain for golf, even though they were very difficult to build.

Taba: It was especially fun for me to meet you

in France last year at the course you designed in Bordeaux, Grand Saint Emilionnais Golf Club. I learned a lot when you talked about how you built the individual holes so they would not only be beautiful and challenging to play, yet you always took into consideration how water would flow. You were so eloquent when you explained how you did this. Perhaps you could say a little more about it here.

Tom: Most architects will tell you the key to good design is drainage, or the more advanced version of that, which is to make the drainage look good [so you don't notice it at all]. I've worked on a lot of sandy sites where you can build features that don't surface drain well, because the soil makes up for it. But when you are working on clay such as in St Emilion, you don't have that luxury. You must be sure that the water flows around the greens, and not across the fairway right where most people will be hitting their approach shots and that runoff doesn't contaminate the bunkers [which is one reason Augusta had way fewer bunkers than Cypress Point].

"You must be sure that the water flows around the greens, and not across the fairway."

The other part of building in St Emilion that was interesting is that the environmental laws are written by the local farmers, and in Bordeaux that's the winemakers. One of their main rules [which I've never dealt with anywhere else] is that you are not allowed to drill a well as a water source. You need to make do with what Mother Nature gives you in the way of rainfall. That's why vintages are so important in Bordeaux wines. If it's too wet or too droughty the grapes won't be at their best. But it also protects the wineries that have the best terroir, and the most complete knowledge of how to blend their grapes differently in a wetter year.

For the golf course, having such a limit on the volume of irrigation water was a challenge. Luckily, the course is all set in one big valley. By building a big pond at the bottom, we capture all the rain that falls on the site and use it. Then, anything that's not taken up by the plants works its way back to the pond so we can use it again. In the spring, the golf course superintendent waters the course less than his peers, because he's always got to be wary that he will run out of water in a dry summer. So, the grasses adapt to drought conditions, and the playing conditions are quite good considering the clay soils.

Taba: Since the subtitle of my book is *A Golf Book for Wine Lovers* perhaps this is a good place to end where we began, playing golf in one of the greatest wine regions in the world. Thanks to you and the Mourgue d'Algue family, you have perfectly illustrated the synergy between golf and wine!

So, this is where we converge by continuing our pursuit of seduction, beauty and pleasure through the language of golf course architecture and playing the game of golf through the puzzles you create for us.

You move our eyes through space and our bodies over the terrain, and then we can celebrate with another living work of art — a luxuriant glass of wine!

David McLay Kidd

Principal, DMK Golf Design

Excerpts from Rolling Hills Country Club video, and Easy Reader newspaper article.

"I was on the point of thanking Chuck for the opportunity and leaving when we reached the highest point of the course and I was able to look down into the quarry. It wasn't a rock quarry. It was a sand quarry."

"Sand is the elixir of life to a golf course designer. Knowing we had hundreds of acres of sand next to the course meant we had the sacred ingredient needed to make a great course," Kidd said.

"Sand is what makes great golf courses great to a golf course designer. It lays under the turf. The average player doesn't know it's there but that's what makes the courses great.

It's the secret ingredient to create great golf. It's what enables me to create a firm, fast golf course that's incredibly natural."

Kidd is known for designing "links" courses. Links is a Scottish term that refers to coastal areas, where the early Scottish golf courses were built on land unsuitable for any other purpose.

Golf according to Kidd:
One afternoon last month, after walking the course with construction supervisor Vaughey, general manager Sullivan, board member Welsh and this reporter, the group seated itself around a low table in the old clubhouse and listened to Kidd's thoughts on golf course design.

"In 2008," Kidd said, "I had an epiphany. Harder is not better. Fun is better. Why did people love the early courses I designed, when I knew so little? And why weren't they returning to play the courses I did 10 years later when I knew so much more?"

"Golf is already one of the hardest sports there is, and you want me to make it harder?

Imagine if tennis had to be played with wooden rackets and skiers had to use straight skis." Kidd, a 6 handicap, said he learned that early on as a golfer.

"But it took me a long time to understand what that meant for a golf course architect," he said. "We've been taught that golf is all about intimidation and playing defense. I'm turning that on its head. I want my courses to breed confidence. Then golf becomes fun."

Kidd traced the divergence between the Scottish links courses he grew up with and America's less forgiving parkland courses to the 1933 opening of Augusta National, the Churchill Downs of golf, with its colorful flower boxes, tree lined fairways and bright white, egg-shaped bunkers.

"Never was the iron gauntlet of challenge more skillfully concealed in velvet," the legendary Bobby Jones said of the course he helped design. "The architect assumes the role of defender against the golfer attacking the course," he wrote in "Golf by Design."

"Every April, golfers watched the Augusta Masters on their color TVs and dusted off their clubs. Groundskeepers looked at Augusta and thought, 'That's my benchmark,'" Kidd said.

"Then Bandon Dunes opened, and American golfers were able to experience the golf I grew up with — its wiry grasses, multiple colors, imperfect nature."

"I spent my childhood at St. Andrews and Gleneagles. That's the only golf I knew." "When I came to Bandon Dunes to meet with (owner) Mike Keiser, I had never played a Pete Dye, an Arnold Palmer, a Jack Nicklaus or a Tom Fazio course.

"I knew Keiser had already talked to Nicklaus and Fazio and didn't think I had a chance.

So, I told him what I thought, that he should keep it simple because the land was already so good. A few weeks later, he called and asked, 'Do you really believe what you said?'"

"He thought golf had gone down a course it wasn't meant to go down and he wanted someone unencumbered by American golf's overcontrolled and overspending look."

"So, he hired someone who didn't know enough to screw it up."

Kidd was 27. As he had proposed, he left the relatively flat, nearly treeless site largely alone, wrapping the fairways around the brown sand bunkers that had always been there. When Bandon Dunes opened in 1990 it triggered a revolution in golf course design in the US

"Whatever else I achieve; I believe Bandon Dunes marked a turning point in my life and I believe it marked a turning point in golf in America. Sophisticated American golfers already understand that," Kidd said.

Like Bandon Dunes, Rolling Hills' fairways will be defined by strips of tall grass rather than trees. Its bunkers will be the brown sand that has always been there.

Kidd concluded, "Course design changes from an engineering exercise to a lot of hand waving, flag planting and foot dragging [to outline the bunkers and greens]. The trick is to make the course look as random as nature. It's whimsy that excites golfers. People look at the old Scottish courses and ask, why is there a hump in the fairway? It's there because it was there. No one shaped it."

Pat Ruddy

Owner, Designer The European Club

Excerpts from our conversation.

Taba: I am with Pat Ruddy in his magnificent library at The European Club. It's such an honor to be here with you in your sanctuary. It's so nice and cozy. I could live in this room.

Pat: It's a warm room. And a perfect place for my books, a bit more than 6,500 now.

Moving along very well.

Taba: At least ten of them you've penned yourself. It's only natural for somebody who loves words as much as loves designing golf holes to collect so many books about golf. When did you get started collecting?

Pat: I got my first personal book in 1958. It was Henry Cotton's My Golfing Album.

Before that I read my father's books. One of my brothers gave me another book, so I had two books. Then I got Tommy Armour's How to Play your Best Golf and was launched on a lifelong expedition of thoughts and images.

Taba: One of the things I remember when I first met you in 2003, was I learned you were from Sligo. What was it like growing up in Sligo? For those who don't know, Sligo is in the west of Ireland.

Pat: I was born in the neighboring county, Mayo, in a town called Ballina. When I was about 6 or 7, my dad moved us to south Sligo. A place called Ballymote, in the province of Connacht. The golf course there was very modest.

Taba: In one of your books, I read about a lady who took care of a golf course with her horse. Please recount that.

Pat: I've never lost the image of this lady. She would tackle up her horse and put leather boots on him to prevent making hoof marks and go along and cut the fairways using a cylinder mower. They didn't always get cut, due to bad weather, and would take a long time to do it. She made the fairways about 20 yards wide, and when our ball went off the fairway, we'd walk up and down, side by side and hope to kick or step on the ball.

Taba: This was an actual course?

Pat: Yes, this was at Ballymote, a nine-hole course. There were fences around the greens to keep the cattle off. She was the first greenkeeper. Life was simple then, post-World War II, and most golf clubs had very modest courses which were established and kept at low cost. Some of today's big spenders could have avoided much pain if they had a taste of history and stayed out of debt.

Typical Pat Ruddy bunkers at European Club with railroad ties.

Taba: Sligo would be considered Yeats country. He considered it his spiritual home. I think you would too. Your spiritual golf home.

Pat: This was the richest part of my childhood. It was heaven for a dreamy child. Lovely landscapes and lovely people. Everyone would make tea for me when I visited, and apple tart.

The golf courses were uncrowded, too. And there was lots of room to hit balls, eat ham sandwiches and drink buttermilk.

Taba: Yeats was born in 1865 and died in 1939. In 1923 he was awarded the Nobel Prize for Literature. Many believe he produced his greatest works after receiving the Nobel Prize.

Pat: We were reared on Yeats, you see. We knew the poem of Innisfree. I cycled down to see it as soon as I had a bicycle. It was Yeats and these men who immortalized the place. It's easily equal in beauty to any place on the planet.

Taba: I read in your book, Holes in my Head, and I quote: "It was at Rosses Point I fell seriously in love with golf. It was the 1950s. I was but a boy. Ever since, as boy and man, I have dreamt of Rosses Point every day. Every day."

You are every bit a poet yourself. You went on to talk about many happy memories there.

You wrote, "I even thought about making arrangements to be buried there near Benbulben." (This is the famous tabletop mountain, formed during the ice age.)

Pat: I was going to be mummified and placed in a standing position under the tenth tee at the County Sligo Golf Club. I would leave them some money to make a window looking down the fairway towards Benbulben, so I could see my friends and their descendants going golfing, and extra cash to keep the window clean. (lots of laughter)

Taba: That's the poet in you. You're so artistic. You have such an incredible imagination.

Pat: Children in the country have a great advantage. They see birds, bees, plants growing, leaves being shed, and storm clouds coming.

If you are a child in the country, you get the rhythm of life.

Taba: Please tell me more about County Sligo Golf Club (known as Rosses Point).

Pat: Every hole at Rosses Point is full of happy memories. Most of all, my father and I going out to play with his friends. Also, the thrill at championship time of watching my heroes like Cecil Ewing (born at Rosses Point, prolific amateur golfer from 1930 to 1955) and Joe Carr (the greatest amateur Irish golfer of all time, first Irishman to play in the Masters and Captain of the Royal & Ancient Golf Club in 1991, inducted into the World Golf Hall of Fame in 2007) perform unbelievable feats.

The thrill of the opening drive! The climb to the second green to stand and drink in the view of the wide Atlantic with almost the entire classic links revealed below. Heaven on earth.

"The climb to the second green to stand and drink in the view of the wide Atlantic with almost the entire classic links revealed below."

Taba: What was the spark that ignited your interest, your obsession with golf?

Pat: It was here that the seeds were sown for a career in golf course architecture. I was told that the links had been designed by a great man named Harry Colt in 1927. That seemed like ages ago, but he became much more immediate when I realized he had died as recently as 1951. Our lives had overlapped.

We lived twenty miles from Rosses Point. The roads were quiet then. There weren't many motor cars.

Taba: You wrote in Holes, "I couldn't get the ball to do what I wanted it to do. I spent a lot of time thinking about how my driver would get from here to there. Then I had to get into position to get around the bunker...would I hit a 5-iron or 7-iron to get on the green?" So, you were sitting in the back of the class trying to work this out.

Pat: Always the back. Colt got me working in the back seat at school, hoping that the teachers

The European Club, beside the Irish Sea.

would not spot that I was off-subject, sketching holes at The Point. I was trying to plot a safe way around the links and how to deal with the Mahon Burn. To me it was the loveliest and deadliest stream in golf, as it demanded shot making and skill and nerve in front of green seven and again in front of green fourteen.

I knew I was plotting against a master. After all, Colt had designed or partly designed a litany of the best courses in the world, including Royal Portrush, Royal County Down, where his main brief was to eliminate some blind shots, and Royal Dublin which he returned to after the links were damaged by the army during World War I. Also, the two courses at Sunningdale and he had input at Muirfield, Pine Valley and Hoylake.

Taba: It's as if you were playing chess with Colt.

Pat: He designed the Dun Laoghaire (pronounced 'done leary') golf course near my house. Harry and I are old pals.

Taba: You wrote, "Imagine my shock and delight in 2013 when David O'Donovan, manager of the County Sligo Golf Club, visited and asked me whether I might be interested in making a submission on possible improvements to their great links. I felt like locking him in the wine cellar so he could not escape." So, you have a wine cellar?

Pat: I have a wine cellar. It is in a 220-year-old house with a large cool basement.

Always full of suspect wine. As a non-drinker I don't know if a wine is good. People keep on giving me presents of wine and I don't know if it's gone off. So, I have a wine competition at The European Club most years. I put up 100 bottles of wine and give it all away. If anyone gets a bad bottle, I replace it, of course.

Taba: You have been such a prolific writer for so long. You said, "Golf courses are much more than mere sports fields. They are a clear expression of landscape art." Music to my ears. Then you wrote, "The architect weaves a magic tapestry, and the fortunate golfer gets to walk and play within." I read that and couldn't sleep!

Pat: It's nice to know you took my book to bed with you. (Laughter)

Taba: You have been in the presence of greatness so often. You witnessed Ireland's greatest amateur golfer, Joe Carr in his prime. I often refer to him as Ireland's Bobby Jones. You hosted Tiger Woods, David Duval, Mark O'Meara and Scott McCarron at The European Club. You set up The European Club perfectly for Padraig Harrington to practise before he won the Open Championship. You were his secret weapon!

Pat: It is a rewarding experience to host the champions of your age — and really frightening. It must be like a person getting a picture hung in a gallery. People coming along, and look at your picture. Frightens the bejeezus out of you. But sometimes I think about people, friends, who died too soon and didn't see it (things I accomplished). That's a sadness.

Taba: Were you ever intimidated while working on any piece of land? Being an artist, you are working in three dimensions. People experience what you have created for them. You said you went out and had conversations with Old Tom, the two Harrys (Colt and Vardon) and James Braid when you were working on different projects. You were communicating with them — these people who are not with us anymore.

"We must treat the land with respect. Adapt the land to your purpose."

Pat: We're doing the same. Like farmer Jones worked the land for his purposes. We must treat the land with respect. Adapt the land to your purpose. Golf just happens to be an occupation which is a ball game. Also, in a big, big way, it occupies a huge section of the life of the person who is playing. They must be in a nice place. They must be safe from each other, safe from wildlife. It's a huge responsibility.

Taba: The whole process blurs through decades and centuries.

Pat: Very true, and it gets very personal. I have one dear friend's ashes scattered out here at The European Club. Sometimes, I go sit on that hill of the twelfth and I'm not sure if I am sitting on his backside or his head. I couldn't sit down for three months. It is nice to go out and commune with him.

I am mindful of all the generations walking before us. Sligo Golf Club is 125 years old. There were men from the early 1900s who I remember seeing when I was a kid. This gives a deep consciousness of 100 years being nothing.

Biblical proof always beats me. Yet I've become conscious that time is so short. It was only yesterday. Twinkle of an eye. Place 25 eighty-year old people nose-to-tail and you have 2,000 years and you are back to the time of Christ!

In Ballymote, it frightened me for a while. In the heart of the town the people of my childhood are mostly gone. There has been a total transfusion. In the span of 75 years there are completely new people there. Same with a golf course. When you get your turn, enjoy it. There will be a new generation of golfers very soon, when you are gone.

Taba: You got your turn at Rosapenna. That was a special experience. That would be a situation where you could be intimidated. You talked about how Old Tom had to travel from St Andrews in those early days by horse and buggy, or train and then by steamer. Then 100 years later you got the call from the current owner to discuss the possibilities for the sand dune system. I love the way you say everything. At the same time, you were working on Ballyliffin. When you got to do Sandy Hills. That was your baby.

Pat: A big one. I went over there first in the 1960s, saw the dunes. I played a good bit of golf on the Old Tom. At that time, I got out into the dunes. They just embrace you completely.

You feel totally gone from civilization. There are long grasses and rabbit paths. It was screaming isolation.

It was screaming golf. One of the miracles. Your time comes, you get the chance. You're in love with the place but not there for decades. Then it comes back into your life. You are given the opportunity to do what you dreamt of, but now you know a lot more.

Frank Casey and his wife are great people. They trusted me to tamper with such a thing. My soul was bursting to get the best possible out of it. Great thrill that they weren't disappointed.

The place had fallen from attention with the advent of air travel and people went to Spain and Florida. The troubles on the border didn't help for decades. Yet my work restored Rosapenna to a point where it enters golf conversations around the world.

Taba: You also wrote, "How fantastic it was to be immersed in the spirit and beauty of the place." You said the dunes were, "handsome and alluring." Who writes about golf like this? Only Pat Ruddy!

Pat: This is a lovely story. There was an old friend of mine, Hector Legge, who was editor of The Sunday Independent. He played tidy golf into his 90s despite a suspect putter. He was a wine lover, too. For thirty years he'd come to our house on a winter's night. We'd do some carpet putting. I had a bottle of wine sitting there, you see, as a prize. He coveted that prize. But he got under the sofa and lost time after time until eventually, after midnight, I would bring him upstairs into the main bedroom and say to my wife, Bernardine, "Okay, you know what's going on here."

We'd putt around the bed, out the door, down the hall, down the stairs, around the table, in the hall, around the lounge. I'd make sure my ball wound up under the sofa and he'd win the bottle. He'd phone me an hour later to gloat that he had made it home safe with the bottle. The essence is, it's all about the love of the moment — transposed to a magnificent landscape.

Taba: Here's a beautiful passage you wrote, "Hills and wetlands and rivers cannot be discounted. It is not land alone but space that counts. Parkland courses are at their best when adorned with a good stock of trees. There is a rush to get rid of them on many classic golf courses and get them back to where they began. How sad this is if brought to the extreme. Trees are beautiful and a high canopy is a marvelous hazard, which I see as a bunker in the sky."

Taba: High canopy? Marvelous hazard as a bunker in the sky? Really Pat, this is such an evocative image!

Pat: Bunker in the sky. Yes, it's the arc of the shot. I love all land. I love all golf courses. But the ball spends 99 percent of its time in the air. The wind and what else is up there, like the canopy of a tree is part of the course. There is a big rush now to clean out trees for light and air. It takes a long time for a good tree to become mature. We must take a long time and consider before you cut it down. People don't think enough sometimes. If a tree takes 100 or 150 years to mature, it should have a chance to have another 100 or 150 years to live.

Taba: It was funny yesterday. While playing at Portmarnock, my lady friend hit a tree with her ball. I did the same thing! It became a hilarious moment. I thought I could get around it. A little later, on the final hole of the Yellow nine (Portmarnock has 27 holes with the Red and Blue nines comprising the championship course), I said to her, "There's another tricky tree out there."

"What tree?" She ignored it completely, hit a perfect shot and reached the green.

Pat: The reward was great.

Taba: You talked about Henry Cotton (Sir Henry Cotton MBE was the leading British player of his generation, winning the Open Championship in 1934, 1937, and 1948). You did more than relax with him over afternoon tea. Tell me about him. Were you in business together?

Pat: We became partners for a while. Great hero and champion in the 30s to the 50s. Went to Portugal for his health, to a place called Penina. We all found our way down to sit at the feet of the great man. He had a donkey named Pacifico as a caddie. The donkey wore a straw hat with his ears poking out, and Henry's clubs were strapped along its flanks. It was a great age then. Anybody who was sincere had the opportunity to meet the great people. Nowadays, if you go to the Players' Lounge, it's best to keep quiet.

In those days you got very close to each other. I did him a favor. (Pat says this is covered on page 62 of Holes and other books.) He was a very canny old guy. We became partners in design. He figured it out. I'd do all the work and he'd get some of the money. Didn't work out great financially, but if you can get one percent of their wiles, you'll survive in the jungle of life.

I was preaching to the local authorities. We should have public courses. We should have putting greens. We went to a few good dinners. He was a lovely man.

Taba: You were promoting golf in the city. You talked about Pitch and Putt courses. (Developed mainly in Ireland since the 1940s. The course is

18 holes, par is 54, only requires 12 to 15 acres. Players are allowed a maximum of three clubs which must include a putter.)

Pat: When I came to Dublin, I was treated very well as Ireland's first full-time golf writer. I was embraced by the clubs. Mary O'Brien would phone me up and say, "Mr Ruddy, you haven't been here in Elm Park for three weeks. Come for lunch." You'd find yourself sitting with the captain and watching very carefully what knife and fork he was using so you'd keep pace. The inner circle has many bonuses. If you're in the club, it's lovely.

But if you're not in the club, it means exclusion. I felt it was a pity so many people couldn't play. It's a difficult thing to set up for everyone. Takes up more space than a football pitch or a tennis court. Trying to overcome that. Pitch and Putt brings people in. More people should be infected young.

Taba: Until I started spending my summers in Ireland, I wouldn't know how prevalent Pitch and Putt courses are. There's like over 400 in Ireland. I think they're brilliant. People in the US don't know about them. There are no holes longer than 75 or 80 yards and they have their own associations, societies, and rigorous tournaments.

Pat: We're building one now at Ballyliffin. The new nine-hole course will be called The Pollan Links. Lots of pressure on me. It better be good. All the kids from miles around can come down and play it. Get a taste of golf. Without the driver — all the rest of golf is there.

Taba: When will it be open?

Pat: We're going to have it in play the second half of next year. I think they will have a very enjoyable game.

Taba: I also remember you wrote that when you were building Sandy Hills, you got on the excavator yourself when you wanted to create a particular effect. You wouldn't have to get on the excavator for the Pitch and Putt, right?

Pat: Oh yes, I do. It is golf after all. Great golf! I always worked excavators on the courses I have designed. I love doing it, and you can deliver what you imagine and sense. At Sligo and Ballyliffin they were very patient waiting for me when my hips were bad again. They helped me get up on the machine. Once I got up, I was okay. Like sitting in an armchair. I can't work after hours anymore, though, like I used to. I'd work until dark. But now I need someone to help me down. An eight-hour day sees a lot of sand shaped.

Taba: Kevin and I plan to be up that way next July. Maybe we'll get to play there.

Pat: They started moving dirt this week for me. The way we do it, I say give me so many tons here and so many tons there, then I go shape it. We're having fun.

"All the kids from miles around can come down and play it. Get a taste of golf."

Taba: This is exciting. You must promise to keep in touch with me about that. We will be staying in Ballina at the Mount Falcon Estate.

Pat: That's just at the edge of the town. One of my great grand aunts used to work as a seamstress in that house. Did dressmaking. Nice place. We stayed in it two or three years ago. I did go there and connected spiritually with it when it was a private house.

It's right on the River Moy. When it was full to the brim with salmon, you could nearly walk across the river on their backs.

Taba: What time of year are they running?

Pat: They run from the months of May to September. Check that. They must get back to the sea while they're young. Amazing how they find their way.

I had an uncle with a boat on nearby Lough Conn and he would always catch salmon. He would cast the fly and catch a salmon. I would just catch a cold. We used to eat lots of salmon and new potatoes. They go well together.

Taba: Please tell me more about your spiritual connection. Almost more than anybody I know in Ireland, you talk about and you truly have, the spiritual connection. In your book about Rosapenna, you wrote, "A person wishing to mix a bit of golf with a spot of meditation or introspection can do no better than to go out here and just live."

After laughter, Pat added this narrative:

Pat: I'd know a lot of the rabbits by name. One hare, we'd be out there the two of us. Harry looked like an elephant. He was so big I thought he could eat me. I'd be worried about him, and he'd be worried about me. I like golf anywhere. Rosapenna has this tranquility and solitude. It's a great place to do some thinking or non-thinking.

It's good here too, and quiet. Bernardine and I go for a stroll. Sit down. Bring a banana or an apple. We don't talk too much. We just listen to the wind and the sea and our dead friends whispering.

Taba: I once wrote a story about playing golf alone. Probably my favorite way to play.

My then editor said you can't do that. He doesn't know that there are courses where you can play alone, rather than being put in a foursome. Perhaps you can't do that in many places. But when you can, it's such a beautiful way to commune with nature.

Pat: I was fortunate to start life as a person with a feeling for life, and the mystique of life. I went for a little while to a monastery to become a priest. I had a huge problem. I was worried, not about getting to play golf, but I was worried about people's souls. Then the three Gs got me.

Bad Grub, no Golf, and what are these things called Girls? So, I got out of there weighing eight stone (112 pounds). I went golfing. Dead simple. Inoffensive.

Taba: My all-time favorite thing that you wrote, "Golf does not just collide with art. It is a high art when handled and presented by the expert designer."

Back to Yeats. I feel that you are in alignment with him. There are two qualities that he valued late in life: passion and joy. That is what I feel from you.

Pat: If you're not happy, at least be content. If you don't feel like being merry every day, feel content. If you have a mad mind, life is okay.

(Lots of laughing, as there always is with Pat)

Pat: I said to Poppy, my granddaughter, "You're very beautiful." Poppy looked up and said, "I know Pat, I know."

I learned so much from her unassuming confidence. So, if someone says, "You must be a genius," you should respond, "I am, but don't get daft notions."

Taba: I saw a photo of Poppy in your latest book. She's playing in the sand of a bunker with siblings Andrew and Lilla.

Pat: It was one of the greatest moments of my life. Some people like bunker play!

Taba: It's definitely one of the perks to owning your own course, when your grandkids get to build castles, like at the beach.

Pat: Today's Golfer, a very fine magazine, wanted me to do a sketch for one of my stories. I had Poppy help me. Going into an international magazine, assisted by Poppy Meehan. She turned sixteen years old last week. We have birthday parties big in our house. The key is to enjoy every nuance.

Taba: Lovely that they are so close to you, geographically and spiritually.

Pat: A few years ago, we were driving down the country. They were in the back seat of the car and they were making some noise. I said, "Be quiet back there."

Then I heard, "Bald headed bastard." I loved that. She produced joy. It wasn't naughty, just a child developing the art of repartee in a safe and loving environment. (Tons of laughter)

Old and young, all golfers are the same. All have their moods. Take the men. Get them reduced to little boys in short pants. There is a little boy in everyone. There is a little girl in everyone. We must be dignified on occasion, but we must not be stuffy.

We must love each other. I have a friend, retired from two clubs. He was getting old and had MS. I told him, "You're a member here now." He got the ball out of the bunker but couldn't get himself out. Great thing, he died golfing. He was shunned away. But everyone should be included if he is intrinsically honest.

And old golfers should be allowed to play while they can still walk.

Everyone loves a bit of praise. There is no one who doesn't like praise.

Author's PS: Previously, I have said that when I die, I'd like my ashes to be spread on a golf course in Ireland. But now, if Pat and the rest of the Ruddys will have me, it is here at The European Club that I want to spend eternity. This way, I can keep on talking and laughing with Pat about golf holes, beauty and poetry. And whatever other hilarity comes to his madcap mind.

The European Club, Ardinairy Beach in the background.

Jason Straka, ASGCA

Principal, Fry/Straka

Excerpts from our conversation.

Taba: It sounds like you have been circumnavigating the world and building courses in all kinds of exotic locations. You even have offices in Brazil and China. I'm lucky to catch up with you.

Jason: We are fortunate to have an active worldwide business. We are currently designing courses in the United Arab Emirates, Vietnam, Brazil, Mexico and here at home in the US, plus we have 'irons in the fire' in numerous other countries.

Taba: You said before that you were doing courses in Italy. You were one of the people, if not the first, who told me I needed to include Castiglion del Bosco in the Terroir book, which I have done.

Jason: I first saw it when I visited with CNN's Living Golf crew. We stayed on the property for several days, touring and filming. It's an incredible place.

Taba: There's so much to their story with the world-class Tom Weiskopf golf course and the winery. You can't describe it without talking about the fact that the Ferragamo family bought an entire village. That's a pretty big deal.

Jason: It is a big deal. Everything that they do is centered around how they manage the land. The chef uses local things that they grow there. It's all about the quality of the land, tied to the land.

Taba: Let's talk about how you were drawn into the game of golf in the first place.

Jason: For me it was a family-oriented sport. My father and uncle introduced me to the game at a very young age. My fondest golf memories will always be of playing with my dad, late in the evenings, heading down the fairway with clubs clicking as we walked, talking about life in general.

My uncle was a golf junkie and was ahead of his time in keeping all his analytics. But keep in mind, this was well before computers were ubiquitous. He'd keep all his playing stats by entering them into handwritten spreadsheets, including what courses he played. It took a lot of effort to do that. Now there are 'apps' for it.

My mother's side of the family were golfers too — the whole family. For some twenty- five years running we have had an annual family reunion centered around golf, in an event deemed 'The Straka Cup'. It's a handicapped event where the winner gets their name engraved on a large silver cup and they get to keep it for the year. It's quite a prestigious event you know. (Laughs).

Taba: What age were you when you started to play?

Jason: I was five or six. My dad would say, "Hey, let's go out and play nine holes — after school and work in the evening, or on the weekend." Golf was woven into our family life. Everything centered on it. We all loved to sneak out and play nine holes. It kept us all really active.

I am the poster child for introductory golf courses. There was a 9-hole, par 3 course that was about ten or fifteen minutes from our house. We'd go there often when we weren't hitting golf balls in our backyard.

When I was good enough, we'd go play a fun 9-hole executive course. It was about 2500 yards. It was quick and inexpensive. Once I graduated from that course, and even though it was pretty rural where I grew up, there were thirty or so golf courses within a half hour of our house. One of the better public courses was just a ten-minute drive away and was the same course where I eventually played high school golf.

Back in those days, there was a junior golf pass for $150 for the entire year. You could play anytime you wanted, other than when leagues teed off on weekday evenings and on weekends, when it was from 2 pm.

Taba: How nice that golf was so accessible for you.

Jason: Accessibility was the big thing. Growing up like that, my friends and I all had the same pass. This was in the sixth, seventh and eighth grades. My mom picked me up from school and dropped me off at the course. My buddies and I would go play golf, and then come home to do our homework.

Taba: Sounds so idyllic to me. What was the spark that ignited your interest in golf architecture?

Jason: I didn't know I was going to do golf architecture. I loved being outside. I loved to fish, hike, canoe, and camp. I had a passion for those outdoor activities. And I really enjoyed the design world. When I played golf as a junior, it dawned on me that I could actually merge the two things. Then I became more interested in landscape architecture, agronomy and horticulture. I realized, "Heck, I could do all of that." Looking back, I used to lay out golf courses around our three-acre property, using empty plant pots for holes. The only problem was that the house was an obstacle and occasionally would get hit. (Laughs)

Taba: So, it was an organic evolution, then?

Jason: For sure.

Taba: I've been an art dealer for forty years. When I started writing about golf architecture, I said that golf courses are living works of art, and golf architects are the Rembrandts and Beethovens of their domain. That's how I think of you. You are an artist. You are painting on the greatest canvas in the world. It's not a painting though. It's three- dimensional. You

Straka designed Ambiente Course at Camelback Golf Club, Scottsdale, Arizona.

are a sculptor. It's the earth. You are sculpting the earth. It's the terroir. I'm trying to lay a foundation here for asking you, how do you go about approaching this gigantic canvas? Has it ever felt intimidating to you when you're just starting to come up with a design?

Jason: Oh, yeah, it's like you are going to be a performer, or public speaker. Right when you're getting ready to start, you have the butterflies. Then you must rely on your training and preparation, plus your creativity. Nervous, yes, but exhilarating.

Learning about the site and the land before you start is most important. What is the vegetation out there? How does it grow? How does it thrive? Does it even belong there? Then you need to do all your subsurface exploration. Is it sand? Is it rock? Is it a combination of the two? You have all this study up front, so you are prepared. Once you start, it does evolve. There are some architects who are very much engineering oriented, and some are much more art oriented.

Taba: Where do you fall in that spectrum of engineering versus art oriented?

Jason: I fall squarely in the middle and tell people this. Pick a favorite painter — Rembrandt, Monet, Jackson Pollock, or whoever. Designing a golf course from a pure engineering standpoint is like recreating a painting from one of those master artists by numbers, where each number is a specific color. In the end, you might have a nice work of art, but you can tell it's painted by number and not an organic work of art — but it still functions well.

I like to do a thorough site investigation and planning up front to make sure the course will function well. But, after we start construction on site, we let our creativity take over, making changes and improvements as we go. Sometimes the most unexpected things, even what you think is a mistake at times, turns out to be a fabulous result. The fieldwork is very organic and that's where the art is.

Taba: It takes a lot of courage to do what you do. It's not like a little painting that started on an easel that went into a corner of a closet. People are out there playing on your course. They're interacting with you as the designer. It's a real test for you.

Jason: Sure. If I had anything that is a leave-behind, first and foremost, I want to serve the client well. But true success is usually driven by having people go out and enjoying whatever product you put out there.

If people go out to play golf and have a great experience, that is the thing I'm going to remember and cherish the most. The time I spent with my son, my father, my family and friends, the conversations. The memories that we had. It's not going to be so much about the score I shot on a given day. I believe my true gift is creating places where people can enjoy a physically and mentally healthy pursuit.

Taba: Makes me think of being in an incredible place, maybe at sunset with a glass of wine. It's like you said, it's more of a feeling. It's more about memories and being happy. That's one of the things about being on a golf course. You're out in nature and having fun — you're playing.

"That's one of the things about being on a golf course. You're out in nature and having fun — you're playing."

Jason: The thing about golf is the canvas is ever-changing. It's not like a baseball field or a soccer pitch. From one place to the next across the world, those are all the same. The fascinating thing about golf is, courses blend into the native environment. If done correctly, you should have a sense of place when you play golf there, because it's tied to the land.

So, whether you're playing golf in the south of France, Italy, Napa, or Ireland for that matter, the course should be unique to the terrain and the vegetation. The materials that the course is built with, everything contributes to a direct sense of place.

Taba: You've answered a question I was wanting to ask. How does the land inform you? You just told me that answer. I really like that.

Taba: Do you have a favorite type of land, soil or terroir, to use the French word?

Jason: My preference, first and foremost, is really to have interesting topography. I like golf to be both an aerial and a ground game. When the ground is firm and fast, the ball rolls a lot, and you've got to read ground contours. It goes back to the quality of the land. It's important to understand the land you are on.

That introduces another element – 'fun'. When you have interesting terrain that is like a crumpled sheet with side hill lies and downhill lies, that provides me a nice canvas to work on.

You not only have to judge how far the ball is going to carry, but also what it will do on the slopes once it lands and starts to roll. Will it roll in multiple directions? How far will it roll? What is the consequence for the next shot? It's all tied to the land.

Taba: If you could build a course anywhere in the world, where would you love your signature course to be — your art statement? There's no budget.

Jason: Ha-ha. Wow. That's a hard question. It depends on what you're putting value on. Taba: What makes your heart sing? It could be Scotland, or it could be Ohio.

Jason: This is cheating. I'm going to pick more than one place. Here in Ohio — it's only because I have so many friends and family here. I've had an opportunity to do new work here in Ohio — friends and family can enjoy the experience of that golf course together. So, a place that is accessible to my friends and family. That would be one answer.

Another would be a non-golf-centric country. Quick example. When we started to do some work in Brazil, we created a little putting course in São Paulo. There were every day, run- of-the mill people peeking around the walls. They were fascinated. Never seen it before. Never played golf before. Suddenly, I'd say, "C'mon over and try it." You could see the joy and the intrigue. They would hit a couple of putts. Then when they hit something halfway decent, you could see the spark. They were hooked.

What would be special and unique is to create an experience for people who were just learning to play golf. That would be a pinnacle in my career as well.

Third answer. Pick any place like Ireland, Scotland, Monterrey — some signature place along the coast. That would be fascinating. So, I cheated.

Taba: (Laughing) Please make sure I'm on the A-list for the opening!

Professional Golfers with Their Own Wine Label

Luke Donald enjoying his claret.

Luke Donald

I found out that Luke Donald was into wine when I stumbled on a story about him having an interest in art. Not just an interest, though. Turns out he is actually a painter. And that's not all, he majored in art theory and practice at Northwestern University, but started painting before he was ten at a private Steiner school in England, where he was born.

Although he had to put painting on the back burner, when becoming the World No.1 golfer and raising a family intervened, his interest in wine continued to grow. Donald's father had a fondness for fine wine, and it rubbed off, to where Donald now has his own wine label.

The Luke Donald Collection includes a California chardonnay, a Viognier and a Bordeaux-style red blend — the Luke Donald Claret, named after the trophy given to the winner of the Open Championship. Donald is intimately involved in all aspects of winemaking, including sourcing the grapes (having tasted wine from over sixty vineyards) and assisting with the label design.

In his Chicago house, Donald built a glass-enclosed wine cellar that holds 800 bottles. He is building a new house in Florida, where the cellar/tasting room will accommodate 1000 bottles. An authentic wine aficionado, Donald keeps fancy champagnes on hand, whites and reds, ranging from light to heavy, and saves some racks in case Sergio Garcia shows up with a case of Vega Sicilia Unico from Spain's del Duero, like the one he gave Donald for his wedding present.

When asked, "What do you like to drink when on holiday?" Donald declared, "Wine from the Luke Donald Collection, of course!" He described his cabernet merlot blend, saying, "Hints of dark berries, good depth, nice aroma (I don't say 'nose'), pairs well with barbecued meats. Complex and interesting flavor. Not heavy, can be drunk in quantity. Ages well."

Donald played on four winning Ryder Cup teams, with an excellent 10-4-1 record, and was vice-captain for the 2018 Ryder Cup Match in France. During 2011, he won the PGA Tour money list and European Race to Dubai to complete a historic double, the first player to ever do so in the same year. Consequently, he was named PGA Player of the Year and the European Tour Player of the Year.

In May 2011, Donald became the No.1 golfer in the Official World Golf Ranking and held the position for 40 weeks. He was later awarded honorary life membership of the European Tour for his achievements in 2011. Cumulatively, Donald spent a total of 56 weeks as the World No. 1 and spent over 200 weeks in the Top 10 on his way to 17 professional wins. He was awarded an MBE in 2012 for services to golf.

Luke serves as the Honorary Chairman of The First Tee of Greater Chicago, a youth development organization that provides educational programs that build character, install life-enhancing values and promotes healthy choices through the game of golf.

Annually, Luke and his wife Diane host 'Luke Donald's Taste of The First Tee' — a wine tasting benefit featuring wines from the Luke Donald Collection and The Terlato Wines Global portfolio. Thanks to their generosity and philanthropic support, Luke and Diane have raised nearly $3 million to support the Chicagoland Chapter, reaching over 50,000 young people through programs in schools, parks and golf courses.

Other charitable initiatives that are near and dear to Luke and Diane include Habitat for Humanity Palm Beach County, Northern University, and Ronald McDonald House Charities Chicagoland and Northwestern Indiana.

Ernie Els

Theodore Ernest Els (b. October 1969) has been winning since 1984, when he won the Junior World Golf Championship in the Boys 13-14 category. Among his 71 career victories are four majors, including the 1994 US Open at Oakmont, Pennsylvania, the 1997 US Open at Congressional Country Club, Bethesda, Maryland, the Open Championship in 2002 at Muirfield and the 2012 Open at Royal Lytham & St Annes.

Other highlights of his career include topping the 2003 and 2004 European Tour Order of Merit (money list) and winning the World Match Play Championship a record seven times. Els was also inducted into the World Golf Hall of Fame in May 2011. The rest of his awards could fill a book.

Yet I would say that none of these accomplishments would bring him and his wife Liezl more joy than having set up their Els for Autism Foundation, as they have first-hand awareness of the difficulties individuals and their families face when living with and caring for a loved one who must battle daily with being on the autism spectrum disorder, as does Ben, their own son.

Since their son's autism diagnosis, Els and his wife have created several fund-raising events like the annual Els for Autism Pro-Am. The couple has also established The Els Center for Excellence, where efforts are directed toward improving the education and quality of life of the students. They invested $6 million of their own money in the center, and helped raise much of the $30 million required to build it.

Ernie Els decided to pursue his developing passion for fine wine in the late 1990s. Along with establishing his base of operations in Stellenbosch (the heart of South African wine country), he chose the gifted winemaker, Louis Strydom, to lead the team.

Ernie himself is passionate about red wine, so naturally there is a classic 'Medoc-style' Bordeaux blend — The Ernie Els Signature Blend. All these vines grow on the north-facing slopes of the Helderberg region within the Stellenbosch appellation.

Another wine in the portfolio is The Proprietor's Blend, which includes all six varieties cultivated on the property. The vineyards thrive at about 250 meters above sea level with the cooling influence of the Atlantic Ocean just 15 km away. The varietal composition is Cabernet Sauvignon 60%, Shiraz 20%, Merlot 5%, Cabernet Franc 5%, Malbec 5%, Petit Verdot 5%. There are now eleven brands within the portfolio and Ernie is involved in the tasting process for all vintages.

In the US, the Terlato Wine Group distributes the entire range of Ernie Els Wines and they also support the Els' work on behalf of autism, making a donation to the Els for Autism Foundation with every bottle of Ernie Els wine sold.

While continuing to play stellar golf, Ernie Els is the driving force in many endeavors including golf course design. His courses span the globe, from Mauritius to Malaysia. He also has a charitable foundation which supports golf among underprivileged youth in South Africa.

Nick Faldo

Sir Nick, as he is often called nowadays, wasn't assigned a moniker in his golf heydays that I know of, but it could have been The Intimidator. Standing at 6'3" and a muscular 195 lb, the steely-eyed Englishman would wear down his golf opponents until they buckled. With his playing days behind him, Nick has risen to the top of his new profession as a leading CBS golf analyst.

Nicholas Alexander Faldo was born 18 July 1957 in Welwyn Garden City, Hertfordshire, England. While a student at Sir Frederic Osborne School, Nick played every sport available to him: soccer, rugby, basketball and cricket. He was also a swimmer, cyclist and ran track.

Golf burst into the Faldo living room when at age 13, Nick's parents, George and Joyce, brought home a new color television. Nick watched Jack Nicklaus competing in the 1971 US Masters and it ignited the imagination of the young sports-obsessed lad. That did it. He was bitten by the golf bug and signed up for lessons. A mere three years later, he qualified to play in the 1974 English Amateur at Woodhall Spa. Successes followed immediately and he landed a golf scholarship to the University of Houston.

Nick found he didn't like being back in classrooms. After just three months of college life, Faldo left school and turned professional in 1976. He skyrocketed to eighth on the Order of Merit on the European Tour in 1977, then placed third in 1978, winning events both seasons. At age 20, Faldo's stellar play led him to becoming the youngest golfer to make the 1977

Ryder Cup team. He would go on to represent Europe a record 11 times, then captained the team in 2008.

In 1983, Faldo finished at the top of the Order of Merit, with five European Tour victories. It's a risky business, making changes to your swing, but Faldo did it in the mid-1980s, working with David Leadbetter. There were setbacks, but the hard work paid off in 1987 when Faldo won the Spanish Open. Just two months later he won his first major, the Open Championship title at Muirfield.

Faldo won his second major championship at the 1989 US Masters and successfully defended in 1990. He was the first player to win back-to-back Masters titles since the man who galvanized him to take up the game — Jack Nicklaus — did in 1965-66.

In 1990, along came Fanny Sunesson. Born into a golfing family in Gothenburg, Sweden, she played at a high standard as a teen. In search of more experience as a competitor, she wound up becoming the most accomplished female caddie in professional golf history and was on Nick's bag from 1990 to 1999. During this time, they won four majors together.

Faldo won his second Open Championship at St Andrews in 1990 and hoisted the Claret Jug a third time in the 1992 Open back at Muirfield. This might have been the only time the stoic competitor displayed visible emotion, trembling, and shedding tears.

In July 1993, Faldo won the Irish Open for an unprecedented third time in a row. Later that month, Faldo fought a memorable duel with Greg Norman in the Open Championship at Royal St George's, with Norman coming out on top.

The tide turned when Faldo decided to focus on playing in the US where he believed he could capture more major titles. The strategy put him in position to collect his sixth major at Augusta in 1996. Faldo was trailing his rival Greg Norman in the final of the Masters. But the golf gods robbed Norman of his six-shot lead as The Intimidator applied the screws and Norman collapsed under the pressure on the back nine.

During his years of dominant play, Faldo was ranked No. 1 on the Official World Golf Ranking for a total of 97 weeks. His 41 professional wins include 30 victories on the European Tour. Only one European golfer, Harry Vardon, who won seven majors in a span between 1896–1914, has had more major victories than Faldo. And only one golfer from outside the US (Gary Player from South Africa) has won more majors than Faldo.

Sir Nick Faldo 2021

For his contributions and service to golf, Nick Faldo received a knighthood from Queen Elizabeth II in November 2009. Sir Nick is the only living British golfer to have received such an honor.

With his playing days waning, Sir Nick turned his attention to other pursuits and partnered with Milton Sandford Wines in 2015 to launch a range of his own. The firm was originally founded by former restaurant owner Stan Park and Michelin-starred chef Richard Sandford.

In a nod to his major wins, each bottle bears the Faldo Shield of six stripes in red and green, representing the Claret Jug of the Open Championship and the Green Jacket of the Masters. The range comprises two whites and four reds, from some of Europe's finest wine regions in France, Italy and Spain. A few of the wines are: an Italian Ripasso Valpolicella, a Barolo from the Piedmont Region of Italy, and a Chateauneuf Du Pape from the Rhone Valley of France.

Other commercial endeavors include Faldo

Design, launched in 1991, which has remodeled or designed dozens of courses across several continents, from the US to Vietnam and India. A proud moment came in 2015 when the firm was presented with the Sustainable Golf Course Architects' Award by Green Planet Architects. It recognizes high quality courses that are economically, socially, and environmentally sustainable.

Another feather in Sir Nick's cap is the Faldo Series, created in 1996, for aspiring young golfers, aged 12 to 21. About 5,000 boys and girls participate annually and the winners of each tournament are invited to join Sir Nick at one of the Grand Finals in Europe, Asia and North America.

Faldo was voted BBC Sports Personality of the Year in 1989, and inducted into the World Golf Hall of Fame in 1997. In 2000, he was ranked 18th greatest golfer of all time by Golf Digest magazine. Also, he was the 2014 recipient of the Payne Stewart Award, presented by the PGA Tour to a player who demonstrates respect for the traditions of the game, a commitment to uphold the game's heritage of charitable support, and professional and meticulous presentation of himself and the sport through his dress and conduct.

When asked in an interview what occurred to initiate his interest in vino, Nick said it started as a lad, and expounded, "On summer holidays in France, my dad allowed me have a little taste of wine to go with our fresh steamed mussels— for all of two Francs!"

Just like watching the US Masters as a young lad, Nick probably stored that memory and used it to fire up his imagination to accomplish every major goal he set for himself, including winning majors. He parlayed it into launching his wine brand and then he applied himself to become a television commentator. Now he's aced that game too.

David Frost

David Frost is the real deal. He is a third-generation vintner whose family has been part of the wine heritage in South Africa dating back to 1693, the year wine farm Saxenburg was founded. Even today, Saxenburg is an established winery in South Africa and one of the oldest wine farms in the country. In February 1932, Henry Laurence was the owner of Saxenburg. He was also the father of Liezel Laurence, mother of David Laurence Frost.

I first came across the David Frost wines at The Marcliffe Hotel in Aberdeen, Scotland.

The owner, Stewart Spence, is a wine connoisseur and passionate golfer himself. The hotel offers an incredible wine list and an entire section, Wine for Golfers by Golfers.

The first entry on the Marcliffe Wine List is David Frost Wine and it informs us that, "Unlike many athletes or celebrities who lend their name to a brand, David Frost and his family have been in the wine business in South Africa for over 60 years. His father's vineyard was the first place he hit balls and the pocket money he made from picking grapes funded his first set of clubs and an ongoing supply of balls. In 1994 the tradition of vineyards in the family continued when David bought a 300 acre vineyard in the Paarl wine region where he produced his first 3,000 cases of Cabernet Sauvignon in 1997."

The David Frost Winery now bottles cabernet sauvignon, shiraz, and sauvignon blanc.

Then there are the exceptional David Frost Merlot Reserves. The 1999 vintage has a LeRoy Neiman painting of the late, great Arnold Palmer on the label. Another bin at the Marcliffe holds the David Frost Merlot Reserve 2001, which is dedicated to the all-time Majors Winner, Jack Nicklaus. The 2000 Merlot Reserve, also with label painted by Neiman, is dedicated to Gene Sarazen.

Frost was born in 1959 in Cape Town, South Africa and was schooled at Paarl Boys High School. He became a professional golfer in 1981 and scored his first win in his home country in 1983. In line with many other Commonwealth golfers, his first move abroad was to the European Tour which he played from 1982 to 1984.

Starting in 1985, he was primarily on the US based PGA Tour where he won ten tournaments. His most prestigious win was the 1989 NEC World Series of Golf where he defeated Ben Crenshaw at the second playoff hole. He made the top ten on the PGA Tour money list twice, placed 9th in 1988 and 5th in 1993 and was ranked in the top 10 of the Official World Golf Rankings for 86 weeks between 1988 and 1994.

Since 2007 Frost has reestablished his career on the European Tour. In June 2013, David won his maiden senior major championship at the 2013 Regions Tradition, by a single stroke over Fred Couples.

Frost won the Sunshine Tour Order of Merit in 1998/99. He was a member of the International Team in the first staging of the Presidents Cup in 1994, and took part again in 1996. In 1997 and 1998 he captained South Africa to victory in the Alfred Dunhill Cup in Scotland.

His teammates were Ernie Els and Retief Goosen.

The Frosty Facts from the Frost Wine website:

- Shattered a 16-year standing record for fewest putts (92) in a 72-hole event at the MCI Heritage Classic in April 2005.
- Is a two-time winner of the South African Open in 1986 and in 1999. 10 PGA Tour career victories.
- Six Champions Tour victories in the last five years. 30 total national and international victories.
- Won the Dunhill Cup for his native South Africa in 1997 and in 1998.
- Is a three-time winner of the Million Dollar Challenge Event, Sun City, South Africa (1989, 1990, 1992).
- Set a modern-day record (65), the Old Course, St. Andrews, Scotland at the 2005 Open Championship.

David shares his two greatest passions, wine and golf, with his native country; and energetically supports a foundation that instills education and life skills for the youth of South Africa. The Raymond Ackerman Golf Academy leads their students to academic success as they mature into respected young adults and become competent and enthusiastic golfers. For every bottle of David Frost Wines sold, a donation is given to the Raymond Ackerman Golf Academy.

On Tour they may call him Frosty but otherwise he is best known for his warm heart.

Retief Goosen

The Goose Wine range is truly unique as it is handcrafted in high altitude vineyards on the northern slopes of the majestic Outeniqua Mountains in the heart of the Garden Route, South Africa. The wine estate is situated in the Upper-Langkloof appellation, arguably one of the coldest wine growing regions at 2500 feet above sea level.

Goose Wines, owned by Retief Goosen and his partner Werner Roux, launched the maiden vintage of The Goose Expression in 2005. A blend of equal parts Cabernet Sauvignon and Shiraz, this wine is produced in a Bordeaux style, aged in French Oak barrels for 18 to 24 months. In 2008, the first single-vineyard white wine followed — The Goose Sauvignon Blanc. The range now includes Chardonnay and Pinot Noir.

The name on the farm's Title Deed is 'Ganzekraal' which means 'Goose Enclave'. The farm and surrounding area was given the name over a century ago when wild geese from the area flew down during the day to rest in the cattle and sheep closures. Now more than 100 years later there are five large ponds on the farm that attract various water fowl, including the Spur-Winged Goose, Africa's largest fresh water goose.

Retief, often called 'The Goose', is known as one of the coolest customers in the world of golf. Fittingly, the wines that carry his name are also produced in one of the coolest regions in the Western Cape with the Indian Ocean just 8 miles to the south.

On the property you'll also find the 'Altitude Tee Box'. With its panoramic views over the valley and mountains, visitors to the farm can practise their golf swings while sipping Goose Wines produced from the surrounding vineyards.

Retief Goosen was born in February 1969 in Polokwane, formerly known as Pietersburg, in the northern part of South Africa. After racking up 30 amateur titles, he turned professional in 1990 following a win in the South African Amateur Championship that year.

Retief's first major victory came in 2001 when he won the US Open at Southern Hills Country Club, Oklahoma. This outstanding year was concluded when he was awarded the European Tour Player of the Year and was crowned 2001 European Tour Order of Merit Champion, winning the Harry Vardon Trophy, and moving into the top 10 of the World Rankings for the first time.

Retief's US Open victory in June 2001 spurred him on to win The Scottish Open at Loch Lomond, Scotland, and then win his third European Tour victory of the season at the Telefonica Open de Madrid. He and Ernie Els finished off the year in style by taking the World Cup in Japan for South Africa in a play-off with Denmark.

In 2004, Retief won his second major when he triumphed at the US Open at Shinnecock Hills, NY. Retief finished the 2004 season in style at Sun City in South Africa where he won the Nedbank Golf Challenge by 6 shots. Multiple wins followed in 2005, 2006, 2007 and 2009. The 2011 season saw Retief experience multiple injuries which eventually led to a back operation in August 2012.

Along with 35 worldwide wins on three tours (PGA, European and South African), and being awarded the European Tour Order of Merit for a second time in 2002, Retief was picked for the President's Cup in 2000, 2003, 2005, 2007, 2009 and 2011. He has represented South Africa in the Dunhill Cup six times (1995 — 2000) and played in the World Cup for South Africa in 1993, 1995, 2000 and 2001. In recognition of his many outstanding achievements Retief was also inducted into the World Golf Hall of Fame in 2019.

Known for his unflappable attitude on the course, Goosen earned the nickname 'The Iceman' on the PGA Tour. His mother attributes her son's calm demeanor to the profound effects of being struck by lightning at age fifteen. Retief took a direct hit while playing golf through a light drizzle with his friend, Henri Potgieter at Pietersburg Golf Club.

Henri was knocked from his feet and when he stood back up, he saw Retief lying on the ground on his back. His clothes had been burned from his body and his shoes had disintegrated. His watch band had melted, and he retains a scar on his wrist from the incident. Yet he doesn't remember the event.

Goosen is married with a son and daughter, and has homes in Virginia Water, Surrey, England, Lake Nona Golf & Country Club in Orlando, Florida, US, as well as two residences in South Africa.

As a result of his long friendship with golf legend Gary Player, Retief regularly plays in the Gary Player Invitational series to help raise funds for needy children in both China and South Africa as well as around the world. Retief has also played in the Nelson Mandela Invitational hosted by Gary Player in South Africa, honoring former South African President Nelson Mandela.

Established in 2010, the Retief Goosen Charitable Foundation, was primarily set up for charitable causes in South Africa. The RGCF also supports Gansies Pre-school which is a non-profit organization situated on the Goose Wine Estate. Gansies means gosling, forming an appropriate connection to 'The Goose'. The school was also initiated in 2010 to help children of young mothers with full time jobs, by providing transportation, three meals a day and good tutoring.

Cristie Kerr

Cristie Kerr's interest in wine developed in the late 1990s when she began playing tournaments in California's Napa Valley. After her early morning practise rounds, she visited vineyards and enjoyed wine tastings with her fellow golfers. Over the course of time, she fell in love with the Napa Valley and became intrigued with the winemaking process.

In 2008, Cristie Kerr launched her first label, Curvature. Kerr Cellars followed in 2014, working with renowned vineyards in Napa and Sonoma Valley. To make her small batch wines, Kerr chose to work with two winemakers who are both women. As she is a self-described detail person, and one who is involved in every aspect of the winemaking process, she is also now a holder of the Level 1 Court of Master Sommeliers certificate.

When creating Curvature, Cristie Kerr partnered with Suzanne Pride Bryan, co-owner of Pride Mountain Vineyard, and a breast cancer survivor. It was, perhaps, by divine intervention that their stars aligned to make great wines and make a difference in all their life-affirming endeavors. Kerr also aligned with Sally Johnson, Pride Mountain Vineyards winemaker since 2007.

Philosophically, both Kerr and Johnson insist on excellence in everything from harvesting to the final expression of the wine. Reaching beyond the Pride family estate atop

Spring Mountain as her fruit source, Johnson includes some of her favorite vineyards on the Napa Valley floor in the making of Curvature. Sally's family has also been touched by breast cancer — two of her aunts are survivors.

Helen Keplinger has been the Winemaker for Kerr Cellars since early 2013. She is widely recognized as one of the top winemakers in California. After graduating from UC Davis with a master's degree in enology she built her resume working with many industry all-stars. In 2006 Helen started Keplinger Wines with her husband D J Warner and since then, Keplinger Wines has sold out of every vintage they produced and received incredible reviews along the way. Helen was named 'Winemaker of the Year' by Food and Wine magazine in 2012 and in 2014 she graced the cover of Wine Spectator magazine's June issue.

Cristie Kerr, born October 1977 in Miami, Florida, is one of the most accomplished professional golfers of her generation. She has 20 wins on the LPGA Tour including two major championships and she was World No.1 in the Women's World Golf Ranking three times in 2010.

Kerr started playing golf at the age of eight and by 1995 was the American Junior Golf Association Junior Player of the Year. In 1996 she played in the Curtis Cup and was the low amateur at the US Women's Open. She turned professional in 1996 at the age of 18 and by 2004 was one of the leading players on tour. She won the 2007 US Women's Open with her second major win coming in 2010 at the LPGA Championship.

Kerr was honored in 2011 with the Muhammad Ali Award for Sportsperson of the Year and is a two-time ESPY winner for Female Golfer of the Year. As of August 2017, Kerr has played in 9 Solheim Cup matches—the most played by an American and is the all-time leading American point scorer.

In 2003, Cristie Kerr founded the non-profit organization Birdies for Breast Cancer. The foundation was created the same year

Cristie Kerr (left) with winemaker Helen Keplinger, discussing soil.

her mother was diagnosed with the disease. Kerr's aunt and godmother have battled breast cancer too. In 2010, Birdies for Breast Cancer partnered with Jersey City Medical Center to create the region's foremost comprehensive facility specializing in women's health issues. The Cristie Kerr Women's Health Center offers breast cancer screening, diagnostic testing and treatment programs available to all women regardless of their ability to pay. The center has seen over 53,000 procedures since opening in 2010. Proceeds from Curvature help fund breast cancer research and treatment.

Jack Nicklaus

The first time I met The Golden Bear was on the Island of Hawaii, in early 2000. I asked him to sign my copy of Jack Nicklaus: My Story, and he graciously did. I'm also the proud owner of a Royal Bank of Scotland £5 note issued in 2005, commemorating his last appearance at the Open Championship at St Andrews. That precious piece of memorabilia features the champion golfer of 1978 in his argyle sweater, embracing the iconic Claret Jug. And yes, Jack autographed the note for me too. It was a thrill to witness him waving goodbye to the thousands in the grandstands, who gave him a thunderous standing ovation, after sinking his final birdie putt on the 18th green. And for me a teary-eyed moment.

My most exhilarating recollection occurred when I had the good fortune to attend the inaugural Concession Cup at The Concession Golf Club in Bradenton, FL. Nicklaus was the captain of the US team and Tony Jacklin captained the Great Britain & Ireland squad.

The biennial event is a competition played between teams comprising leading male Mid-Amateurs, Senior-Amateurs and Super Senior-Amateurs from the United States and GB&I. The tournament took place at the club, named as a tribute to a 1969 Ryder Cup incident. Jack Nicklaus conceded a 2-foot putt to Tony Jacklin to square the match. This pure act of sportsmanship defines the essence of Jack Nicklaus, the golfer and the gentleman.

During the Q&A at the gala dinner, Jack was asked to narrate the scene. He said, "Tony was the reigning Open Championship winner and there was no way I was going to let him miss that putt." That might sound ridiculous to some, but any putt is missable under a variety of circumstances (pressure being #1). Just ask Doug Sanders, who only needed to sink a 3 foot putt on the 72nd hole at St Andrews to defeat Jack Nicklaus in 1970. He missed it. Then famously said he only thinks about it, "once every four or five minutes."

Those were the days when golfers wore metal spikes, which tore up tufts in the greens.

Furthermore, the putting surfaces were much bumpier to begin with, rather than the pristine condition of most in this modern age. The putt was a slightly downhill left to right slider. Doug's mind was probably racing ahead. He just didn't get the line and speed right. Doug's ball, and his chance to win a major, slipped by.

To hear both Tony and Jack recount the details of that head-to-head contest, how it meant halving the hole, halving the match, and halving the Cup, was fascinating. But equally riveting was hearing Barbara Nicklaus speak about the Nicklaus Children's Hospital that they created to provide world-class pediatric medical care from birth through adolescence. Later that same night, during the build-up to the live auction, Barbara said, "Children are not just small adults, and they must be treated with special care and compassion." It was then I understood what the deeper Nicklaus legacy was all about. Another teary-eyed moment.

Jack William Nicklaus was born 21 January 1940, in Columbus, Ohio. During the 1967 US Open at Baltusrol in New Jersey, Australian sportswriter, Don Lawrence, described the Germanic golfer as a Golden Bear. At the time, Lawrence was witnessing the exploits of a strong, burly young man with a thick mane of golden hair. The moniker stuck.

Coincidentally, Nicklaus attended Upper Arlington High School, whose nickname and mascot are the Golden Bears.

The debate will continue for centuries, but for now, many believe Jack is the greatest golfer of all time. During a span of 25 years, Nicklaus won 18 major championships and finished second 18 times! He is one of only five golfers who have won the grand slam (all four majors).

Nicklaus knew how important it was to win majors and he set himself up to do just that. He played a selective schedule that included competing in 164 major championships — more than any other player. He captured 73 PGA Tour victories and is third on the all-time list behind Sam Snead (82) and Tiger Woods (82).

Jack took up golf at the age of 10, under the influence of his father, Charlie, a scratch golfer. The young cub shot a 51 at Scioto Country Club for his first nine holes ever played. Jack was coached at Scioto by club pro Jack Grout, who became his lifelong golf instructor.

Nicklaus attended Ohio State University from 1957 to 1961 and planned to follow his father's footsteps into the pharmacy business. His life trajectory changed dramatically when he gave up the idea of winning the Masters as an amateur and turned professional in late 1961.

By then he had married Barbara Bash (b.1940), a nursing student at Ohio State. Jack Jr, the first of their five children was born in September 1961. Given their intended career paths and love of children, it's clear why they established their Nicklaus Children's Health Care Foundation and created the Nicklaus Children's Hospital.

At the 1962 US Open at Oakmont, Nicklaus and Palmer were tied for the lead. The crowd was clearly cheering for Palmer, their local hero who had grown up in nearby Latrobe, PA. Nicklaus won the 18-hole playoff, and became the youngest US Open champion since Bobby Jones claimed the honor at age 21 in 1923.

This was the beginning of one of the greatest rivalries in golf. And like a helping tailwind, television brought the gladiators into the national spotlight. In 1963, Nicklaus won two more majors —the Masters and the PGA Championship. There is no doubt that he was setting the world on fire with these victories coming in his second year as a professional.

Winning big early in his career enabled Nicklaus to capitalize on significant endorsement opportunities. Nicklaus joined Mark McCormack's IMG (International Management Group), which also managed Palmer and Gary Player. McCormack cleverly marketed the 'Big Three' and even set up a series of televised golf matches around the world with his star athletes.

Everybody benefited from the exposure. Then, in the early 1970s, Nicklaus left IMG to set up his own management agency, Golden Bear Inc.

"At age 46, Nicklaus became the oldest Masters winner in history, a record that still stands."

There are more magic numbers in the long list of Nicklaus' stellar statistics — the sixth Masters title at age 46. The Golden Bear is known for accomplishing many things, but for this feat he is eternally revered. More numbers. In 1986, Jack shot a six-under-par 30 on the back nine, carding a 65. Nicklaus played the final ten holes seven under par, with six birdies and an eagle. At age 46, Nicklaus became the oldest Masters winner in history, a record that still stands.

This victory was his 18th and final major title. It was described by renowned golf writer Herbert Warren Wind (who coined the phrase 'Amen Corner' for holes 11, 12 and 13 at Augusta) as, "Nothing less than the most important accomplishment in golf since Bobby Jones' Grand Slam in 1930."

Back in the mid-1960s, Pete Dye was designing a course in Columbus, Ohio, Jack's hometown. He asked the highly acclaimed golfer to take a look at what he was doing and offer any suggestions. A new passion was born, and Nicklaus and Dye teamed up to design Harbour Town Golf Links in Hilton Head, SC.

Four decades later, with son Jack Nicklaus II as president, Nicklaus Design has over 400 courses open for play in 39 states and 45 countries. One of the most famous is Muirfield Village Golf Club in Dublin, Ohio, where Jack has hosted the Memorial Tournament every year since 1976.

Also notable is that Nicklaus was inducted into the World Golf Hall of Fame in the inaugural class of 1974, and the Canadian Golf Hall of Fame in 1995.

In November 2005, the Golden Bear was honored by President Bush with the Presidential Medal of Freedom, the highest honor given to any US civilian. A few weeks later, Golf World magazine named him its Newsmaker of the Year. Jack is a five-time winner of the PGA Player of the Year Award, was the PGA Tour's leading money-winner eight times and runner-up six times. He played on six Ryder Cup teams, captained two other Ryder Cup teams, and served as US captain for the 1998, 2003, 2005, and 2007 President's Cup teams—going unbeaten in his final three captaincies.

A partnership between Terlato Wines and Jack Nicklaus

At the same time Jack was collecting major golf titles, he began collecting wine. Perhaps it started after his 1972 Masters win, when Augusta National GC chairman, Clifford Roberts, gifted him some cases of 1947 and 1952 Chateau Lafite Rothschild. Sometime later, Nicklaus decided to pursue this new passion. He toured the Chimney Rock and Rutherford Hill wineries in Napa Valley with his sons Jack II and Gary, and in partnership with Terlato Wines, they created a range of reds and whites.

In 2010, they produced the Jack Nicklaus Private Reserve (a red blend), Cabernet Sauvignon and Private Reserve White (a white blend). In 2012, Golden Bear Reserve, a Bordeaux-style red blend, was released to mark the 50th anniversary of his first major championship victory at the 1962 US Open.

The fortuitous partnership between

Jack and Barbara Nicklaus and the Terlato family, both celebrated for their philanthropic efforts, continues to expand their charitable contributions with the Jack's House Foundation. A percentage of net proceeds from every bottle purchased is donated to the Foundation and also distributed to The Nicklaus Children's Health Care Foundation, Judi's House, and Sepsis Alliance.

Arnold Palmer who rose to challenge The King became his best friend and greatest admirer. And now it is Nicklaus, along with fellow elder statesman and member of The Big Three, Gary Player, who carry the torch like two Olympians into the new age of golfdom. It is hard to imagine that any other threesome in a modern golfing era will ever be their equal.

Greg Norman

The King. The Bear. The Black Knight. Everybody who plays golf knows who they are. They also know The Shark. Greg Norman earned his nickname, The Great White Shark, when he burst upon the scene at Augusta in 1981 at age 26 to play in his first Masters. Sporting a head of long, blond hair and a taut surfer's body, he captured fourth place at 5 under as well as many swooning ladies' hearts.

It isn't known for sure if he earned his nickname for his aggressive style of play, or because great white sharks habitually cruise the waters off Australia's east coast, not far from where Norman grew up. Then again, it might be because great whites have an extra sense that enables them to detect the heartbeat of their prey and Norman would turn many of his competitors into chum when he was in the field.

After claiming his first European victory in his rookie year as a professional at the 1977 Martini International in Scotland, Norman went on to win 91 international tournaments including 20 PGA Tour events and two majors. Norman won the Open Championship in 1986 at Turnberry, Scotland and in 1993 at Royal St Georges, England. He also earned thirty top-10 finishes and was runner-up 8 times in majors throughout his prodigious career.

Born Gregory John Norman, 10 February 1955 in Mount Isa, Queensland, Australia, he played rugby and cricket as a youth. Then, at age 15, after caddying for his mother, a single-digit golfer, he took up the game. Within about 18 months he was down to a scratch handicap.

Norman's powerful and precise play catapulted him to No.1 in Official World Golf Rankings in the 1980s and 1990s for 331 weeks. His record was finally broken by Tiger Woods in 2004, long after The Shark was inducted into the World Golf Hall of Fame in 2001.

When Norman began his foray into golf course design, his first course in America was for Wente Vineyards in The Livermore Valley of the East Bay region of San Francisco, California. By the time the course opened for play in July 1998, Norman had developed a taste, literally and figuratively, for the intoxicating combination of golf and wine, and started his own wine label.

In 1987, GNGCD (Greg Norman Golf Course Design) was established, and the company has been responsible for creating over 100 golf courses across 34 countries and six continents.

After launching his wine label in 1996, Greg Norman Estates (GNE) now produces 14 different varietals sourced from wine regions in Australia, California, Argentina and New Zealand. He has achieved accolades from both Wine Enthusiast and Wine Spectator magazines. The range of reds include Pinot Noir, Cabernet Sauvignon, Shiraz and Malbec and the whites, Chardonnay and Sauvignon Blanc, are all highly regarded. Two in particular mentioned in an article by Michael Corcoran in the GOLF.com April 2019 issue are the Shiraz McLaren Vale Reserve 1998, and Shiraz South Eastern Australia Reserve 1999. Wine Spectator singled out the 1998 Reserve Shiraz as No.8 in the Top-100 Wines in the World.

Norman was first introduced to the appreciation of a good bottle of wine back in the 1970s while playing golf in France. His GNE now controls 60% of the market share of all premium Australian wine in the US.

In 2000, Andrew Hales was appointed the chief winemaker for the GNE portfolio.

His experience was acquired in the premier Barossa, Clare, and Hunter Valley wine regions of Australia and stretches to distant vineyards in France and Sicily. He brings his expertise and strong understanding of wine making techniques to the brand so the wines can best express the regionality of each vineyard.

Norman's passion for fine living, fine dining and fine wine was taken up by his daughter, Morgan-Leigh. After graduating from Boston College, she spent time in both Italy and Australia to learn more about food and wine, eventually earning a culinary degree in South Florida. From there, she went on to become a chef in the Napa Valley and then joined GNE where she has been involved in every aspect of the wine business for more than six years.

Along with serving as the Chairman and CEO of a diverse global corporation, with a portfolio of companies in fields like apparel, real estate, private equity, golf course design and wine, Greg finds time to engage in several philanthropic endeavors.

In 1987, Greg and his father Merv formed The Greg Norman Foundation. It provides professional guidance and instruction throughout Queensland to students and those in other educational establishments, children with specific physical disabilities, and junior members of golf clubs.

Norman has also donated to and established numerous charities and charity events such as the QBE Shootout that benefits the CureSearch for Children's Cancer fund. The QBE Shootout, (formerly known as the Shark Shootout), is a PGA Tour team golf event that Greg himself hosts. It is played at the Tiburón Golf Club in Naples, Florida. The shootout benefits the CureSearch National Childhood Cancer Foundation.

The Environmental Institute for Golf, the philanthropic arm of the GCSAA (Golf Course Superintendents Association of America), is a collaborative effort of the environmental and golf communities, dedicated to strengthening the compatibility of golf with the natural environment. Norman became a trustee of the Institute and a member of its advisory council in 2004.

Norman received the Golf Writers

Association of America's Bartlett Award in 2008 for his philanthropic endeavors. In 2009 as part of the Q150 celebrations, Greg Norman was announced as one of the Q150 Icons of Queensland for his role as a 'sports legend'.

All in all, even though there is a decline of the shark population in Australian waters, you would have to say the Great White Shark of Golf needs no federal protection. His proprioceptors are still firing on all cylinders, and he is as strong and fearless as ever.

Arnold Palmer

The minute you step inside Arnold Palmer's Restaurant in La Quinta, CA, you are immersed in memories from his amazing six-decade career. Masters flags, photos of triumphant moments, and display cases full of his trophies take you deep into Arnold's world. It's not every museum where you can get a full dose of an iconic golf legend's history and great meatloaf — an AP favorite.

In the main dining room, situated in front of a marble fireplace, is a round table with a place card that reads, 'Reserved for Arnold Palmer'. Even though he passed away on 25 September 2016, you can still feel his infectious magnetism and hear his hearty laugh.

Arnold Daniel Palmer was born 10 September 1929 in Youngstown, PA. His father, nicknamed 'Deacon', was the golf professional and grounds superintendent at Latrobe Country Club. Growing up in this scenario and under Deke's tutelage, "Hit it hard, boy. Go find it and hit it hard again," young Palmer racked up 26 amateur wins and earned a golf scholarship to Wake Forest College in North Carolina.

From there, he enlisted in the US Coast Guard and served for three years (1951-1954).

At the Cape May, NJ training center, Palmer drew a plum assignment to build a nine-hole course. Somehow the golf gods knew this Pennsylvania prodigy was destined for greatness, and gave him a small parcel of land where he could continue to hone his golf skills while completing his military service.

After his enlistment, Palmer won the 1954 US Amateur in Detroit. That victory instilled the confidence for him to turn professional in

November of that year. Probably the biggest prize of that pivotal time was capturing the heart of Winifred Walzer. Winnie, a constant companion for 45 years until her death in 1999, was a big part of the Palmer legacy. Starting with the Arnold Palmer Hospital for Children, continuing with the Winnie Palmer Hospital for Women & Babies, Winnie generously gave her time and energy to these institutions. In addition, she served on the Arnold Palmer Hospital board of directors for more than 10 years.

Arnold Palmer and sculpture unveiled at Laurel Valley Golf Course, Ligonier, PA, on September 10, 2009

Millions of words have been written about Arnold Palmer, but he is also the author of 12 books, including Go For Broke! Written in 1973 with William Barry Furlong, the title defines his fearless style that led to 62 PGA Tour victories from 1955 to 1973 and 92 national and international championships overall.

Palmer won seven major titles, including four Masters (1958,1960,1962,1964), two Open Championships (1961, 1962) and the US Open at Cherry Hills in Denver 1960. Only a handful of golfers have won more majors.

Palmer also represented the US in Ryder Cup Matches as either a player or captain seven times. Among the countless awards recognizing his golfing exploits are 'The Athlete of the Decade' for the 1960s by the Associated Press, and Sports Illustrated Sportsman of the Year, in 1960.

When Palmer burst on the scene, the ground shook, literally and figuratively. Whether he was hitting supersonic irons on the practice range or competing with his reckless escaping-from-the-trees spellbinding golf, Palmer the showman played to the crowds.

They loved his full-out attacking style. It was the way he lived life and legions of fans — known as 'Arnie's Army' — followed their swashbuckling hero's every scintillating success, and heartbreaking failure.

Nicknamed the King, Palmer's ascendancy to golf stardom coincided with the dawn of the television age. His swagger and charm were irresistible. No autograph seeker was ever disappointed. His eyes locked on yours and you were under his spell. On or off the course, the King was gracious, fair and always a true gentleman.

In 2000, Palmer was ranked the sixth greatest player of all time in Golf Digest magazine's rankings, and by 2008 had earned an estimated $30 million. He was the first golfer to be awarded the Presidential Medal of Freedom in 2004 and the second golfer, after Byron Nelson, to be awarded the Congressional Gold Medal.

He also won the PGA Tour Lifetime Achievement Award in 1998, and in 1974 was one of the 13 original inductees into the World Golf Hall of Fame.

The licensing, endorsements, spokesman associations and commercial partnerships built by Palmer and Mark McCormack of the sports-entertainment conglomerate IMG, included deals with companies like Ray-Ban, Pennzoil motor oil, Hertz, Rolex, United Airlines, and many others. Probably one of the best-known branding arrangements was with the popular mass-produced beverage, the Arnold Palmer, a blend of sweetened iced tea with lemonade.

However, Palmer also developed an avid interest in wine during his sports career. He regularly played at the Transamerica Senior Classic at the Silverado Resort in Napa during the 1980s and 1990s. Wine dinners and winery visits were part of the festivities. It was during that time that Palmer met Mike Moone, the then President of Beringer Winery.

In 1996, when Moone started Luna Winery in Napa Valley, Palmer was eager to be part of the project. Luna soon created Arnold Palmer Red, a blend of 50% Sangiovese, 40% Merlot, and 10% Cabernet Sauvignon, plus Arnold Palmer Pinot Grigio.

In 2005, the winery launched Arnold Palmer Wines featuring a Cabernet Sauvignon and a Chardonnay. Luna Vineyards still produces Palmer's wines, aging them in a barrel room across the street from Silverado. Of the 15,000 to 16,000 cases released each year, most are sold directly to country clubs, restaurants and wine-club members. However, a sizable quantity probably winds up in the 2000 bottle Wine Room at the Arnold Palmer Restaurant!

"Palmer's education started with helping his father maintain the course at Latrobe Country Club. Coming full circle, Arnold bought the club in 1971."

As president of Arnold Palmer Enterprises, Palmer supervised the design and development of more than 300 golf courses in 38 states, 25 countries, and five continents. Palmer's education started with helping his father maintain the course at Latrobe Country Club. Coming full circle, Arnold bought the club in 1971. There's something sweet about the King ending up owning the course where as the superintendent's young son, he would have to sneak out to hit balls.

For more than a half century, Arnold Palmer was one of the best-known sportsmen and he was equally successful in the corporate world. He co-founded and was consultant to The Golf Channel, a firmly established cable network entity now owned by NBC Sports Group.

Automotive aficionado, master tinkerer, devoted family patriarch, and pitchman for numerous products, Arnold was a world-famous public figure. However, when it comes to aviation, his passion almost rivaled that of his love for golf. Along with piloting his own Lear Jet and a series of different Cessna Citations, Palmer got to man the controls of an Air Force Thunderbird F-16, test a Boeing 747, and a McDonnell Douglas DC-10. On May 19, 1976, he even set a world record by circumnavigating the globe in a Lear 36 in less than 58 hours.

Arnold Palmer died just after his 87th birthday. Like the title of his last book, published the following month in October 2016, *A Life Well Played: My Stories*, Palmer exemplified how to treat people kindly and do things the right way. Often seen in a classy polo or his trademark cardigan, Arnie even proved that real men wear pink!

Gary Player

I met Gary Player in Hawaii the same year I met Jack Nicklaus. He came to participate in an exhibition match with Hale Irwin for the opening of a golf course called Hokulia on the Big Island. Nicklaus had designed the course and he would explain his objective for each hole throughout their round.

The next time I saw him was in 2003. Gary was jogging on the streets of Sandwich before the Open Championship at Royal St George's Golf Club in Kent, England. He waved as he ran in place at a stoplight. That moment defines one very important aspect of Gary Player. Even now at the age of 86 he is devoted to keeping fit and does crunches with a 100 lb weight on his chest. His full regimen includes push-ups, planks, squats and lots of core strength work.

Gary Player was born 1 November 1935, Johannesburg, South Africa. Dozens of South African lads have followed in his footsteps, but none have logged as many air miles. Keep in mind, when Gary first starting coming to the US, it took 40 hours to fly from Johannesburg, through Zimbabwe, Congo, Accra and Dhaka before reaching Boston. Gary reckons he has been traveling by air for 64 years.

Several South African golfers including Ernie Els, Retief Goosen, Trevor Immelman, Charl Schwartzel and Louis Oosthuizen, have scored major victories following in the footsteps and the slipstream of their idol. It should be noted that Player was preceded by the incredible Bobby Locke (1917–1987) who won the Open Championship four times (1949, 1950, 1952 and 1957) and had 74 professional wins around the world.

Gary was the youngest of three children. When he was eight years old, his mother, Muriel, died of cancer. His father, Harry, toiled long hours in the gold mines but took a loan to buy a set of clubs so Gary could begin to play golf. When he played his first round at age 14, Gary parred the opening three holes. When he was just 16, he announced that he would become No.1 in the world. At age 17, he became a professional golfer and married his wife, Vivienne (Verwey) four years later.

Gary's drive stems from having to fend for himself while his father labored 8,000 feet below the surface of the earth. His brother went into the military at 17 while his sister went away to boarding school. Young Gary had to take a bus and tram home from school to a dark house, cook his own food, iron his clothes, and be up the next morning at 5 am. His passion to lift himself up, and become a champion is an amazing journey. Over the course of the next several years Gary's family grew to include six children. The entire entourage, including a nanny and a tutor, traveled with him and Vivienne to each tournament.

Player's extraordinary grit and determination led to his first of nine majors at Muirfield at age 23. He then completed the career grand slam at just 29 years of age in 1965. Only four other golfers can claim this achievement, but Gary is the only non-American to accomplish the feat.

It was Gary Player himself who created his Black Knight nickname, which is now a global brand. He said, "When I first came to America, there was a series on television called Have Gun, Will Travel. The hero was always dressed in black and had a silver holster. If people were in trouble, he gave them a card that said, 'Call on me if you need help.' I liked that, so I decided to start wearing black!" However, once in a while the Black Knight deviates and wears all white.

Along with Arnold Palmer (The King) and Jack Nicklaus (The Golden Bear) the Black Knight is often referred to as one of 'The Big Three' golfers of his era from the late 1950s through the late 1970s. Golf was becoming ever more popular in the US and around the world, and this triumvirate benefited greatly from the expanded television coverage.

During his career, Player won nine major championships on the regular tour and nine major championships on the Champions Tour. This staggering set of statistics adds up to Player winning 163 tournaments on six continents over seven decades.

In addition to his impressive record of tournament wins, Gary Player has received numerous awards and accolades as below.

Gary Player was inducted into the World Golf Hall of Fame in the initial class of 1974. He won the World Match Play title five times, the Australian Open seven times and the South African Open 13 times.

Player was the PGA Tour leading money winner in 1961, was honored with the Bob Jones Award in 1966, and the Payne Stewart Award in 2006

Player was the captain of the President's Cup teams in 2003, 2005, and 2007.

In 2000, Player was voted 'Sportsman of the Century' in South Africa and Golf Digest magazine ranked Player as the eighth greatest golfer of all time.

In 2002, Player was voted as the second greatest global golfer of all time by a panel of international media, golf magazines and fellow professionals conducted by the leading Golf Asia magazine.

In April 2009, the Black Knight played for the last time in the Masters — a record 52 times.

At age 73 in July 2009, Player competed in the Senior British Open Championship at

Sunningdale Golf Club, 53 years after capturing his first European Tour victory at that venue.

Starting in 2012, Gary joined Jack Nicklaus and Arnold Palmer — The Big Three — as an honorary starter at the Masters.

Player has also authored or co-written 36 golf books.

Black Knight International is owned and operated by Player's eldest son, Marc Player.

The company exclusively represents Player in his commercial activities, including all endorsements, licensing, merchandising, and real estate development. The golf course design company has more than 400 design projects on five continents throughout the world. The Gary Player Stud Farm breeds thoroughbred race horses, and produced the 1994 English Derby winner Broadway Flyer.

It is Marc Player that led the way into the wine business. Apart from wanting to honor his father and select a wine that reinforces Player's South African roots, Marc decided to extend the Player brand since they were already supplying apparel, luxury homes and golf courses and wine to fit with their baby-boomer audience.

"Gary Player's aptly named Black Knight Wines are produced by the Quoin Rock winery in the Stellenbosch area of South Africa."

Gary Player's aptly named Black Knight Wines are produced by the Quoin Rock winery in the Stellenbosch area of South Africa. The first step in creating this synergy between great golf and great grapes was to bring Andrew Smith on board as the general manager. Andrew was instrumental in developing an outstanding premium wine.

The label launched with the Muirfield 1959 vintage, part of the 'Gary Player Major Championship Series'. The series is set to release 18 new vintages over the next two decades.

Winemaker Carl van der Merwe's 2003 blend of Merlot, Cabernet Sauvignon, Pinotage and Shiraz, was chosen to commemorate the first in the series, Player's 1959 Open Championship victory at Muirfield.

The stylish packaging of the series commemorates Player's major victories, captured in striking labels by South African artist Athol Moult. Drawing inspiration from press clippings and iconic photos from the Player archives, Moult has produced a modern design that integrates black and white photography.

Father, husband, and humanitarian, Gary is the inspiration behind The Player Foundation.

Originally formed to address the education crisis in their home country of South Africa, the Player family soon realized the need for quality education for less fortunate children around the world. Since its establishment in 1983, the foundation has provided over $64 million dollars to build and operate facilities such as the Blair Atholl Schools in Johannesburg, South Africa.

The school has educational facilities for more than 500 students from kindergarten through eighth grade. The students receive nutrition, medical and dental care and can participate in sports, join a choir, and learn to play violin and piano. The Foundation also provides transport and adult education and training.

Gary Player is a role model to millions of people around the world. Always smiling, always oozing love, he is the very vibrant picture of excellent health— body, mind, and spirit. Sharp as a tack, body made of steel, his true grace is his giant heart of gold which eclipses all South Africa.

Annika Sörenstam

Annika. The name is synonymous with quality. Ultra-high quality, that is. Everything she has turned her hand to, be it a clothing line, golf course design, or wine, is always first-rate.

Annika Sörenstam was born October 1970 in Bro near Stockholm, Sweden. As a child, Annika was an exceedingly all-round talented athlete. She excelled at soccer, skiing, and was a nationally ranked junior tennis player. At the age of 12, she took up golf and shared her first set of clubs with her younger sister Charlotta. Annika was so shy as a junior player that, by her own admission, she deliberately three-putted when playing a final match so she wouldn't have to give a victory speech. Eventually the officials noticed and changed the protocol so that both the winner and the runner-up had to give a speech. That's when Annika figured she might as well go ahead and win.

A coach spotted Annika playing in a collegiate event in Tokyo and recruited her to play golf at the University of Arizona in Tucson. She won seven collegiate titles and in 1991, became the first non-American and first freshman to win the individual NCAA Division I Championship. Annika turned professional in 1992 and went on to become one of the best female golfers of all time.

The winner of a record eight Player of the Year awards, and six Vare Trophies (given to the LPGA player with the lowest seasonal scoring average), Annika is the only female golfer to shoot a 59 in competition. In 2003, Sörenstam played in the Bank of America Colonial tournament, becoming the first woman to

Annika Sörenstam during pro-am before the 2008 LPGA Championship

play in a PGA Tour event since 1945. To honor her numerous outstanding achievements, the World Golf Hall of Fame admitted Annika to the Class of 2003. She holds various all-time scoring records including the lowest season scoring average of 68.7 in 2004.

During her years of dominance, Annika represented Europe in the Solheim Cup on eight occasions between 1994 and 2007, and she was the event's all-time leading points earner until her record was surpassed by England's Laura Davies during the 2011 Solheim Cup.

In 2008, at the top of her game, Annika stepped away from competitive golf, having won 90 international tournaments as a professional, making her the female golfer with the most wins to her name. She has won 72 official LPGA tournaments including 10 majors and 18 other tournaments internationally.

Sörenstam began the transition from professional golfer to entrepreneur during the later years of her career. In 2007 she created the ANNIKA Academy as a platform to share her passion for golf and fitness. That same year, Annika became engaged to Mike McGee, the managing director for the ANNIKA brand, and in January 2009 they were married.

During this exciting time, Annika teamed up with Wente Vineyards in Livermore, CA, to create fine wines. Working directly with Karl Wente, whose family-owned winery was established in 1883, was great fun for Annika. She described the joyous experience of creating her blends as if they were in a chemistry lab.

The first release of 635 cases of Syrah became available in May 2009. Fifth generation winegrower Carolyn Wente characterized Annika as an amazing woman who wanted her wines to be beautiful. What else could they be, but a natural reflection of her style?

Annika Sörenstam, photo by Robert Kaufman

The grapes for Annika's wines were grown and vinified on Wente's meticulously-kept vineyards.

Their attention to detail made Wente the ideal partner to assist Annika in the creation of a vintage that would meet her standards for perfection.

Along with the launch of the Chardonnay varietal, Annika became pregnant with the couple's first child, Ava, and in 2011, they welcomed their son, William, into the world.

Annika's passion for creating superb wines for the luxury market was ultimately superseded by becoming a mother. Having her own wine label had to take a back seat to raising her two young children. The timing was unfortunate. It was awkward for Annika to promote drinking wine while she was pregnant.

Although Annika's wine label was short-lived, she remains involved in a diverse array of other projects and philanthropic endeavors. In 2007 Annika became a National Ambassador for Make a Wish Foundation. That same year she also established the ANNIKA Foundation with the goal of developing women's golf around the world and encouraging children to lead healthy, active lifestyles. The focus is on fitness and nutrition, and the Foundation enables aspiring junior golfers to pursue their dreams.

The golfing world has continued to celebrate Annika's impact on the LPGA and Ladies European Tour and in 2015 she became one of the first female members of the Royal & Ancient Golf Club of St Andrews, along with Laura Davies, Renee Powell, Belle Robertson MBE, Lally Segard and Louise Suggs.

In 2018, Annika was voted Top Female Golfer of All-Time by PGA.com and she was also ranked the No.1 Female 'Most Dominant' Athlete by ESPN The Magazine.

It seems there is always a headline somewhere about the indefatigable Annika. Recently I read about the 8th ANNIKA Invitational Europe that offers the best European female junior golfers a chance to compete against others from 23 different countries. But it's not just that they earned a spot in the field, with Annika as their host, they are treated to decades of wisdom.

Annika is someone who didn't just learn how to win in sports. She learned how to win in life and gives so much inspiration and encouragement to others. In my book, and this is after all my book, I deem her Dame Annika.

Jan Stephenson

She is formally known as 'Lady Jan' and was born in Sydney, Australia, 22 December 1951. She was awarded the Order of Australia medal in March 2018 for her contributions to the game of golf. Along with her extraordinary achievements in the world of sports, Jan has been involved in a wide range of charitable endeavors and touched countless lives.

Not only is Jan an honorary chair of the National Multiple Sclerosis Society, Tri Cities of Texas Chapter, she is an ambassador for blind and disabled golfers through ISPS Handa. When Jan acquired Tarpon Woods Golf Club in Palm Harbor, Florida through her Crossroads Foundation, it enabled her to provide initiatives for blind/disabled and wounded veterans and first responders.

Jan has stated her mission as 'Giving to Those that have Given so Much'. She was awarded recognition by the Military Order of the Purple Heart in October 2017. Her foundation was awarded the Charity of the Year by the Palm Harbor Chamber of Commerce in September 2018.

One of Stephenson's early charitable endeavors, Jan For Juniors, is a non-profit organization that offers opportunities for Australian female junior golfers to travel to the US and experience an LPGA Tour event. However, Jan's ultimate passion project is Tarpon Woods where she is devoted to creating a golf facility for veterans. Jan not only conducts special clinics for blind golfers, her overarching objective is to provide assistance and emotional healing to those who have served in the military.

Stephenson's passion for golf was ignited when she was growing up just seven miles north of Sydney, where she lived, near a course by the ocean. At the age of 10, she tagged along with her father, toting a canvas bag with some sawn-off clubs. Right then and there, Jan fell in love with golf.

Beginning in 1964, while a teenager, Jan won six consecutive State Schoolgirl Championships in Australia. She followed that up with three straight wins in the New South Wales Junior Championship. A two-time winner of the NSW Amateur, Stephenson was named the 1971 NSW Athlete of the Year.

Jan turned professional in 1973 and joined the Australian LPGA. She won the Wills Australian Ladies Open that year, and captured the title again in 1977. In her first season on the LPGA Tour in 1974, Stephenson was named LPGA's Rookie of the Year. She went on to lead an impressive career with 41 professional victories, including 16 on the LPGA Tour, and 10 LPGA Legends Tour wins — a tour Jan helped to found with Jane Blalock, Hollis Stacy, and Sally Little, among others.

In 1981, Jan won the World Ladies Championship in Japan, becoming the first Australian woman to win a golf tournament there. Her competitive fire propelled Jan to win three LPGA Major Championships including the Peter Jackson (Canadian Open) Classic (1981), The LPGA Championship (1982), and the US Women's Open (1983).

Her statistics, including an astonishing 15 holes-in-one (9 in LPGA competition) are incredibly admirable, but they do not begin to describe Jan's resilience and fortitude in the face of adversity. While Jan was enjoying her best year in 1987 as the leading money winner, following the third round of the St Petersburg Classic, ahead by five shots, a driver ran a red light and crashed into Jan's car. She sustained serious head and back injuries and broke several ribs on her left side.

Tragedy struck again in 1987, when Jan's brother-in-law was killed in a car accident and her father, Frank, was diagnosed with prostate cancer. Frank had been a big part of Jan's career, and even caddied for her on the LPGA Tour in 1981 and 1982 during her two major championships in those years. When Frank lost his battle with cancer in December 1988, it was a massive blow. That same year her trusted caddie since 1982, Rick White, also died of cancer.

It took until 1990 for Jan to find the spark to get back to playing a full golf schedule. In her first two events, Jan finished in the Top 10, but then was brutally mugged in a parking lot on her way to an NBA basketball game. Her left ring finger and hand were broken in five places, and her right shoulder was dislocated. Devastated, Jan was sidelined for months.

At this point, finding a way to play golf again was not easy. But Jan reconnected with a friend in Australia, a well-respected instructor, Gary Edwin, who was teaching a system that emphasized the right side. (Gary's technique is called 'The Right Sided Swing' and addresses the cause of motion. His philosophy focuses on weight transfer, and he describes how in our backswing, we coil and during the swing the right hip pushes the left hip around to get to our finish.) With grip changes and Gary's guidance, Jan worked to overcome the debilitating injuries in the hope that she could return to professional golf.

When Jan developed arthritis in her left hand, she felt compelled to lend support to the Arthritis Foundation by creating an arthritis instructional program. She also leads a group of athletes called PACE (People with Arthritis Can Exercise).

After struggling with her game, Jan turned her attention to golf course design. She attended courses at the University of Georgia on turf grasses and began work with Dye Designs. In the late 1990s Jan won a bid to design her first golf course in Mims, Florida. She named it the Walkabout Golf Course as a tribute to her homeland of Australia.

Even though Jan had experienced remarkable

success as a golf course designer, she missed playing full-time and wanted to the give the LPGA one more shot. She called Gary Edwin and persuaded him to come to the US to coach her with his Right Sided swing method. Jan went on to compete on the LPGA tour year in 1999 with two second place finishes, including a playoff loss to Rosie Jones at the Firstar LPGA Classic.

Jan's numerous accolades include induction into the Sport Australia Hall of Fame in 1985, and she was named among GOLF Magazine '100 Heroes' during the 1988 Centennial of Golf in America celebration. Jan was also recognized during the LPGA's 50th Anniversary in 2000 as one of the LPGA's Top 50 players and teachers. She is, without a doubt, revered as one of the most well-known and influential women in professional sports. Capping this remarkable career, Stephenson was inducted into the World Golf Hall of Fame, Class of 2019.

It is indeed impressive that Jan has remained undaunted by multiple setbacks. Her vision and energy have been channeled into a music production company, and now her love for fine wine has lead her to develop her own line of Jan Stephenson Signature Series Wines.

Jan's winery is in Paso Robles, California and she has taken a hands-on approach to wine making. Jan makes frequent visits to the winery. During harvest season, she gets into the vineyard and harvests grapes, crushes, and supervises all aspects of the wine making process.

Jan's winemaker, Chris Cameron, is also from her home country of Australia. Chris has been recognized as winemaker extraordinaire by many wine rating groups. Jan is currently producing Cabernet Sauvignon, Reserve Cabernet Sauvignon, Chardonnay and a very fine Merlot. Next to come is a red blend called 3 Majors.

Jan is an incredible inspiration to me. Her busy schedule keeps her always on the go. She is like a human comet. I hope she'll be able to find the time some day, so we can meet up and do an orbit around a golf course, and then share a glass of her wine.

Golf Clubs with a Strong Wine Culture

Hole #2 at Adare Manor Resort.

Adare Golf Club

County Limerick, Ireland

Where do you start with Adare, the golf or the wine? After J.P. McManus bought Adare Manor in December 2014, the entire property was closed for a full 21 months to complete an extensive makeover, including the golf course. From top to bottom, today this is an extraordinary place to eat, drink wine, play golf — or all the above.

Golf membership is currently capped at 300, according to Andy McMahon, Director of Golf Operations. He hails from Scotland, so you can be sure he knows his golf. Andy also points out that guests at the hotel have access to the course, with the ideal being a stay and play experience.

The Golf Course at Adare Manor is located along the banks of the River Maigue and was originally designed by Robert Trent Jones Sr in 1995. For over twenty years it has been highly respected as one of the last two courses RTJ Sr designed in Europe — the other one being at Celtic Manor, Wales.

The golf course at Adare Manor was the venue for the Irish Open in 2007 and 2008 and it also played host to the J.P. McManus Invitational Pro-Am in 2005 and 2010. While raising the profile of the course, with professional golfers like Tiger Woods and celebrities such as the actor Hugh Grant participating, the events also raised millions for multiple charities.

When Adare Manor began its spectacular redevelopment project in 2015 — 2017, they decided the golf course also deserved a comprehensive redesign. Renowned American golf course architect Tom Fazio was hired to take on the project, reimagining the course at Adare Manor quite literally from the ground up.

Although Ireland is known for its links courses, this is a unique and pedigreed parkland course. Fazio, with over fifty years of golf design experience, brought his prodigious expertise to Adare and used the original RTJ Sr layout to maximize the existing topography and natural beauty of the site.

While the order of holes remains the same, everything else has been transformed.

Each green and tee has been rebuilt and the Pure Distinction greens boast tightly mown low-cut A4 bentgrass surrounds. The impressive result has led to Adare Manor being named the venue for the 2026 Ryder Cup.

Along with significant underground installations for drainage, new irrigation and water delivery systems, Adare Manor is now one of just a handful of courses worldwide to have the patented Sub Air technology beneath every putting surface, providing constant air movement for aeration and to moderate the temperature in the root zone. Every bunker has been replaced with the latest Capillary Concrete liner drainage technology and all fairways and roughs are sand-capped for the driest playing conditions. But that is all invisible technical stuff, and doesn't begin to describe how much fun it is to play the course.

The elegantly renovated Carriage House now incorporates the locker rooms, the pro shop and offers several dining options. The bar is cozy and stylish with rich leather and dark-stained oak furnishings, in contrast to the terrace, which features Breccia Violetta marble

The eighteenth green at Adare Manor Resort.

table tops and a whole wall of glass, overlooking the putting green and lush landscaping.

Whatever dining experience you choose, it will be complemented with a fine bottle of their wine. With such an extensive wine list, you may require the assistance of Jurica Gojevic, the Head Sommelier. The members of Adare Golf Club and guests of the hotel are twice lucky with this incredibly knowledgeable and friendly human asset. Before you ever set eyes on the 650-bin cellar (which houses only 40% of wines on hand, the rest are in storage two miles away), you will see numerous bottles of wine on display throughout the clubhouse and the Manor.

Just a few of these bottles include vintages of Taittinger Champagne — all presented in elegant cases with sophisticated lighting. But Mr Gojevic is only in the initial phase of building the collection, which includes a selection of all the best vintages of Château Pétrus.

Once inside the Cellar, which has the feel of an ancient cave, when your eyes adjust to the low light, you'll discover the handy port tongs. They rest on a table with all the necessary accoutrements for use at a moment's notice and are put into service whenever a precious and expensive older bottle needs to be opened without having to disturb the cork.

In Ireland, or anywhere for that matter, this exceptional property exemplifies the best of both golf and wine worlds.

Adare Manor, wine cave long table

Aerial view of Castiglion del Bosco.

Castiglion del Bosco

Tuscany, Italy

Great wine, fabulous food, centuries-old history, and rich culture — all of what you would expect in Italy. And world-class golf too? Yes! In the heart of Brunello wine country, members of The Club at Castiglion del Bosco enjoy a superb golf haven.

Italy's only private golf club, CdB is owned by Massimo and Chiara Ferragamo. For some insight into the visionary proprietors, let's look back in time. Massimo's father, Salvatore (1898–1960), was born in Bonito, Italy and studied shoemaking in Naples. He migrated to Boston in 1914, and with his brothers, moved to California, where they set up shop to create custom-made shoes for the Hollywood stars.

In 1927, Salvatore returned to Italy and settled in Florence. He married Wanda Miletti in 1940 and together they built the world-renowned Ferragamo brand into an iconic luxury goods company, making shoes, bags, eyewear, silk accessories, perfumes, and ready-to-wear clothing.

Massimo, Chairman of Ferragamo USA, and his wife Chiara, live between New York City and Tuscany. Massimo has always loved

Tuscan wines and he has always had the desire to get into the wine business. One sunny morning, their exploration led them to an abandoned borgo (village) within Vald d'Orcia, a UNESCO protected landscape in Tuscany. It was love at first sight and in 2003, they wound up buying Castiglion del Bosco, a 5,000 acre property.

The Ferragamo family has a strong tradition of participating in significant restoration projects. One example is the famous Fountain of Neptune in Piazza della Signoria in Florence. Made of marble and bronze, commissioned in 1565, it has been restored to its former glory, including an overhaul of the water pump system. The project cost 1.5 million euro, funded by the Florentine fashion house Salvatore Ferragamo SpA.

Another example is the funding of a massive project in the Uffizi Gallery, spearheaded by Ferruccio Ferragamo. The work was carried out on the oldest areas of the Uffizi overlooking the river Arno. The renovation involved eight rooms (numbers 25 to 32 of 101 rooms), which held the Medici foundry in the last two decades of the 16th century. Before the renovation, these rooms held 16th century Florentine, Veneto, Emilion and Lombard paintings by artists like Lotto and Michelangelo.

Massimo and Chiara are respectful of their ancestry and take their role as custodians of the 800-year-old estate very seriously. First and foremost, the couple wanted to preserve and share the heritage of such a deeply rooted age-old Tuscan village. Within The Club at Castiglion del Bosco, they restored a historic farmhouse, which they converted into a rustic but elegant clubhouse, using reclaimed stone and roof tiles. It now houses locker rooms, sauna and steam room, and the pro shop.

Just as carefully as Massimo and Chiara meticulously restored and repurposed old buildings to create a beautiful and relaxing hub for the golf members, they selected Tom Weiskopf to design the golf course. Weiskopf had a hugely successful career as a player, winning 16 PGA Tour titles, and 28 professional wins

The Hilltop Resort.

overall, including the 1973 Open Championship at Royal Troon in 1973.

A golf course designer since 1985, Tom Weiskopf has created courses in the United States, Scotland, South Africa, Asia-Pacific and the Caribbean. He was charged with the task of creating something unique, and aesthetically pleasing. He has masterfully blended the rolling Tuscan hills and valleys of the Val d'Orcia landscape into a beautiful 18 hole course, alongside the topography that yields the ripe delights of acclaimed Brunello wines.

Although the club is private, Massimo and Chiara restored the ancient Borgo, creating a 5 star resort, which is managed by Rosewood Hotel & Resorts since 2015. The 23 sumptuous suites and 11 villas, configured from 17th and 18th century farmhouses, feature exposed wooden beams, antique furniture, genuine textiles, and all the latest technology to create the ultimate comfort for guests.

Castiglion del Bosco is also a superb culinary destination. It features a leading Brunello di Montalcino winery, two restaurants, organic vegetable garden, and a cooking school.

What a perfect place for total immersion into the world of Tuscan wine with 153 acres of vineyards located within the estate.

The Brunello di Montalcino wine is elegant and deeply rooted in local tradition — ruby red, intense and complex, with golden yellow hues or burgundy overtones. The terroirs of the arid, breezy heights of Capanna and the wetter hills to the north around Gauggiole are captured in three different labels, each telling of soil rich in clay, sandstone, and typical Tuscan marl.

These elements nourish the Sangiovese grapes of the single-cru Campo del Drago Brunello di Montalcino DOCG, The Millecento Riserva Brunello di Montalcino DOCG, and the Rosso di Montalcino DOC. The harvest, a two-stage hand selection process and barrel-aging in the 43,033 sq. ft. winery are rituals supervised by enologist Cecilia Leoneschi.

Castiglion del Bosco is in the northwest of Montalcino, where the rocky soils are perfect

Presidents Cup Dinner in Winery Ageing Cellar.

for yielding wines of superb structure and complexity. Within the estate's 5,000 acres, 153 acres of vineyards are planted exclusively with Sangiovese, the historic grape. There are two distinct vineyards defined by unique aspects, soils, and weather conditions: The 50 acres of Gauggiole just beneath the Borgo and the 103 acres of Capanna, where the top wines are produced.

The on-site winery hosts an array of

wine-tasting seminars, and an annual harvest event takes place in September. The Castiglion del Bosco Wine Experience is a seminar where participants visit the vineyards, cellar and aging room with an expert guide. The tour concludes with a tasting of six Castiglion del Bosco wines and a delightful culinary surprise.

From there you can participate in the Cheese and Wine Pairing and learn how to match different types of Italian cheeses with Castiglion del Bosco wines. Afterwards, the Vertical Tasting of seven remarkable Brunello di Montalcino vintages.

A fact that is of particular interest for true wine connoisseurs is that in 1967, Consorzio del Brunello di Montalcino was established with Castiglion del Bosco as one of its founding members. The organization was created as a voluntary association of producers who regulate and control the quality of Brunello di Montalcino production. In 1966, it became one of the first Italian wines to achieve the DOC (Controlled Denomination of Origin) title and in 1980 earned the DOCG (Controlled and Guaranteed Denomination of Origin) status.

(Note: The regulations for DOCG wines are tighter and more restrictive. Each wine must pass in-depth technical analysis and tasting to receive the official DOCG seal of approval from the Ministry of Agriculture).

You could spend an entire summer discovering the multi-layered landscape that is Tuscany. Within Castiglion del Bosco, beyond the ancient castle ruins that date back to 1100 AD you can also discover the medieval San Michele Church in the village in the heart of the Borgo. In the immediate surroundings you can revel in local history and drink in the cultural sights, while traveling through a patchwork of fields that form a living canvas. You can also visit the Roman settlement from the Augustan age (tombs 1st century BC — 1st century AD) and wander along the cypress-lined roads that used to be a route traveled by merchants and pilgrims on their way from Canterbury to Rome.

There's much more to enjoy. Massimo and

The lush fairways of Castiglion del Bosco.

Sangiovese vines at Castiglion del Bosco

Chiara Ferragamo also own a 25 acre estate called Prima Pietra in Riparbella, located on the Tuscan coast near the Bolgheri wine area. The vines face the Tyrrhenian Sea at an elevation of 1475 feet. The site enjoys abundant sun and ventilation, and the rocky, iron-rich soil ensures wines of superb structure. After in-depth soil and climate research, Merlot, Cabernet Franc, Cabernet Sauvignon, and Petit Verdot were planted. In fact, these varieties flourish in this terroir, producing wonderfully expressive wines, with power and elegance.

To top it off, if you are really lucky, you'll be able to catch a concert with Andrea Bocelli, performing under the Tuscan stars in a natural amphitheater.

Castiglion del Bosco owner Massimo Ferragamo and course designer Tom Weiskopf.

16th hole at Grand Saint-Emilionnais Golf Club, with 12th century church in the background.

Grand Saint-Emilionnais Golf Club

Gardegan-et-Tourtirac, France

Just a few miles from the picturesque medieval village of St Emilion, surrounded by legendary vineyards and chateaus, a new golf course, designed by the world renowned architect Tom Doak, is the centerpiece of Grand Saint-Emilionnais Golf Club (SEGC). Founded by the Mourgue d'Algue family, the patriarch Gaëtan, established the Trophée Lancôme in 1970, and was the top French player of his generation. Along with son André, (who once halved with Tiger Woods in a team match between Paris and California) they identified the land and managed the complex project.

Golf and wine run deep in the DNA of all the family members, who have won more than 80 golf titles worldwide. Mother Cecilia, born in Sweden, holds one of the most distinguished French amateur records ever. Kristel, Gaëtan's daughter and André's sister, is the only French individual winner of the NCAA championship in the United States and is a former Ladies European Tour player with one win on Tour. She is married to Pierre Lawton, the 8th generation of leading traders in first growth Bordeaux wines, and a passionate golfer who is

110 yards off the tee, the par 3 15th at Grand Saint-Emilionnais.

an overseas member of Portmarnock Golf Club in Dublin, Ireland. Andre's wife, Philippine, the granddaughter of Bordeaux wine producers, is herself a Junior and College French Champion. Fabian, the oldest brother, with his years of international financial experience, completes the team.

Tom Doak and his talented group at Renaissance Golf Design, laid out the fun and engaging course that spreads over 242 acres of gently rolling terrain. Just like Bordeaux's regulations relating to viticulture, natural rainfall is the only source of water allowed for maintenance on the course. According to Doak, every drop of rain naturally flows downward toward the pond at the ninth hole. Seven acres of lakes were also built to assure that all available water would be captured and retained. Tom is especially proud of how the design of the course respects the laws and spirit of this Old World wine region.

On your approach to SEGC, vineyards are visible in every direction as far as the eye can see. Although the course is often bordered by centenary oaks and towering pine trees, vineyards are in view on several holes, including the first and eighteenth, which sit just below the charming clubhouse. The warm welcome, sumptuous food and outstanding selection of wines from just next door at Chateau de Pitray and other nearby wines, Château La Gaffelière being just one of the notable ones, create one of the most delightful golf experiences you can have in France.

And where else will you see 150 yard markers made from the characteristic gnarly grape vines?

Mayacama wines and wine cabinets.

Mayacama Golf Club

Sonoma County, Northern California, USA

If there was a rating system for 'Golf Clubs with a Strong Wine Culture', Mayacama would have to be in the top three. Set on 675 acres of Sonoma County in northern California, the club was founded in 1999 when David Wilhelm and his partners purchased the land from Marv Soiland and Peanuts cartoonist, Charles M. Schulz.

Schultz, known affectionately as Sparky, was a founding member. To this day, Mayacama hosts the Schultz Celebrity Golf Classic, focused on providing charitable support for children's organizations throughout the county.

As fun as that tournament must be, the All Vintner Cup & Pour event is especially inviting for those who indulge in the dual passions of golf and wine. Each year, all vintner members, currently forty-two, pour their new wines while participants enjoy the sumptuous array of lavish food.

And who might these vintner members be? Only some of the best in the business including DuMOL, Foley, Harlan, Kistler, Joseph Phelps, and Marcassin. And, according to Jeff McCarthy, the Director of Wine at Mayacama, they also have a number of small

The Wine Room at Mayacama.

artisan winery members. Their following grows rapidly when Mayacama wine enthusiasts bring in bottles of their new discoveries to their favorite restaurants (very much encouraged in California) and subsequently, the proprietors wind up buying a significant number of cases to offer to their discerning clientele.

No wonder the founder of Mayacama calls it a 'Wine Club with a Golf Course'.

Although that sounds like a fair description, the Jack Nicklaus Signature Course is not just a pretty backdrop to those sipping their wine on the clubhouse terrace. The 6,761 yard layout, beautifully woven into rolling hills and valleys, carries a 150 slope rating, making it a serious challenge.

Even with a good bit of elevation, the club takes great pride in maintaining the walking tradition of golf, so they enlist the same kind of caddie program used by Augusta National. They do keep a limited number of carts on the property for members who have a physical handicap/injury or are seventy-five years and older. However, with most of the membership (around 500) leading such a health-conscious lifestyle, the carts sit idle much of the time.

Of the many formal tournaments Mayacama organizes for its members (eg, the annual Vintner's Cup in May), when the members are thinking about draining their glasses as much as draining their putts, the Vintner Members become the 'pros' in a pro-am, and magnums of wine are presented as the tee prizes. Overseeing all the competitions is Head Golf Professional, Ted Antonopoulos, who's quite familiar with all the protocols of conducting a serious tournament, as he's on the PGA Rules Committee. His devotion to the Junior Golf Program at Mayacama led to him being named the 2017 Golf Professional of the Year by the American Junior Golf Association.

At a club where there are more wine lockers than golf lockers, this is a place where the synergy of wine and golf is in full force. The 40,000 square foot Mediterranean style clubhouse, along with a spa, fitness center and three dining rooms, has a two-story wine cellar, allowing the club to offer 750 selections on their wine list, which changes daily!

Besides hanging out in the wine cave, to do private wine tastings or take a blending seminar, members can participate in Wine Tour Field trips, organized around each of the prominent AVAs such as Russian, Dry Creek, Sonoma and Napa. For example, when visiting Foley Estates, guests are regaled with the fascinating story of the winery's laborious conversion from the stables of what was once a thoroughbred horse ranch.

If that doesn't sound like heaven, then what does? Maybe being part of the Private Residence Club where the pantry and refrigerator are stocked, prior to arrival in a villa or casita, and you can wander over to the practice area and putting green where your golf clubs are already waiting for you?

Entrance Hall lined with wine cabinets.

Real Club Valderrama

Sotogrande, Cadiz, Spain

If you ask golfers to name the most memorable course in Spain, the majority will answer Valderrama. Like Augusta National Golf Club, known simply as Augusta, or referred to as the National by locals, rarely does anybody say, or need to say, Real Club Valderrama, the royal title granted by King Juan Carlos I toward the end of his reign in 2015.

Located in the Andalusia region of southern Spain, Valderrama opened in 1974 and was first named Sotogrande New, to distinguish it from Real Club de Golf Sotogrande, which opened in 1964. In 2015 the Club obtained Royal Status from his Majesty the King Juan Carlos I.

Like Sotogrande, Valderrama was designed by Robert Trent Jones Sr. Throughout his career, RTJ Sr designed or remodeled about 500 courses in 35 countries and Sotogrande was his first course in Europe. His outstanding creation made him the natural choice to lay out the course farther up the hill, renamed Las Aves in 1981.

When Jaime Ortiz-Patino acquired the course in 1985 he changed the name to Valderrama.

Redesigned and expanded by RTJ and later

in 2008 by Kyle Phillips, this elite club, now member-owned since late 2017, only grows more spectacular, while maintaining its immaculate condition through the efforts of Adolfo Ramos, the Head Agronomy Engineer.

Thanks to continuing enhancements like the new irrigation system, Valderrama reaches new heights in its bid to be the best. With the construction of another area adjacent to the current practice range which resembles the playing conditions of the actual course, Valderrama solidifies itself as the ideal venue for many top European championships.

"The iconic layout has hosted over 23 world-class events, including the Volvo Masters, the Spanish Open, The Andalucia Masters, and the World Golf Championship"

The iconic layout has hosted over 23 world-class events, including the Volvo Masters, the Spanish Open, The Andalucia Masters, and the World Golf Championship. The 1997 Ryder Cup, captained by the greatest continental golfer of all time, Severiano Ballesteros, may well be its crowning glory. Seve Ballesteros, born 1957 in Pedreña, Spain, won five majors: the Open three times and the Masters, played at Augusta twice, along with more than 90 international tournaments in his career. The importance of Seve serving as captain cannot be overstated.

This was a momentous occasion as it was the first time the Ryder Cup matches were contested in continental Europe. Earlier in 1997, Tiger Woods, then a 21-year-old rookie, was playing in his first Ryder Cup. He had recently won his first major championship by a record 12 strokes at the Masters. Even with all the American firepower, the European team won by a margin of 14-1/2 to 13-1/2, igniting a streak of six consecutive victories at home by Europe that remains intact through 2018.

Along with the grand reputation of a club that is mighty enough to host some of the most

Valderrama par-3, hole 6.

prestigious golf events in the world, one could easily surmise that Valderrama would have a strong wine culture. The minute you step on the property you'll recognize that you are actually in a cork forest.

According to the General Manager, Javier Reviriego, there are 5,600 Cork Oak trees on the property. Not that these Cork Oaks would ever be stripped of their deeply fissured outer skin. However, they are regularly pruned to gently

Head green keeper Adolpho Ramos shows cork below the bark.

allow more light to enter and movement of air, which improves the health of the plant. These beautiful gnarly trees also produce an enormous number of acorns.

Valderrama is a superb steward of its highly esteemed course and its precious Cork Oak trees. They even go to great lengths to make sure that the vast number of acorns are harvested (for free) and used to feed the prized Iberian Pigs. That is just one aspect of being a course with the Audubon Certification, which has a strong commitment to take care of and manage all their flora and fauna.

The wine cellar of Valderrama is refreshed by a consultant sommelier three or four times a year, and averages 5,000 bottles. Although it is composed of mostly Spanish wines, the sommelier also chooses some great wines from France, Italy, Portugal, Chile, Australia and even Napa Valley. Some of the examples from France (at the time of this writing) include Codoulet de Beaucastel 2016 (Cote du Rhone), La Jannasse 2012 (Chateauneuf-du-Pape), and Chateau Les Forts de Latour 2008 (Pauillac).

Attesting to the strong wine culture of the club, the Viña Arana Reserva is a special house wine made just for Valderrama. This winery has a certain parcel in the estate-owned vineyards where the grapes for this wine are grown exclusively in some of the finest terroir of Rioja.

Fittingly, several of the members are owners of some of the best wines in Spain.

Although their names are kept very private, one member is affiliated with Cosme Palacio, which launched its iconic brand in 1899 bearing the name of the founder, Cosme Palacio y Hermanos.

Their early wines are believed to be the precursor of modern Rioja, but the winery now has an entire family of highly rated wines.

When asked if the club uncorked the most prized bottles to celebrate the Ryder Cup victory, Mr Reviriego implied that they did, but explained that they get special requests from their wine aficionado members all the time. Thanks to a couple of outstanding suppliers, he said they always succeed at finding them!

Whereas others might have coveted a bottle of the Vega Sicilia Unico that Sergio Garcia gave to Luke Donald as a wedding present, I was absolutely delighted when Adolfo Ramos gifted me two large chunks of cork oak after my round at Valderrama.

Valderrama Club House.

Royal Wimbledon Golf Club

London, England

Rarely do you find the words 'royal' and 'common' just an inch apart in a sentence or on a map, but in the case of Royal Wimbledon Golf Club, you do, since the club is situated on Wimbledon Common.

Like many clubs founded in the 18th and 19th centuries, RWGC started humbly and followed a circuitous route. Records from 1864 of the London Scottish Rifle Volunteers reveal that after one particular shooting match, they had the idea to create a 7 hole golf course on ground known as Wimbledon Common. At the time, these original 7 holes encircled a windmill, which is still a prominent feature of the Royal Wimbledon logo. This distinctive landmark, built in 1817, now has another useful purpose as a museum, demonstrating how grain was milled to produce flour.

The Common, which includes ponds, streams, and nature trails, is the largest expanse of heathland in the London area. The green space, wooded and boggy in some places, spreads out over 1,100 acres and features football, cricket and rugby pitches for local schools and clubs. But in its earlier life, it was a popular place for staging duels!

One such duel was fought on Putney Heath

in May 1652 between George Brydges, 6th Baron of Chandos, and Colonel Henry Compton. The outcome was tragic. The swordsmen engaged in a ferocious battle. At the end of the violent thrusting and cutting, Compton was punctured by the Baron's blade and fatally lacerated. Then more tragedy when Chandos was found guilty of manslaughter and died of smallpox while in prison!

"At the end of the violent thrusting and cutting, Compton was punctured by the Baron's blade and fatally lacerated."

In the late 18th century, the combatants most likely used matched pistols. Fortunately for future quarrelers, the medieval code of chivalry evolved into a trend where 'the enlightened society' resolved their disagreements by dueling with words in the newspapers.

RWGC currently resides on a 240 acre piece of land known as Warren Farm. And now, duels of a different nature are waged about a mile away on the grass courts where the weapon of choice is a tennis racket at the All England Lawn and Tennis Club. If you are wondering, "Isn't that where they play the oldest, most prestigious tennis tournament in the world, known simply as Wimbledon?" you'd be right.

In 1907, when the RWGC moved to the land adjoining the Common, the course they played on was laid out by the highly respected golfer, Willie Park Jr. By 1924, the great golf architect Harry Colt, who learned his golf at Wimbledon, was hired to develop a new layout.

Long before the course acquired the distinction of such a renowned architect as Colt, the Royal title was conferred on the club in June 1882 by none other than Queen Victoria.

However, the first royal patron was The Prince of Wales, later King Edward VII.

As cited in Scott Macpherson's weighty tome, *Golf's Royal Clubs*, many captains and members distinguished themselves in the world of golf. Perhaps one of the most famous was Dr William Laidlaw Purves. He, along with other Royal

Purple Heather in bloom at Royal Wimbledon.

Royal Wimbledon windmill painting. Original oil painting by Frederick Cotman.

Wimbledon members, Henry Lamb and William Anderson, founded St George's Golf Club in 1887 on the linksland of Sandwich in Kent. The royal prefix was included some years later, granted in May 1902 by King Edward VII. To this day, there is a close alliance between the two clubs, with Sandwich, as it is commonly called, having hosted the Open Championship fifteen times.

Considered a 'sister club', and one where The Claret Jug has been hoisted many times by the winner of the Open, the wine culture there is legendary.

According to the Secretary of Royal Wimbledon, Mr Robert Brewer, a number of RWGC members have significant wine cellars. They are encouraged to bring in a bottle from their private collection to enjoy at the club whenever it strikes their fancy.

Judging by the exceptional wine list of the club, they may not have much need to dip into their personal cellar very often. Nowadays, club member Tim Atkin, an award-winning writer and Master of Wine, advises the House Committee on their wine selection, which is prominently featured on their website.

Not only are the choices diverse and reasonably priced, the succinct descriptions are both witty and whet the appetite. An example includes the 2016 Mytilus Albarino, Rias Baixas that is 'an intense, crunchy, lime-scented white from Spain's North.'

One would expect there to be a solid medium-bodied wine from France, and there is. It is the 2014 Chateau Beaumont, Haut-Medoc. 'This vintage is a leafy, refreshing, elegant claret with notes of graphite, mint and cassis.'

Another wine that makes the list is a 2012 Geoff Merrill Pimpala Road Shiraz from South Australia. From the multi-award-winning vintner, 'it is a spicy, brambly, mature red' created by a legendary winemaker who is also a RWGC member.

Since Geoff's first release under his own label in the early 1980s, Geoff Merrill Wines has vineyards in three of Australia's classic viticultural regions: Pimpala Vineyard and Wickham Downs in McLaren Vale, Graymoor in the Coonawarra, and the Pogue vineyard in the Goulburn Valley.

There is perhaps the most unique wine-related tradition at Royal Wimbledon ever conceived by a golf club that has what's known as a 'roll up'. The much-loved institution, which is very common in Britain, encourages members to just show up, in this case on any Saturday morning, without booking a tee time in advance.

However, in addition to the modest ante for the best Stableford score on the day, there is also a booby prize — The Wine Waiter. This poor soul is the individual finishing with the fewest number of points in the group. So, whether a banker, diplomat or school teacher, after much ribbing, the lowest-scoring player must don the dreaded apron to take and serve the orders for a full round

Royal Wimbledon Wine Waiter.

of drinks from the bar. The only consolation is the winner of the kitty picks up the tab.

So if you are a Londoner and want to escape to a club with a highly regarded golf course where you can also share a superb bottle of wine, amble on down to Royal Wimbledon. In the words of Bernard Darwin, author of *The Golf Courses of the British Isles*, "A wonderful place is this new Wimbledon course, for as soon as we are on it all signs of men, houses and omnibuses, and the other symptoms of a busy suburb disappear as if by magic…"

The Golf Gods are not endowed with the power to grant membership, but one can always hope to be an invited guest. And if you are so fortunate, along with your smart golf attire and bonhomie, be sure to bring a fine bottle of wine for your host!

San Lorenzo Golf Club

Algarve, Portugal

There may be a few other golf clubs in Portugal with a strong wine culture, but none have a more congenial Director of Golf than San Lorenzo Golf Club in the Algarve.

After our round on the stunning pine-tree-fringed course, António Santos, Director de Golfe and Master of Hospitality, invited me and my partner, Kevin McGrath, to have lunch. Even though we planned to get right on the road for our long drive to a hotel north of Lisbon, we just couldn't say no. We thought we'd have a quick bite to eat and be on our way, but when António asked, "Would you like to have some wine?" How could we say no?

That is how our magical post-round lunch began, on the lovely stone patio outside the clubhouse.

Framed with umbrella pine trees, palms, flowering bushes, and green fairways in the distance, it was an absolute haven of peace and serenity. How did it come about?

Let's start with Portugal and then we'll get to the Algarve. Portugal is the western-most country in mainland Europe. Its coastline along the Atlantic Ocean is 1,115 miles, so it's not

7th Hole from the forward tee.

surprising that the country has a rich seafaring heritage. As a comparison, the general coastline of California is 840 miles long.

In the late 15th century, after Christopher Columbus set out across the Atlantic to search for a route to Asia, although he was not Portugese-born or sponsored, he married a Portuguese woman and obtained nautical charts from his father-in-law, who was the governor of the island of Porto Santo in Madeira. He was also employed as a navigator by John II (João II), the King of Portugal, who reigned from 1481 until his death in 1495. In 1500, Pedro Álvares Cabral discovered and claimed Brazil for the Portuguese Crown on his way to India. Remember these explorers? In the US we learned about them in 5th grade.

Now we get to the historical significance of the Algarve, which is the southernmost area of Portugal. The Romans, along with other cultures, sought to control the region. They brought their viticultural practices and their cultivars to the Iberian Peninsula along with the Phoenicians and the Greeks. You know those Romans, they couldn't go very long without their wine!

Also in the 15th century, Prince Henry the Navigator based himself near Lagos and conducted various maritime expeditions and established the colonies that comprised the Portuguese Empire. Also from Lagos, Gil Eanes set sail in 1434 to become the first seafarer to round Cape Bojador in West Africa. The voyages of discovery brought Lagos fame and fortune. Now it is golf tourism and the wine that bring the fame and fortune.

Trade flourished and Lagos became the capital of the historical province of Algarve in 1577 and remained so until the catastrophic Great Lisbon earthquake of 1755. Seismologists today estimate it had a magnitude of 9 on the Richter scale. In the Algarve, destruction was monumental.

The accompanying tsunami destroyed or heavily damaged coastal fortresses, towns and villages. Except for Faro. Why was this city spared? Located only about five miles as the crow flies from present day San Lorenzo GC, Faro was protected by the sandy banks of the Ria Formosa lagoon. To underscore how precious this system of barrier islands is, consider that in nearby Spain, the tsunamis swept the Andalusian Atlantic Coast and nearly destroyed the city of Cadiz, killing one-third of the population.

We are now zeroing in on our particular spot on the southern coast of the Iberian Peninsula. Since this is precisely where San Lorenzo is situated, in the southeast corner of Quinta do Lago, bordering the Ria Formosa Estuary and salt water lagoons. Now do you see why this place is so special?

Although the British introduced the game of golf to Portugal in the 19th century, when a group of wine exporters formed Oporto Niblicks Club in 1890, it was Sir Henry Cotton who started the Portuguese golf boom with The Penina. Dating back to 1966, it is the oldest course in the Algarve and it is renowned as the venue for the Portuguese Open on numerous occasions.

Cotton proved to be a catalyst for the creation of

many golf courses and hotels in the Algarve, which became a popular destination for the Germans, Dutch, and Irish. In recent years, it has developed into a great golf playground for Europeans, Canadians, Americans, and Australians.

Many of the courses were designed by famous architects such as Robert Trent Jones Jr, Jack Nicklaus, Arthur Hills, and Arnold Palmer. One thing the courses all have in common is their environmental quality and the harmonious way in which they blend into the natural surroundings.

Perhaps none blend more than San Lorenzo, designed by Joseph Lee and his younger associate, Rocky Roquemore, in 1988. Joe Lee began his career working with Dick Wilson, a rival of RTJ in that era, and his portfolio included more than 250 courses in his 25 year career. San Lorenzo, a challenging test that is both demanding and dramatic, is a real standout. It is by far one of the most famous golf courses in the Algarve, available to guests of Dona Filipa Hotel, and of course, to those who are lucky enough to be private members.

The round begins with an enjoyable par 5, and continues to the three following holes along rolling, lush, green fairways. The par 3 fifth and sixth holes begin pointing toward the seaside. But it was the exhilarating 7th hole that jumped up and stunned me. I was almost disoriented at first with the exquisite beauty of the views over the Ria Formosa estuary.

The scene was so dazzling, it was hard to settle down to hit my tee shot. I felt like I was leaving the golf environment and entering a magic zone full of sand, wetlands, little fishing boats, birds, and blue lagoons.

The eighth hole turns back inland where you have to navigate around two lakes. Every shot requires full engagement to steer clear of all the water. Whether or not it was a good ball-striking day, one had to enjoy the sheer magnificence of the course and appreciate the attention to detail of the meticulous maintenance.

We were euphoric after finishing our round. When we met up with the exuberant António, he was keen to usher us to a beautifully appointed outdoor table. After we chose several delicious dishes from the menu, our generous host began our extraordinary wine experience by instructing the servers to bring some special bottles from the cellars. It quickly became clear that we were not just having some ordinary wine with our meal.

António presented and poured each vintage with such knowledge and finesse. The wines he chose included the Esporão, Reserva 2014, and two that were private label JJW Hotels & Resorts (a red and a white).

But António wasn't finished. Next he treated us to one of his personal favorites, Lavradores de Feitoria. This was the first time I'd ever experienced a wine from the Douro Valley. He chose the Branco 2017 vintage. It was everything you would want, if you enjoy Sauvignon Blanc, fresh and fruity with a hint of citrus. The label was just as elegant, with a simple 1/2 inch wide line snaking gently across the white background, suggestive of the rich river gorge.

To add to San Lorenzo's charm, several beautiful birds joined us for lunch. The first one I noticed was the Ibis, quietly poking around the grass on its long spindly legs. I had never seen a live one before, and I could barely contain myself trying to get a photo without scaring it away.

With great pride and awareness, António said, "To us, the abundance of wildlife we have around the club all the time is the proof that we are good stewards of a healthy environment."

Some other birds that flitted around looked to be either the Calandra Lark or the Lesser Short-toed Lark. The most astonishing of all was the Iberian Magpie. What a sight! Intense black head, light grey iridescent body, and stunning azure blue wings and tail. It was magnificent just perched on the back of a chair. But when it took to flight and fanned out its beautiful blue wings, I nearly fell off my own chair.

Explorers, conquerors, earthquakes, and golf enthusiasts have all left their mark on the Algarve. And they've discovered that the sanctuary of San Lorenzo is heaven on earth. Next time, before we go and the wine starts to flow, we will know to book a room at the Dona Filipa Hotel so we don't have such a long drive ahead of us!

Long view of the Wente golf course.

The Course at Wente Vineyards

Livermore, California, USA

At Wente, the golf and wine cultures come together in a brilliant tour de force. One would have to believe that the original founder of Wente Vineyards, Carl H. Wente, would be quite pleased to see how his family masterfully blended grape growing with the golf culture. By family, we are talking five generations, as Wente Vineyards is the oldest continuously operating, family-owned winery in the US. In fact, the Wente Estate is registered as a California Historical Landmark.

In 1883, Carl Wente parlayed his training with Charles Krug, one of the pioneers in winemaking in the Napa Valley, into establishing his own vineyards when he bought 47 acres of excellent soil in the Livermore Valley.

Establishing the Wente Vineyards just 50 miles east of San Francisco was only the first smart move. In 1912, second generation winegrower, Ernest Wente, took cuttings from the University of Montpellier viticultural nursery in France to plant what is now famously known as the Wente Clone. This development was so important that a number of other wineries have adopted the Wente Clone (certified by the Foundation Plant Materials Service of the University of California, Davis) as source material for their Chardonnay plantings.

In viticulture a 'clone' refers to vines descended from a single plant by taking a cutting or bud. In theory, each vine grown on a clone is genetically identical to the original vine. And now, about 75% of Chardonnay in the US is based on the clone the Wente family brought over from Burgundy in 1912.

"About 75% of Chardonnay in the US is based on the clone the Wente family brought over from Burgundy in 1912"

Karl Wente, fifth generation winegrower, has two masters degrees from UC Davis, one in viticulture and one in enology. In an interview with Christopher Barnes of *Grape Collective* magazine (September 2016), Karl described himself as very lucky to oversee 2,000 acres of vineyards in the Livermore Valley and also 1,000 in Arroyo Seco, Monterey.

He stated, "My family was the first to varietally label wines — after Prohibition. Now you look at the shelves across most stores, a high percentage of those wines were varietally labeled. In 1932, we put Sauvignon Blanc on the label and in 1936, we were the first to varietally label Chardonnay."

The significance of varietal labeling was to let the consumer know the wines coming from Wente Vineyards in 1934 were from the finest grape varieties delivering the highest quality.

In another stroke of genius, the Wente family realized the Livermore Valley was not only perfect terroir for growing grapes, it was also ideal for a world-class golf course. In 1994 they hired Australian two-time major winner Greg Norman to design The Course at Wente Vineyards. It was his first course in the US, and now it is one of over 100 that he has designed across 34 countries and six continents.

Construction began in 1995 and after a long grow-in period, the course opened for play in July

View of the Par 5 fifth hole completely surrounded by vineyards.

1998. The fairways are framed beautifully by the vineyards, and the course has matured into a premier Bay Area golf destination. Featuring three distinct topographies, native woodlands, mature vineyards and rolling hills of natural grasslands, the course has proudly played host to the Livermore Valley Wine Country Championship. This event became part of the PGA Tour's Nationwide Tour and now the Web.com Tour, which is the primary pathway for those seeking to earn their PGA Tour card.

To say the Course at Wente is unique is an understatement. According to Carolyn Wente, "Each hole is shaped in the vineyards, so when a player's ball strays off the fairway, they find themselves up close and personal with the grapes and exposed to wine country in an extraordinary way."

Although it is primarily an upscale, daily-fee golf course, about 350 people avail themselves of two golf membership options, taking advantage of wine tastings from Wente's outstanding portfolio. On Sundays, members can also participate in wine and cheese pairing events in the historic sandstone caves, with artisanal cheeses sourced from local and sustainable cheesemakers.

In 1986, The Restaurant at Wente Vineyards opened, and Carolyn Wente launched the annual 'Concerts at Wente Vineyards' series that features top entertainers and adds a new twist to the wine country experience. Since he is a musician at heart, Karl Wente and his Front Porch Band host an all-day music festival at the winery, attracting a new generation of music lovers to the Livermore Valley. Karl's day job is winemaking, and he introduced the Nth Degree,

View of the heavily bunkered Par 3 third hole framed by vineyards and the mountain

a line of limited-production, ultra-premium handcrafted wines. The focus of this small lot program is to create stellar wines that reflect the distinctive terroir of the family's estate vineyards.

In addition to striving for the highest quality grapes, in 2010 Wente Family Estates received certification of sustainability for vineyard, winery and company practice from the Certified California Sustainable Winegrowing Alliance. That hard-earned status is a direct result of striving for a healthy ecosystem, where egrets, hawks, owls, squirrels, gophers, turkeys, and deer are all attracted to the Livermore Valley.

That same year, in January of 2010, the course earned Audubon International Certification, which focuses on small habitat restoration projects and replanting of perennial native and drought tolerant plants. When fourth generation Carolyn Wente gushes with excitement about how the flowers they have planted are bringing back the Monarch butterflies, you know their commitment to creating the best expressions of more than eight varietals is equaled by their devotion to being the best stewards of their precious land.

"2018 brought another important milestone for Wente, as the 135th anniversary of being a family-owned and operated wine company."

As a tribute to all their outstanding achievements, it's no wonder that in 2011 the Wente Family Estates was awarded American Winery of the Year by *Wine Enthusiast*.

In 2012, the Wente family celebrated the 100th anniversary of the Wente Chardonnay clone.

While 2018 brought another important milestone for Wente, as the 135th anniversary of being a family-owned and operated wine company, it is impossible to list all these

Wente Vineyards Tasting Lounge

extraordinary achievements without feeling like the entire family has the Midas touch.

Fate intervened when I was researching Annika Sörenstam for another chapter in this book, that led me to Wente in the first place. Annika, who made history in 2001 as the first female to ever shoot the magical number 59 in competition, had partnered with Wente to create her own wine brand.

Just like Annika's scorecard, one birdie led to another. Although I initially thought I should have only one California profile for this chapter, when I heard the passion in Carolyn's voice, I felt that to exclude the Wente story would be an unforgivable omission.

Like the Chardonnay cuttings they brought from France, the entire family seems to clone their genius.

Wente Vineyards fringing the course.

"Dragonflies" by Mark Hill.

The Hills Golf Club

Arrowtown, New Zealand

The Hills came to my attention long before I began writing this book. I had heard of this extraordinary place that is essentially a sculpture park, while it was originally conceived as a private members golf club in New Zealand.

It was the vision of Sir Michael Hill, who bought a former deer farm and asked his good friend, John Darby, to help him build his own putting green. That turned into three greens with bunkers and several different tees. They must have really enjoyed the process. The Harvard- trained course designer then brought an entire team from Darby Partners to the project, and it expanded to become a 7,000 yard championship course.

That certainly sounds like the brainchild of someone who is always figuring out ways to think bigger, which is the title of one of Sir Michael Hill's fascinating books on how to succeed in business. It relates how setting goals is the key to great accomplishments while creating intrinsic happiness along the way.

Young Michael created his first golf course at age 11 on the lawn of his family's house at Whangarei, in northern New Zealand. He mowed little circles for greens and used baked bean tins for the holes. The enterprising boy collected fees from the neighborhood kids who were eager to play his course. He even ran mini tournaments, each offering a prizes to the winners.

As a teenager, Michael Hill aspired to be a concert violinist, but he soon realized that he hadn't started early enough to become a professional musician. Instead, he took a job at his uncle's jewelry store. Michael not only excelled as a salesman, he had a gift of creating effective advertising and his brilliant business acumen earned him promotion to manager. While working in the store, Hill met Christine Roe and they married in March 1965. Son Mark came along in 1969.

In 1971, daughter Emma was born. Then, on 1 October 1977, the house that had taken the Hills four years to build was destroyed in a fire. Only great reserves of firmness of purpose could see them through this disaster. The setback changed the trajectory of Michael Hill's life. He first tried to buy his uncle's business, but when his uncle refused to sell, Hill simply opened his own jewelry store.

Like the three little greens that grew to become a championship course, Hill applied his tenacious philosophy to building an empire, starting with the goal of seven stores in seven years. In 1986 he exceeded that. In the subsequent years his vision expanded, and Michael Hill Jewelers now has 300 stores.

In 1990, Hill was awarded the New Zealand 1990 Commemoration Medal. In the 2002 New Year Honors, Hill was appointed a 'Companion of the New Zealand Order of Merit', for services to business and the arts. Sir Michael was promoted to Knight Companion of the same order in the 2011 New Year Honors, also for services to business and the arts.

The Hills Golf Club, which spreads over 280 acres opened in 2007. It has been the venue for the prestigious New Zealand Open nine times, starting in 2007, with the 2019 event celebrating the 100th NZ Open. Along with

"Emergence" by Mark Hill.

hosting other world-class golf events like the NZ PGA Championship in 2012 and 2013, The Hills has evolved as a unique environment, replete with natural beauty. It is the home of numerous works of site-specific art.

The rugged glacial valley is the setting for more than a dozen large-scale contemporary sculptures. The five massive cast iron horses by Max Patte are particularly compelling. They stand by the 7th tee and are imbued with the majesty of sacred standing stones. But another piece by Patte is one of my favorites. Titled Solace in the Wind, the larger-than-life-size standing man leans so far forward, he appears to demonstrate immeasurable strength in every fiber of his being. Naked, chest protruding, the work exudes a spiritual or even metaphysical quality.

Other monumental works include the recently commissioned 12-foot-tall piece by British artist Sean Henry. A bearded, seated man, his folded arms resting on a suitcase, gazes in contemplation toward the snow-capped mountains. He appears to be in deep, serious thought as he ponders unknowable questions.

Perhaps the most astonishing work of all, is not one piece but 110 enormous cast iron wolves created by Chinese sculptor, Liu Ruowang. The 'Wolves are Coming', installed on the course in 2012, features a giant, oriental sword-wielding warrior, encircled by a pack of vicious, blood-thirsty beasts. The warrior alone weighs 3.3 tons. When the artist came over to see the site that was chosen, he said, speaking through an interpreter, "Site too small. Not natural. Wolves are starving, coming onto golf course very hungry." An alternate site was chosen and now the grouping is situated alongside the 18th fairway. It is safe to say the wolves add a peculiar degree of danger and could be blamed for a bogey or worse.

The famous New Zealand professional golfer, Sir Bob Charles, who won more than 70 titles throughout his stellar career, jocularly said of The Hills, "One must beware of the course's scenic charm," warning how it has the ability to lull

"Solace in the Wind" by Max Patte.

players into a false sense of security, destroying the "very concentration needed to avoid disaster." As an art dealer myself, I have to say, I'd be too preoccupied walking around this grassy museum with a golf club in my hand. I'd probably do a lot better to have a camera instead.

Yet I haven't even mentioned the fact that The Hills, situated in the Central Otago wine region, is surrounded by dozens of wineries, and is home to some of the world's best Pinot Noir.

Many of the wines are featured in the award-winning clubhouse, designed by Auckland- based architect Andrew Patterson. This clubhouse, two-thirds of it underground, won the New Zealand Institute of Architects Supreme Architectural Award in 2008, and was a finalist in the World Architecture Festival that same year in Barcelona. Along with creating a building in complete harmony with the alpine landscape, it certainly is ideal for the wine cellar as well.

The club keeps an abundant mix of local wines on hand along with a great selection that they know their members love to drink, like the Te Mata Coleraine Cab Merlot Franc. Other popular wines on their list include Akarua Chardonnay and Pinot Noir. Several Pinots from Valli, and Dry River Syrah round out the reds. Some wineries featured on the wine list I must include because I love the names: Wild Hare, Grasshopper Rock and Wooing Tree. Other outstanding choices include wines from Burn Cottage, Felton Road, Gibbston Back Road, Gibbston Valley and the Pisa Range Estate.

Sir Michael has the heart of an artist. His son, Mark, inherited these extra special genes. Several of Mark's works grace The Hills course. His tree-like Corten steel piece, Kelp, and his giant Dragon Flies that appear to skim the surface of a pond, are perfectly placed for maximum visual effect and enjoyment. Hill's daughter, Emma, who succeeded him as chairman in 2015, apparently inherited the business brains. Now her father is freed up to devote more time to his philanthropic endeavors like the biennial Michael Hill International Violin Competition. The winner receives a substantial cash prize, a recording deal for international distribution and a 'Winner's Tour' in which he or she performs in concert halls around New Zealand and Australia in the year following the competition.

There is a great energy and legacy here. Both the golf members and family members have a magnificent playground to pursue their passion for art and practice their religion, of golf and wine, that is. They even have a new Par 3 course called 'The Farm', which is very appropriate since they own the surrounding farmland, stretching their total holdings to about 500 acres.

Interestingly, about 20 years ago, when I'd first become fascinated with golf but wasn't actually playing the game, I came up with an idea I called the 'Museum Course'. I envisioned monumental works by Henry Moore, David Smith, Alexander Calder and other well-established artists placed in strategic spots all around a golf course.

And now, what was just a dream for me, has been actualized by Sir Michael Hill. I doff my golf cap to him.

Whistling Rock, metallic gold ball with rock outcropping.

Whistling Rock Country Club

South Korea

Whistling Rock Country Club has a team of wine sommeliers. However, it also has a tea sommelier and a water sommelier which indicates of how extraordinary this golf club is. Every aspect of the name is fitting. Whistling Rock, carved out of dense woodland in the mountainous area of Chuncheon, about a 90 minute drive northeast of Seoul, is tucked away in sublime seclusion. It is breathtakingly beautiful, and the wind literally whistles through the trees.

The financial power of the Taekwang Group is the driving force, and all the creative entities involved were thoughtfully selected to curate and carry out the building of both the sleek, rectilinear clubhouse, and the spectacular 27 hole course.

It may sound like hyperbole to compare the monumental 167,000 square foot travertine clubhouse to a world-class modern museum, or the mountainous landscape that comprise the three nines as a monumental living work of art, but I guarantee you, it's not.

Francine Houben of Mecanoo Architects is the singular genius behind all the exquisite structures including the tea houses: Cocoon, Temple, and Cloud. Each of the three nine-hole courses has a distinct feeling and are named for their tea houses.

Houben founded her firm in Delft in 1984 and she oversees a staff of 90 professionals.

Her work is based on both analysis and intuition, weaving social, technical and humane sensitivities to reach a design completely in tune with each site. Houben's trademark is to create balance, even luxury, with environmental consciousness, while honoring her commitment to sustainability.

Towering evergreens, a broad array of hardwoods, flowering plants, boulders, streams and dramatic waterfalls, Whistling Rock has it all. California-based Ted Robinson Jr was ultimately the golf architect selected to create the routing plan. To build his vision, more than five million cubic meters of material were moved or blasted to shape the course out of rocky, tilted terrain. After a three-year construction period, the course opened for play in 2012.

Robinson also suggested hiring Pinnacle Design Company to create a plant palette to blend the golf holes into the native forest. They carefully salvaged nearly 8,000 specimens of evergreens and deciduous trees including Korean Maple, Cornel Dogwood, Mongolian Oak and Japanese Flowering Cherry. Pinnacle planted an additional 7,200 trees including White Birch, Gingko and Flowering Crabapple to frame the course. But that is the equivalent of painting with a broad brush, compared to how they artfully incorporated an understory of flowering shrubs like azalea and barberry. There is almost no end to the detail that went into every square inch of Whistling Rock.

In 2014, the club initiated an evaluation of the golf experience and in 2015 hired Eric Iverson, a Senior Associate with Renaissance Golf Design, to make some modifications to the greens and surrounds. Beginning in 2016, the painstaking work was carried out over a two-year period.

Along with an incredibly diverse collection

The Wine Dining Room at Whistling Rock Country Club.

of large-scale artwork inside the clubhouse, WR has placed several sculptures outdoors such as the gleaming 'Golden Horse' near the south entrance.

Nine colorful metallic balls ranging in size from 1.4 to 2.3 meters in diameter are playfully integrated into the golf courses. They inspire delight, joy, and magic. Their perfect spheres even subliminally relate to a round of golf.

If your visit or your membership includes the privilege of a Michelin Star experience, Whistling Rock dazzles further with several different rooms for fine dining, including the one appropriately called the Wine Dining Room. It faces an interior garden on one side, and the three other walls hold hundreds of wine bottles on glass shelves.

This is merely a hint to the 30,000 bottle wine cellar and the 10,000 bottle tasting room on the lower level. The wine list is extensive, and the golf shop carries a selection of wines for sale, ranging from a Poderi Luigi Einaudi Barolo (2003), a Chateau de Cayx, Cahors Malbec (2011), to Buena Vista Pinot Noir (2012) from Sonoma.

Yet none of these descriptions and numbers express the essence of this club! There is a much deeper meaning to every single thing. For instance, take the concept of the Balls, excerpted from the WR website:

The concept of the Balls starts with the idea that the journey of a round of golf is parallel to the journey of life. The seven colors of the spectrum can be found in the main parcel of the property, the 'life' section, and in the isolated valley on the other side of the tunnel, the 'afterlife' (also called 'The Glen'), where the colors are metallic.

Another key is revealed in the elegant WR hardcover history book photographed and published by Joann Dost Golf Editions, in what is a magnificent, harmonious culmination of art and nature: "The aesthetic charge delivered by the golf course at Whistling Rock — fairways seemingly airbrushed onto the hillsides, waterfalls cascading down the sides of mountains — tends to obscure the subtle challenge of the game that is the raison d'être of every hole."

To play the course on the undulating fairways, framed with such beauty, was overwhelming for me. It was nearly sensory overload. There is such a powerful artistic rhythm to the course and a strong spiritual dimension emanating from each tea house, that I felt like I was transported to a parallel universe. The intoxicating mixture of an ancient culture, combined with a state-of-the art clubhouse and its collection of modern art, is truly breathtaking.

If you ever have the opportunity to visit, or best-case-scenario, play a round at Whistling Rock, absolutely, positively, do not pass it up.

Whistling Rock Country Club clubhouse

Acknowledgements

My most profuse "thank you" goes to my sweetheart, Kevin McGrath, who has had as much fun as me... always ready to sample wines and golf courses on any continent. Thank you for being my adventurous companion and eagle-eyed caddie for over 15 years.

Two of my first test subjects were Jack Mettler and Lonna Wais. While Kevin and I were having dinner with them at The Vintage Club in Indian Wells, California, I ventured my theory that with both grapes and golf, everything begins with the ground. And as with wine and golf courses, the result is a work of art. They identified with the concept, and I knew I'd connected the dots in a unique way.

Cori Brett grew up at Diablo Country Club in the San Francisco Bay Area, not far from the famed wine country of Napa Valley. I still remember her inspiring words, "There is such synergy between golf and wine. You are onto something Taba!" Thank you, Cori.

An article about Greg Anderson in *Golfweek* magazine was the next crumb along the path. Greg is a Lifetime Member of the PGA of America, and a wine sommelier. He was pictured holding a glass of deep red wine. When I spoke to him on the phone, I knew I had met a kindred spirit.

I must thank the immensely talented early supporters, Trish Meyer, Deborah Ann Marshall, and Scott Paccie, who with their trained eyes gave *Terroir* some visual form.

Special thanks to Mike Sweeney who invited me to see his private wine cellar of nearly 8,000 bottles. That was another seminal experience. He and his wife are also members of Saucon Valley in Pennsylvania and Stone Canyon in Tucson, Arizona. Their interest and encouragement gave me extra incentive to follow my dream.

A super-special thanks to Charlie Stott, Laurie Rae, Frances Hough, and Dr Anthony Parker for the expertise, observations, and critiques regarding The Claret Jug chapter.

The one time I mentioned this book to another writer, it was Roger McStravick, when we met for a coffee at his club in St Andrews. He told me to think big and follow my dream. That had me floating on air. Thank you, Roger, for fueling my fire.

I was introduced to golf course photographer Dave Sansom by golf architect, Jason Straka. Dave gave me excellent guidance, and always found a way to reassure me that I was getting my message across.

Another golf course photographer, the world-renowned Joann Dost, went out of her way to connect me with the legendary golfer Jan Stephenson. Their friendship went back to the days they played professional golf together on the Australian Tour.

In addition to those named, I want to give my profound thanks to many other friends, clients, and golf enthusiasts, architects, winemakers, Club Secretaries and GMs who gave me their time and encouragement while on this journey.

Enormous thanks to Cliff Carle, my brilliant editor. He shows me where the commas belong and is continually teaching me to be a better writer. Plus, his genius encompasses incredible knowledge about the complex publishing world, which is not easy to navigate without such a seasoned mentor.

Finally, Graeme Ryan of Ryan Publishing was an extraordinary visionary in shaping the book's stunning look and feel while working with Luke Harris, his endlessly patient book designer. I cannot thank you both enough for your wisdom, guidance, and talent.

Author's Notes

It has been a long, fascinating journey writing this book. I have made many discoveries along the way, and hope I can give you tantalizing glimpses of golf and wine cultures. Since my 'lightbulb' moment while playing golf at The Machrie when the phrase 'Terroir of Golf' came into my head, there are some updates to report now that we have lived through the COVID pandemic. I hope we are all on a new, elevated platform from which to view the wide world of golf and wine.

Early Chapters:

Turnberry: Angus Watson is now Director of Sales at the Old Course Hotel, St Andrews.

The Machrie: The Machrie Hotel & Golf Links has undergone a complete renovation and expansion with 47 rooms, suites, and lodges. There are now almost 50 bunkers on the course, following a redesign by golf course architect and former European Tour player David J Russell.

There is also a new distillery on Islay called Portintruan set to start distilling from early 2024.

The murmurs mentioned about a new course on Jura turned into the 18-hole Ardfin on the island's southern tip. It was designed by Bob Harrison and it is now ranked #74 in *Golf Magazine*'s Top 100 in the World Rankings. Ardfin was the seat of McDonalds and then Campbells for hundreds of years. There have been extensive restorations to the country house on the estate.

Eden Mansion is now a private residence.

Kingsbarns Golf Links mourned the passing of developer Mark Parsinen, who died in 2019.

Machrihanish Golf Club has completely rebuilt the clubhouse that tragically burned down in December 2018. The new building is modern but not overly so. The upstairs restaurant has spectacular views over the opening hole and the sea with outdoor seating.

Winemakers Talk Terroir

Andrew Keenleyside: After being nominated New Zealand Winemaker of the Year by *Gourmet Traveller Wine* in 2020, Andrew Keenlelyside joined the Terra Sancta team from the 2022 vintage. In the Global Wine Challenge of 2022, Keenleyside won the Pinot Noir Trophy and Red Wine of Show for his 2020 vintages while at Akarua. This challenge is accessible by invitation only and is restricted to the top 120 wines of each country competing — Australia, Canada, New Zealand, South Africa, and the US.

Designers Talk Turf

Jan Bel Jan: Among many other accomplishments, Jupiter Island Club, Hobe Sound, FL, Pelican Marsh Golf Club, Naples, FL, the two courses at Pelican's Nest Golf Club in Bonita Springs, FL, and 27 holes at Boca Lago Country Club, Boca Raton, FL have been completely overhauled by Jan Bel Jan. In 2023, she will have revitalized the 100-year-old Miami Springs Golf Course. Jan continues to give back to golf through her volunteer work with the *National Alliance for Accessible Golf, Women In the Golf Industry,* and *Women of Color Golf* as well as the ASGCA, GCSAA, and USGA.

Bill Coore: Projects (with Ben Crenshaw) include the South Course of Te Arai in New Zealand, which just opened in October 2022, Cabot St Lucia in the Caribbean, and other new courses due to open in 2023: Brambles Golf Club in Napa, CA, Torch Cay, Bahamas. The Coore & Crenshaw team was also chosen to reimagine The Pines course of The International outside Boston. The course will be closed for the 2023 golf season and will reopen in the summer of 2024.

Tom Doak: As well as designing St Patrick's Links in Donegal, Ireland, which opened in June 2021 and is now ranked #55 in *Golf Magazine's* Top 100 Courses in the World, Doak also created a reproduction of The Lido, Charles Blair Macdonald's original course (on Long Island) and also designed Sedge Valley, both in Mike Keiser's Resort at Sand Valley, Wisconsin. He also finished the routing for the second course at Cabot Highlands (companion to Castle Stuart). The North Course of Te Arai in NZ is under construction and due to open in October 2023. Doak was also named designer of the new 10th course at Pinehurst, which is expected to open in late spring of 2024.

David McLay Kidd: Kidd has designed Mammoth Dunes, the second 18 at Sand Valley Resort. Dormie Network recently announced that David Kidd will lead the design and construction of an 18-hole course, GrayBull, in the Nebraska Sandhills. He has also created his first course in mainland Europe, one hour south of Lisbon in Portugal. The Dunas Course at Terras da Comporta will open in June, 2023. Along with his Gamble Sands course in Brewster, WA, Kidd is set to create another masterpiece in Washington. Westport Golf Links is planning a grand opening in the summer of 2025.

Pat Ruddy: Ballyliffin Golf Club in Ireland has opened a new nine-hole par-three course designed by Pat Ruddy.

Jason Straka: With design partner Dana Fry, designing new holes and renovating others at the Cove Club. The facility will be renamed Cabo Del Sol Golf Club when the project is completed in 2024.

Served as the ASCGA president in 2022. During his term, the European Institute of Golf Course Architects (EIGCA), dedicated to golf and climate change, signed the pledge to commit to climate action in golf at the 2022 Annual Conference in Iceland. Other participants in the program included the R&A, the ASCGA, the Society of Australian Golf Course Architects (SAGCA) and the GEO Foundation.

Other projects include renovations at Sand Barrens Golf Club in Swainton, NJ, Kenwood Country Club in Cincinnati, OH and Chenequa Country Club in the Village of Chenequa, WI.

Professional Golfers With Their Own Wine Labels

Luke Donald: Named Europe's Ryder Cup Captain for the contest in Rome 2023.

Ernie Els: It was announced in November 2022 that Ernie would receive the 2023 Francis Ouimet Award at the Francis Ouimet Scholarship Fund's annual banquet on 3 April 2023. It was also recently announced that the Els for Autism Foundation will host a global autism conference in 2023 at The Els Center for Excellence in Jupiter, Florida.

Nick Faldo: Sir Nick Faldo retired from broadcasting as CBS Sports leading golf analyst in August 2022.

Retief Goosen: Elected to the World Golf Hall of Fame, class of 2019.

Cristie Kerr: Nominated as one of 12 finalists for admission into the World Golf Hall of Fame, class of 2024.

Jack Nicklaus: Awarded Honorary Citizenship of St Andrews in July 2022.

Frank Nobilo: We want to give a nod to Frank Nobilo, who played professional golf for many years, is an astute golf commentator, and an ambassador for leading New Zealand winery, Nobilo Wines.

Greg Norman: Named CEO of LIV Golf League in 2022.

Annika Sörenstam: Returned to competitive golf following 13 years of retirement to win the US Senior Women's Open in 2021 at Brooklawn CC in Fairfield, CT.

Jan Stephenson: Inducted into the World Golf Hall of Fame, class of 2019.

Golf Clubs With a Strong Wine Culture

Adare Manor in Ireland was named as venue for the 2026 Ryder Cup which will now be held in 2027 due to the COVID pandemic.

New Head Sommelier is Jonathan Jønsson.

Castiglion del Bosco: In November 2022, Campo del Drago, the Italian restaurant in the heart of Rosewood Castiglion del Bosco's *medieval* borgo, won its first Michelin star. Located in the countryside of Montalcino, in the heart of the UNESCO World Heritage Site of Val d'Orcia, the gourmet restaurant is set within one of the oldest and best-preserved estates in Italy.

Tuscan-born Executive Chef Matteo Temperini, Maître D' Maikol Calosci with their kitchen and service teams, offer guests an epicurean journey through this fairytale region's gastronomic culture in a warm, intimate atmosphere.

Tom Weiskopf has been elected to the World Golf Hall of Fame, Class of 2024.

The course is currently being renovated by architect Phil Smith, who collaborated with Weiskopf on the original design in 2012.

Mayacama Golf Club: New Wine Director is Carey Vanderborg.

The Course at Wente Vineyards: The Web.com tour is now known as the Korn Ferry Tour.

About the Author

Taba Dale established her golf themed company, Scottsdale Collection, in the early 1990s. Building on her expertise as a fine art dealer, she became the first to specialize in selling golf art online, offering both graphic works and originals.

Her company was invited to be a vendor at the prestigious 1997 US Open at Congressional Country Club in Bethesda, MD. Taba's innovative style of merchandising broke all sales records in her categories, including golf prints, original paintings, photography, memorabilia and books.

The enormous commercial success led to Scottsdale Collection becoming a vendor at the 1998 US Senior Open at Riviera Country

Club in Pacific Palisades, CA. Here, Taba met the Director of Golf, Michael G. Miller, who resigned after the tournament to paint full-time and Scottsdale Collection became his exclusive agent. Two highlights that resulted from this dynamic association were Taba curating a one-man show for Miller at The World Golf Hall of Fame in St Augustine, FL, in 2000, and another at the United States Golf Association in Far Hills, NJ, in 2001. Miller is the only artist to have one-man shows at either institution.

In 2005, Taba partnered with Dublin-born Kevin McGrath to form a golf travel company, arranging custom-tailored luxury golf trips. They also travel worldwide themselves, frequently visiting the 'trophy' courses, and playing hidden gems all over the world.

All these extraordinary golfing experiences have led to the publication of three books: A *Summer in Ireland, Life and Golf on the Emerald Isle, A Stroll on the Old Lady,* which is primarily about playing golf in Scotland and *Golfers, Scotland is Calling.* All three books have been well reviewed on Amazon and *Stroll* was honored with an Outstanding Achievement Award in 2016 by the International Network of Golf. Taba's latest book is *Terroir of Golf, A Golf Book for Wine Lovers.*

Taba Dale has been featured in over fifteen magazine and newspaper articles. In addition to her TV interview on Out of Ireland, she is frequently a guest on six syndicated radio shows.

For a comprehensive list of all media appearances, please visit:

www.ScottsdaleCollection.com.

CPSIA information can be obtained
at www.ICGtesting.com
Printed in the USA
LVHW071243270423
745292LV00026B/433

9 781876 498849